THE SYNTAX OF COORDINATION

CROOM HELM LINGUISTICS SERIES

The Syntax of Coordination

ROBERT R. VAN OIRSOUW

CROOM HELM
London • New York • Sydney

© 1987 Robert R. van Oirsouw
Croom Helm Ltd, Provident House,
Burrell Row, Beckenham, Kent BR3 1AT
Croom Helm Australia, 44-50 Waterloo Road,
North Ryde, 2113, New South Wales

Published in the USA by
Croom Helm
in association with Methuen, Inc.
29 West 35th Street,
New York, NY 10001

British Library Cataloguing in Publication Darta

Van Oirsouw, Robert R.
    The syntax of coordination.—(Croom Helm
    linguistics series).
    1. Grammar, Comparative and general—
    Coordinate constructions
    I. Title
    415   P299.C6
    ISBN 0-7099-2639-1

Library of Congress Cataloging in Publication Data

ISBN 0-7099-2639-1

Typeset by Leaper & Gard Ltd, Bristol, England
Printed and bound in Great Britain by
Biddles Ltd, Guildford and King's Lynn

EDITORIAL STATEMENT

CROOM HELM LINGUISTICS SERIES
Chief Editor
Professor John Hawkins, University of Southern California

Consultant Editors
Professor Joseph Aoun, University of Southern California
Professor Bernard Comrie, University of Southern California
Professor Edward Finegan, University of Southern California
Dr Richard Hudson, University College London
Professor James Hurford, University of Edinburgh
Professor Douglas Pulleybank, University of Southern California

The Croom Helm Linguistics Series does not specialise in any one area of language study, nor does it limit itself to any one theoretical approach. Synchronic and diachronic descriptive studies, either syntactic, semantic, phonological or morphological, are welcomed, as are more theoretical 'model-building' studies, and studies in sociolinguistics or psycholinguistics. The criterion for a work's acceptance is the quality of its contribution to the relevant field. All texts published must advance our understanding of the nature of language in areas of substantial interest to major sectors of the linguistic research community. Traditional scholarly standards, such as clarity of presentation, factual and logical soundness of argumentation, and a thorough and reasoned orientation to other relevant work, are also required. Within these indispensable limitations we welcome the submission of creative and original contributions to the study of language.

The editors and publisher wish to draw this series to the attention of scholars, who are invited to submit manuscripts or book-proposals to:

Professor John Hawkins, Department of Linguistics, University of Southern California, Los Angeles, CA 90089-1693, USA: *or to* Jonathan Price, Linguistics Editor, Croom Helm Publishers, Provident House, Burrell Row, Beckenham, Kent BR3 1AT, UK.

Contents

For Claire

Acknowledgements

The ideas in this book have benefited from many helpful criticisms from a number of people at various departments of linguistics and linguistics conferences in the past two years, and I am grateful to my fellow linguists from the Linguistic Association of Great Britain, and from the universities of Amsterdam, Leyden, Groningen, Utrecht, the Massachussetts Institute of Technology, the University of California at Berkeley, the University of California, Los Angeles, and the University of Southern California for their comments and suggestions.

I am especially grateful to Pieter Seuren and Bernard Comrie, whose unstinting encouragement and perceptive comments have greatly improved earlier versions of the ideas presented here. I have also benefited from very informative discussions on the material presented here with James Pankhurst, Jack Hawkins, Tim Stowell, Paul Schachter, Ken Hale, George Lakoff, Joseph Aoun, and Marc Authier. Naturally, they are absolved from all responsibility for my views and my mistakes.

The Netherlands Foundation for the Advancement of Pure Research (ZWO) provided financial support for this work, and the University of Utrecht relieved me of my teaching duties for a year. I am furthermore very grateful to the departments of linguistics of the University of California, Los Angeles, and the University of Southern California, for the hospitality they have extended to me as a visiting scholar.

And I owe a great debt to Carol Sommer and Simon Varey — for their friendship, their hospitality, and the intellectual and gastronomical haven that their home has been to me.

'Oh innocent devil,' cried the other. 'Oh, candid
if infernal soul. Go back to the earth and walk up and down it
again. For these people have co-ordinated,
Mephistopheles.'

E.M. Forster

Introduction

There are several reasons for writing a book on the syntax of coordination. The most important of these reasons is that because coordination is a syntactic construction that probably occurs in all languages, it is an area of considerable interest to linguists. Indeed, coordination has received a lot of attention in the last 30 or so years in books, papers, squibs and doctoral dissertations. It has been a fruitful area of research, and also a controversial one — and that is the second reason for this book. In Chomsky (1957), coordination is used as a test for constituenthood, and as an argument against Phrase Structure Grammar and in favour of Transformational Grammar. It has also been used as an argument in favour of Phrase Structure Grammar, and against Transformational Grammar, for instance in Gazdar (1981). Furthermore, it has been used to support and to attack a host of different linguistic theories and analyses.

But there is a distinct discontinuity in linguistic writings about coordination. The late sixties witnessed a fairly long debate on whether coordination should be accounted for by means of PS-rules, or by means of transformations. This inconclusive debate fizzled out and gave way to a fascinating discussion about deletion of identical verbs in coordination which has more or less ended with the publication of Neijt (1979). After Neijt, transformational linguists seemed to lose interest in coordination: in Pesetsky (1982) there is some discussion of Gapping, but in Chomsky (1981) there is only one cryptic reference in a footnote which is connected with co-ordination, and in Chomsky (1982) there is one single suggestion about the proper representation of coordination. At the same time, there was a considerable upsurge of interest in coordination in Generalised Phrase Structure Grammar (Gazdar, 1981; Sag *et al.*, 1985), and that discussion has yielded some very good and novel insights. At the same time, however, it explicitly excluded Gapping: the deletion of verbs was excluded from sentence grammar and relegated to some misty realm of 'discourse'.

In spite of this discontinuity, a few ideas keep recurring in the discussions about coordination — directionality, peripherality, deletion, identity, and recoverability, for instance. Very often, one finds that different authors who seem to be unaware of each other's work develop roughly the same ideas seemingly independently: Schachter and Mordechay (1983), for instance, develop a mirror-image rule which coordinates peripheral strings: however, without referring to Ross (1970), who also addressed the 'mirror-image' formulation of rules pertaining to coordination, and without referring to Langendoen (1975), who had already pointed out the importance of peripherality in co-ordination. It is the third objective of this book to bridge part of this discontinuity and to draw together the major ideas of the last two decades about the syntax of coordination.

The fourth reason for this book is that the discussion about coordination so far has made use of a remarkably limited range of data: usually only English declarative sentences are discussed. The resulting influence on the theories based on these data has not been beneficial. I shall extend the empirical basis for theories of coordination phenomena with a detailed analysis of Dutch and German coordination, and I will provide some data from a small number of other languages.

The fourfold purpose of this book dictates that considerable space should be devoted to previous approaches to coordination. This is what I do in Chapter 1, which traces the development of the most important approaches to coordination and provides critical comments about their relative merits and shortcomings. The sheer bulk of writings about coordination precludes a full discussion of all the relevant work of the last three decades. It is a fairly brief discussion of the most salient points that have emerged in the literature of the last 30 years, and for this discussion I have attempted to be representative rather than comprehensive.

Chapter 2 takes up the thread of earlier work, and demonstrates that the most fruitful approach to coordination will be a deletion-based one. I develop a theory of coordination and especially reduced coordinations that does not fall firmly within only one particular type of grammar: it is compatible with most theories of grammar that allow deletion rules. The theory is novel in that it makes crucial use of one obvious property which all sentences of all languages share and which has not been adequately exploited in the literature before, namely that the constituents of all sentences must appear in some linear order. I demonstrate in considerable detail that it is this left-to-right linear order of constituents which determines the application of deletion, and that deletion is not dependent on the structural configurations in which deletion targets or their antecedents appear. This new approach brings to light facts about English, Dutch and German as well as facts from a number of other languages which have not been noticed or discussed before in the literature. It also makes it possible to define an extremely simple and unitary account of coordinate constructions, which is empirically greatly more adequate than previous accounts and makes use of very minimal assumptions.

The third chapter explores four questions which arise naturally within an approach that deletes identical material under identity. First of all, we have to define identity: a thorny question which has hardly been addressed at all in the literature on deletions (with the favourable exception of Sag, 1976). I demonstrate that identity should be defined as nondistinctness relative to a discourse. This has a number of interesting consequences and leads to some novel observations, notably about obligatory disjoint reference in partially reduced coordinations. The second question is what 'deletion' means: I take the position that deletion means total absence of the deletion target, and demonstrate that there are no obvious advantages and some disadvantages to assuming that there are empty pro-verbs, pro-VPs and pro-NPs left behind at the deletion site. This raises the third question: how should one recover deletion (i.e. 'undo' the deletion) once it has taken place? I demonstrate that the recovery of deletion, which has always been assumed in deletion accounts but hardly ever formulated with any degree of precision, can be effected quite simply by reversing the deletion rules of Chapter 2. Lastly, I address the question of where in a model of grammar we should place the coordinate deletion rule, and demonstrate that it must be a late, 'surfacy' rule. I end this chapter with a few observations about coordinate deletions across languages, and conclude that they are quite restricted in very specific ways, which lends further support to the deletion account advocated in this book. Throughout Chapter 3, there is critical discussion of earlier work which has addressed the same four issues: Chapter 3 in this way supplements Chapter 1.

Although the theory presented in this book addresses many questions, and often provides new solutions, it also leaves many questions unanswered. Notably absent from the discussion is the work primarily relevant to the semantics and the pragmatics of coordination (e.g. Keenan and Faltz (1985), Lakoff (1971),

Lang (1984), to name three). It is impossible to address all coordination-related issues in language within the space of one book, and I beg the reader's indulgence for these omissions — this is primarily a book about the *syntactic* patterns found in coordination.

1

The Treatment of Coordination: 1957-1985

1.1 EARLY DAYS

1.1.1 Transformations vs. PS-rules

Although it would be clearly wrong to say that coordination did not begin to be studied until 1957, I shall skip all earlier work on coordination[1] and take, as a convenient starting-point for this book, p. 35 from Chomsky (1957). The second paragraph of a chapter entitled 'Limitations of Phrase Structure Description' starts as follows:

> One of the most productive processes for forming new sentences is the process of conjunction. If we have two sentences Z+X+W and Z+Y+W, and if X an Y are actually constituents of these sentences, then we can generally form a new sentence Z−X+Y=W ... If X and Y are, however, not constituents, we can generally not do this. (Chomsky, 1957:35)

This brings us straight to a problem which recurs with monotonous regularity in the discussion about coordinated structures, namely whether coordinations should be generated directly, by means of some sort of PS-rule, or whether they should be derived from coordinated simplex sentences by means of some sort of deletion rule. The shape of PS-rules and transformational rules has undergone substantial revision in the last 25 years, but this controversy is one which persists, as we shall see later in this chapter.

Let us first of all address the transformations vs. PS-rule

problem in Chomsky (1957). In that same chapter, we also find
the following passage:

> ... if X and Y are both constituents, but are constituents of
> different kinds ... then we cannot in general form a new
> sentence by conjunction ... In fact, the possibility of conjunc-
> tion offers one of the best criteria for the initial determination
> of phrase structure. (Chomsky, 1957:36)

The problem will be clear: coordination is always coordination
of constituents in Chomsky (1957).[2] This coordination of
constituents can be achieved by a rule that collapses two or
more *sentences* which are identical except for the constituents to
be coordinated, and which thus creates the sentence with the
constituent coordination in it. Given this description, such a rule
could not be a PS-rule: therefore PS-grammars could be taken
to be inadequate for the description of coordinated structures.
The implied assumption is that there could not be PS-rules of
the type:

1. $X ======> X_1 .....$ and X_n, where X = any constituent

A rule of this type could obviously account for the data which
Chomsky discusses in as adequate a fashion as the transformational rule he gives. Postulating such a rule will leave us with
two competing hypotheses, both of which are equally adequate
from a descriptive point of view.[3] PS-rules of this type have
been proposed by, *inter alia*, Dougherty (1970, 1971),[4] Gazdar
(1981) and Sag *et al.* (1985); these proposals will be discussed
in detail later on in this chapter.

1.1.2 Gleitman (1965) and Smith (1969)

Chomsky's (1957) proposal received its fullest elaboration in
Gleitman (1965), which is an article written in the *Syntactic
Structures* tradition, and harbours quite a few peculiarities of
that model. The long and awkward conjunction rule is very
similar in outline to what Chomsky (1957) proposes. The basis
for Gleitman's account is the essential 'reduction-based'
proposal, a proposal that has survived the last three decades

remarkably well, albeit of course with considerable modifications. Given that generative grammars describe sentences using S as an initial symbol, and that identical common symbols at some level for the basis of coordination, one can conjoin all sentences of English by virtue of the topmost common symbol S. All other coordinations should then be describable in terms of such a coordination: they are all derived from an initial coordination of grammatical sentences by means of deletion, reduction, ellipsis, wiping, or whatever one wants to call such rules which serve to shorten sentences. Coordinated sentences can be shortened to give coordinated constituents, and Gleitman gives us the appropriate rules. In addition to a rule deriving constituent coordinations from coordinated sentences, Gleitman also gives us a rule which produces what she calls 'conjoined tags'; this is a rule which essentially deletes an identical V and following identical material, and generates such sentences as (2) and (3); constructions which later came to be known as the result of a VP-deletion rule (see e.g. Sag, 1976, discussed in section 1.3.9 of this chapter).

2.   John can come but Mary can't Ø.
3.   John may have wanted to come but Mary may not Ø.

I shall not discuss Gleitman's rules in detail, but restrict myself here to repeating some of her most salient observations. She observes, for instance, that for some reduced predicates, the addition of *too* or some such adverbial is necessary; compare:

4.   *John came but Mary did Ø.
5.   John came, but Mary did Ø too.

She also observed that *but* as a coordinator is rather different from *and* and *or*: it allows only two members in the coordination, and demands some sort of implicit or explicit contrast between these:

6.   *John is ill but Mary isn't but Bill has a broken leg.
7.   *John but Mary arrived.

A third observation is that although in principle any sentence can be conjoined with any other, to conjoin fully identical

7

sentences, or sentences that are totally unrelated, is pointless.[5] This issue was later taken up again in Lakoff (1971).

8. ??? I could not decipher the rest of the message and I could not decipher the rest of the message.
9. ??? I wrote my grandmother a letter today, and six men can fit in the back seat of a Ford.

Although Gleitman does not discuss rules that one could compare to Gapping (deletion of identical verbs) or Right-node Raising (deletion of the antecedent occurrence of a rightmost constituent), she does observe that deletion rules may operate in such a way that a nonconstituent coordination results, and that such nonconstituent coordinations may be perfectly acceptable in English. This is clearly a problem for the suggestions in Chomsky (1957):[6] coordinate deletion rules need not always reduce coordinated sentences to coordinated constituents. Gleitman's sentences of the type (12) are classic instances of Gapping, while sentence like (10) and (11) are taken to constitute strong evidence for a rule of Coordinate Deletion; see e.g. Williams (1978).

10. I gave the girl a nickel and Ø Ø the boy a dime.
11. He took John home and Ø Ø Mary to the station.
12. The man was haggard and the girl Ø sick with exhaustion.

Lastly, on the basis of her observations, Gleitman rejects a proposal by Smith (1969), who wants to introduce conjoined nominals by means of a PS-rule. Smith suggested doing so in order to account for the fact that sentences like:

13. John and Mary bought the new book by John Steinbeck.

can be interpreted as John and Mary buying one copy together, or as John and Mary each buying one copy separately. Secondly, and more importantly, Smith observed that for sentences like (14) we have no source if all coordination is to be derived from grammatical sentence-coordination in the way that Chomsky (1957) suggests:

14. Jimmie and Timmie are a pair of fools.
15. *Jimmie is a pair of fools and Timmie is a pair of fools.

These observations can be accounted for by allowing NPs to be introduced as coordinations in simplex sentences (to use the *Syntactic Structures* terminology) on the one hand, and to also allow the deletion approach advocated by Chomsky on the other. Gleitman (whose paper was published before Smith's, although it was written later) makes a few salient observations on this proposal. First of all, plural nouns allow for the same type of ambiguity of interpretation as was observed for sentence (13):

16.   The girls bought the new Steinbeck novel.

Secondly, words like *couple* and *pair* are peculiar anyway, and some sort of number agreement arithmetic is required to get them right. Just allowing PS-coordination does not solve the problem:

17.   *Smith, Brown, and Jones are a happy couple.

This is especially clear in cases like (18):

18.   Two and two is/are four.

To sum up: The early analyses of coordination left us with a few well-defined problems. Clearly, not all coordination is constituent coordination. Neither can all coordination be derived from coordination of grammatical sentences: PS-coordination is also necessary. Nevertheless, the PS-coordination approach has some clearly identifiable problems. The PS-oriented approach is advocated, in various degrees of purity, and in a number of different frameworks, in e.g. Dik (1968), Dougherty (1970, 1971) Schachter (1977), Gazdar (1981), and Schachter and Mordechay (1983). A transformationally oriented approach can be found e.g. in Tai (1969), Ross (1970), Koutsoudas (1971), Maling (1972), Jackendoff (1972), Hankamer (1972, 1973, 1979), Stockwell *et al.* (1973), Harries (1973), Langendoen (1975), Walter (1976), Kuno (1976), Sag (1976), Williams (1978), Levin (1979) and Neijt (1979).

1.1.3 Lakoff and Peters (1969)

Some of the questions discussed above were taken up in a very influential paper by George Lakoff and Stanley Peters (1969),[7] who argue against an approach in which all coordination is derived from coordination of sentences. Starting from the observation that there is no grammatical coordination of sentences which could be the source for (19), they propose that at least for NPs there should be a PS-rule schema which expands NP into a coordination of NPs:

19. John and Mary are alike.

Given that we now have two ways of introducing coordinated NPs, namely transformationally and by means of PS-rules, Lakoff and Peters argue that these differences in generation are systematically correlated with differences in interpretation. PS-coordination, which is base-generated as a unit, will be interpreted as a unit; transformationally derived coordinations have been derived from separate simple sentences, so they will be interpreted as non-units. PS-coordinations, in other words, are interpreted as [+joint], while non-PS coordinations are interpreted as [−joint].

The first thing that strikes us about the Lakoff and Peters argument is a general point of method: although it is a perfectly reasonable supposition that there should not be more rules or structures than is absolutely necessary, and that indeed a grammar which provides only one structure for an unambiguous sentence is preferable to a grammar which makes a number of possible structures available[8] for that sentence, it does not necessarily follow that if we need more than one structure to account for a syntactic distribution, there will always be different semantic interpretations for the different structures; even if we assume a model of grammar as in Chomsky (1965) this will not be so.

Secondly, the [+joint] distinction which Lakoff and Peters suggest still leaves some matters of interpretation unexplained. Take, for instance, the acid test which Lakoff and Peters employ for PS-coordination vs. transformational coordination: *both* and *together*. *Both*, they claim, is typically [−joint], and will therefore only occur with transformationally derived sentences, while *together* is typically [+joint], and will occur with PS-coordinations. This indeed correlates quite nicely with the interpretations in (20,21):

20. Shakespeare and Marlowe wrote plays together.
21. Shakespeare and Marlowe both wrote plays.

However, in this case the [+joint] reading entails the [−joint] reading: (20) entails (21). This fact is unaccounted for, and it makes this sentence different from e.g. (19). In fact, it is even possible to find sentences where the [+joint] and the [−joint] readings entail each other, as in:

22. Becker and Curren are playing in the men's singles final at Wimbledon this year.

The Lakoff and Peters framework does not provide any suggestions as to why such entailment relations can hold between two such essentially different sentences: in fact, in a binary feature system such as they employ, [+joint] should entail [−joint], and vice versa. Furthermore, although *both* is a crucial test for S-derived coordination, it cannot occur in a coordination of full Ss:

21. *Shakespeare both wrote plays and Marlowe wrote plays.

These observations cannot be accounted for in the Lakoff and Peters framework.

Thirdly, as Gleitman (1965) observed in reaction to Smith (1969), plural NPs and conjoined NPs allow the same range of [± joint] interpretations, but there is no obvious internal structure for plural NPs that could be parallel to conjoined NPs and so account for this similarity.

Fourthly, the [+ joint] interpretation gives rise to some rather unlikely arithmetic — in a sentence like:

23. George and Bill speak five languages.

the number of languages spoken could vary from five to ten — but to claim that it is structurally embedded in natural language that speakers will systematically select one number of languages (five) as opposed to an unspecified number of languages (between five and ten) is intuitively unsatisfactory. They themselves observe, furthermore, that the ambiguity does not extend to coordinated NPs co-occurring with stative verbs and adjectives, which strongly suggests that the [± joint] distinction is not a structural aspect of coordinated NPs: we can conclude, therefore, that the [+ joint] ambiguity which Lakoff and Peters postulate for coordinated NPs is not adequately supported by the facts of interpretation.

Although there is arguably no semantic motivation for the [± joint] distinction, there could still be a syntactic motivation for the distinction which Lakoff and Peters propose. They themselves observed that sentences like (24):

24.   John and Harry went fishing.

could be paraphrased by means of either (25) or (26):

25.   John went fishing with Harry.
26.   Harry went fishing with John.

In order to account for this fact, they propose two rules, *Preposition Adjunction* and *Conjunct Movement*, which apply only to sentence-initial, topmost PS-coordinated binary branching NPs. These rules delete *and*, adjoin *with* to the right of one NP, and then adjoin *with NP* to the right of the VP. Thus they account for the fact that both (25) and (26) are paraphrases of (24): for Lakoff and Peters, the order of coordination, both PS-coordination and derived coordination, is apparently irrelevant. Although there might seem to be some motivation for this proposal at first sight, it faces some significant problems: there is, for instance, no obvious reason why (27) should not be derived, by the same method, from (28):

27.   John and Bill went to the pub with Sue.
28.   John, Sue and Bill went to the pub.

Secondly, the rule gives intuitively the wrong results in quite a number of cases: consider (22), which will yield:[9]

29.   Becker is playing with Curren in the men's singles final at Wimbledon this year.

Even if we correct the preposition to *against,* this does not resolve the fact that such prepositional phrases are considerably less 'agent-like' than the corresponding coordinated NPs; consider:

30.   Becker is playing Curren in the singles final.

in which the object-role of Curren is even clearer than it is in (29).

Thirdly, and most significantly, this pair of rules constitutes an unwarranted violation of Ross's (1967) *Coordinate Structure Constraint,* which states that in a coordinate structure, no conjunct may be moved, nor may any element contained in a conjunct be moved out of that conjunct. We can conclude that the Lakoff and Peters proposal, although a clear step forward, is still suspect from both the semantic, and from the syntactic point of view.

This, however, still leaves us with the problem that there is no source from which we can derive sentences like (14,18,19) if we wish to derive constituent coordination from the coordination of grammatical sentences quite obviously, coordinations are either *sentence-paraphrasable* or *non-sentence paraphrasable.* Let us see if there are any clear differences between these two types.

Lakoff and Peters suggest that coordinations are symmetrical, i.e. that the actual order of conjunction is irrelevant to semantic interpretation. This must be incorrect, since there are many cases like (31) where, if we reverse the order of coordination, the interpretation will change radically:

31.   She died, and we buried her.

Actually, that the order of coordination matters will be obvious from the fact that it can be *referred* to by means of e.g. *in that order, not necessarily in that order* or *vice versa*:

32.   John arrived and Mary left.
33.   John arrived and Mary left, in that order.
34.   John arrived and Mary left, though not in that order.

But what we find is that it is *not* possible to refer to the order of coordination in a non-sentence paraphrasable coordination: only in S-paraphrasable coordinations can we refer to order:

13

35.   *John and Mary are alike, in that order.
36.   *Jimmie and Timmie are a pair of fools, though not in that order.
37.   *Two and two make four, or vice versa.

One construction which makes crucial use of the order of coordination is *respectively* which, roughly stated, relates the first term of a set of coordinately conjoined terms to the first term of the second set, the second term to the second term of the second set, and so on. We would therefore expect that non-S-paraphrasable coordinations will not allow *respectively*, while S-paraphrasable ones will. This expectation is borne out:

38.   *John, Bill, Harry and Paul are a good team and a fine pair of friends, respectively.
39.   John and Mary live in Fowlmere and Duxford, respectively.

We can therefore conclude that one crucial difference between S-paraphrasable and non-S-paraphrasable coordinations is that S-paraphrasable coordinations have an inherent order of coordination which is potentially (though not necessarily) relevant to interpretation, while non-S-paraphrasable ones do not. It should be noted, though, that 'Non-S-paraphrasable' is not a *structural* property of the coordinated constituents themselves, but are selectional properties of the predicates in question. Certain predicates, like *be alike* or *make four* simply require a plural or a conjoined subject, and in their interpretation, they are not 'distributive' (see Hoeksema, 1983). The properties of the predicate do not apply to all the members of the subject conjunction: the same applied to plural subjects that co-occur with a symmetrical predicate. S-paraphrasable coordinations are distributive, and it is precisely this quality of 'distributiveness' which makes them S-paraphrasable. As semantics gained a more prominent place in linguistics, this characteristic of distribution came to be recognised as one of the strong points of the deletion-based approach. McCawley (1981) puts this as follows:

And and *or* have an important characteristic ... namely, that when they conjoin propositions that are the same but for one item, the conjoined proposition may be expressed in the form of a simple sentence with a conjoined part ... The relationship ... corresponds to the grammatical transformation of *Conjunction Reduction*, whereby conjoined clauses that differ only in one item can be replaced by a simple clause that involves conjoining that item. (McCawley, 1981: 17-18)

1.1.4 Summary

In the period after the publication of Chomsky (1957), and before and around the publication of Chomsky (1965),[10] the progress made in the description of coordination can be characterised as follows: initially it was assumed that all coordination is coordination of constituents, which could be derived transformationally from coordinations of grammatical sentences. Convincing evidence to the contrary soon emerged: not all coordination is constituent coordination, nor can all coordination be derived from coordination of grammatical sentences. A detailed attempt, by Lakoff and Peters, to associate PS- and transformational sources for coordination with differences in interpretation, can be deemed unsuccessful. This leaves us with the following state of affairs: there are two types of coordination, namely S-paraphrasable, which allows reference to the order of coordination, and is distributive in interpretation, and non-S-paraphrasable, which has neither of these characteristics.

1.2 EARLY UNITARY APPROACHES

The debate on whether coordinations should be derived by means of PS-rules or by means of transformational rules continued, with increased vigour, after the publication of Chomsky (1965). Two very good examples of theories of this period are Tai (1969) and Dougherty (1970, 1971). The former opts for the transformational approach, the latter for the PS-rule approach. It is interesting to note, in this connection, that neither Dougherty nor Tai advances a principled reason for opting for one approach rather than the other. Both have the same goal, namely to account for the correct distribution of grammatical and ungrammatical sentences involving coordinating conjunctions: that they have selected different means to do so seems entirely coincidental. Both types of account faced major problems.

The main problem for a PS-rule approach within the Standard Theory framework as it was set out in Chomsky (1965), which allows transformations like Passive to operate on Deep Structure, is the following, as was pointed out in Gazdar (1981): if there is a coordination of an active and a passive VP as in (40):

40.   John kicked the dog and was bitten by it.

then, given that the output of the PS-rule component is the input to the PS-rule component, it will be impossible for PS-rules alone to handle (40), since in that model PS-rules cannot generate passive VPs directly.

The main problem for the transformational approach will be to restrict deletions, and to recover the deletions that have applied: Deep Structure is the input to semantic interpretation and to T-rules, so that rules which derive non-S-coordination from S-coordination will have to be recoverable somehow.[11]

1.2.1 Tai

Tai (1969) proposes a theory of coordinate constructions in which non-S-coordinations are derived from S-coordinations transformationally. The important contribution Tai has made is the extension of Ross's (1970) observation that the directionality of *branching* of verbs is the inverse of the directionality of *deletion* of verbs: if a verb is on a right branch, then the leftmost occurrence of the identical verb will delete, while if it is on a left branch, then the rightmost occurrence will delete.[12] Tai follows Sanders (1969) in extending this constraint (henceforth the *Directionality Constraint*, DC) to all coordinate deletions. It is easy to see how this would work for English. Let us take a structure like (41) as the deep structure for sentences (42-44):

16

41.

42. John kicked the dog and John hit the cat.
43. John kicked the dog and Peter kicked the cat.
44. John kicked the dog and Peter hit the dog.

The constraint on directionality of deletion will now make the following predictions: Subject NP and verb will delete forwards (i.e. the *subsequent* occurrence of the identical constituent disappears), and the object NP will delete backwards (i.e. the *antecedent* occurrence of the identical constituent disappears). Deletions which do not obey the DC will be ungrammatical. These predictions turn out to be correct:

45. John kicked the dog and Ø hit the cat.
46. John kicked the dog and Peter Ø the cat.
47. John kicked Ø and Peter hit the dog.
48. *Ø kicked the dog, and John hit the cat.
49. *John Ø the dog, and Peter kicked the cat.
50. *John kicked the dog, and Peter hit Ø.

In addition to proposing this extension of the Directionality Constraint, Tai proposed the *Highest Identical Constituent Constraint* (HICC), to account for the following two observations: in sentences which have an identical subject as well as an identical verb, one cannot delete the verb before the subject has been deleted, and in sentences with identical objects and identical verbs, verb and object have to be deleted together, and one cannot delete either the verb or the object separately:

51. John kicked the dog and Ø kicked the cat.
52. *John kicked the dog and John Ø the cat.
53. *John kicked the dog and Peter Ø the dog.
54. *John kicked Ø the Peter kicked the dog.

The HICC stipulates that only the highest identical constituent can be deleted in a coordination, where 'highest' is defined as 'nearest to the topmost S node'. Thus, identical subjects will be deleted before identical verbs, and not vice versa, and identical VPs will be deleted before the identical verbs and objects that they immediately dominate.

Although the HICC accounts quite neatly for sentences (51-54), it faces some problems if the identical constituents (let us call these the *deletion target constituents, deletion target sites,* or *deletion target* for short) do not form a continuous string. Sentence (55), for example, can be reduced to (56), (57), or to (58), and none of these are bad. The HICC predicts that (57) should be bad in the same way that (52-54) are bad:

55. John kissed Mary and John hugged Mary.
56. John kissed Mary and Ø hugged Mary.
57. John kissed Ø and John hugged Mary.
58. John kissed Ø and Ø hugged Mary.

There are also some problems for the Directionality Constraint. In a sentence with both direct and indirect objects, we can derive the following directionality conflict: if the indirect object follows the direct object, then an identical verb and an identical object will delete forwards together. Identical direct objects, if accompanied by identical indirect objects, will delete backwards together. Identical verb plus identical indirect object will delete forwards — which is a problem for the DC, which predicts that the identical direct and indirect objects, which are on right branches, should always delete backwards:[13]

59. John gave a present to Mary, and Peter Ø Ø to Sue.
60. John gave Ø Ø, and Peter sold a record to Mary.
61. My father gave me a record, and my mother Ø Ø a book.
62. *John gave Ø to Mary, and Peter Ø a present to Sue.
63. *My father gave Ø a record and my mother Ø me a book.

Neither the DC nor the HICC, therefore, is perfect. Of course, the transformational approach advocated by Tai also faces the problems observed by Smith (1969), namely those cases where a non-S coordination contains a symmetrical predicate and therefore cannot be paraphrased by means of a coordination of grammatical sentences. In his attempt to overcome this difficulty, Tai proposes a set of rules to account for non-S-paraphrasable sentences which illustrates quite clearly (though not intentionally) the futility of such an approach. The derivation of a sentence like (64) goes as follows (Tai 1969:99):

64.   John and Bill conferred.

Identity Deletion applies to the input sentence (deep structure) (64a) to yield (64b):

64a.   John conferred with Bill and Bill conferred with John.
64b.   John conferred with Bill, and Bill Ø with John.

Optional restructuring (regrouping) of subjects and prepositional phrases applies, together with obligatory *respectively*-insertion, to yield:

64c.   *John and Bill conferred with Bill and John, respectively.

Each-Other-Pronominalisation (still a respected rule in those days) applies to (64c) to give us:

64d.   *John and Bill conferred with each other, respectively.

Respectively, inserted obligatorily under (64c) is now deleted obligatorily, and thus constitutes a reprehensible case of what Pullum (1976) has very aptly called a 'Duke of York' gambit:

64e.   John and Bill conferred with each other.

A rule called *Prep-each-other-Deletion* then deletes the reciprocal pronoun inserted under (64d), and that will give us (64).

This laborious approach shows quite a few of the less desirable idiosyncrasies of some of the work done in the Standard Theory: an *ad hoc* rule is invented to introduce an element which triggers another rule, only to be deleted subsequently by yet another *ad hoc* rule. Obviously, this is a system of rules which has very little to recommend it.[14] Equally obviously, deriving non-S-paraphrasable coordinations from deep structure S-coordinations almost necessarily commits one to also deriving plurals from underlying S-coordinations: as Gleitman

(1965) observed, plurals and non-S-paraphrasable coordinations occur in precisely the same environments. This is what Tai does: the machinery outlined above, augmented with a rule of *Plural Formation*, is used to derive (66) from (65):

65.   One man came and another man came.
66.   Two men came.

Needless to say, this approach will fail for most plurals, namely all those cases in which the number of underlying sentences in the coordination cannot be established,[15] as in:

67.   Most of the men stayed at home.

Nor will this machinery solve the problem it was designed to account for; a sentence like:

68.   Two and two make four.

will not have an underlying structure, unless it is the hopelessly tautologous and intractable:

68a.   One and one and one and one make one and one and one and one.

We can conclude that the transformational approach can account quite neatly for some facts, but, as it now stands, provides an inadequate and highly counterintuitive description of non-S-paraphrasable coordinations.[16]

1.2.2 Dougherty

Dougherty (1970, 1971), written before Tai (1969), but published later, takes a completely different line. Dougherty recognises that not all coordination can be PS-derived (active and passive VPs are one obvious problem for base coordination in a Standard Theory approach), but he wants to limit the role of transformations as much as possible. He assumes that there is a conjunction transformation, but that this is a substitution transformation rather than a deletion transformation. PS-rules generate a dummy symbol in the places where lexical material will have to be inserted by the conjunction substitution rule, in a way that will become clearer below. For Dougherty, all coordination is coordination of major categories in the base by means of a PS-rule of the following general form (Dougherty, 1970:864).

$$X ====> (Q) X^n (Adv.)$$

where Q = distributive quantifier: each, all, both, either, neither.
   Adv. = distributive adverb: at once etc.
   X = major category: S, NP, VP

Semantic interpretation of a coordinate conjoined node is accounted for by features assigned to the node.

The first thing that we need to observe is that Dougherty's approach will fail to account for any coordination which is not major category coordination: only major categories can be coordinated in the above schema. Sentences like:

69. John ate rice and Bill fish.
70. Richard gave a bunch of flowers to Marianne, and a button-hole to Sue.

are clearly outside the domain of Dougherty's approach, and some sort of deletion rule will have to be invoked to account for them. This, of course, also makes vacuous the claim that only major categories can be conjoined: if one leaves non-constituent coordination out of consideration, then quite obviously there will be little force to the generalisation that only major categories can be conjoined. Dougherty's approach, although much more detailed than Tai's, and much better worked out, is therefore rather more restricted in scope.

Nevertheless, the two theories cover a sizeable amount of comparable data, and can therefore be fruitfully compared. To illustrate how Dougherty's rule of *Conjunction Substitution* works, we shall examine the derivation of sentence (71), a sentence which in Tai's (1969) account would be derived by simply forward-deleting the identical subject NP:

71. John kissed Mary and was reprimanded by her father.

Dougherty's account of such a sentence would run more or less as follows (1970:865-6): first of all, the VP is coordinated *n* times in the matrix sentence, and an equal number of matched sentences are generated independently by the base rules. This gives, for (71), the following structure:

71a.

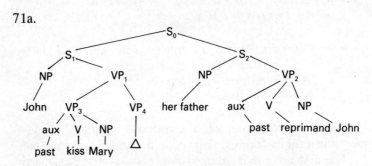

The actual coordination is under VP_1; VP_4 terminates in the dummy symbol $\triangle$. S_2 is generated independently from S_1. The first operation which now takes place is *Passive*, which converts the string under S_2 into:

71b.

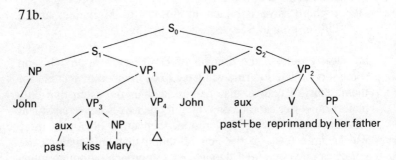

Then the conjunction Substitution Transformation replaces the dummy VP with the real VP, giving us the following structure:

71c.

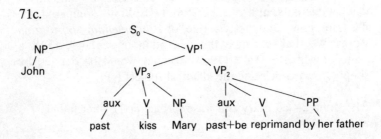

It will be clear from this sequence of structures that Conjunction Substitution does rather more than what Dougherty claims it does.[17] It has not only substituted, it has also deleted. In (71b), there are two occurrences of *John*, while in (71c), there's only one. The deletion has taken place in accordance with the Directionality Constraint outlined in section 1.2.1: the identical subject NPs are on left branches, so deletion operates forward. Had deletion operated backwards, then the result would have been unacceptable:

71d.   *Kissed Mary and John was reprimanded by her father.

Dougherty does not mention the deletion observed here, nor does he refer to the Directionality Constraint. But the DC is important also for the Conjunction Substitution transformation; a considerable problem for this particular approach is the number and position of dummy VPs. The only place where they may occur is coordinated to the leftmost lexical VP: had the dummy VP_4 in (71a) been coordinated to VP_2, then the result would have been:

71e.   John was reprimanded by her father and kissed Mary.

This is perfectly grammatical, but it does not mean what (71) means: Dougherty's claim that the interpretation of a coordinated node is determined by the features that appear on that node will have to be supplemented somehow with a statement about the order of coordination, since only coordinations that co-occur with symmetrical predicates are unordered.

Thirdly, consider sentence (72):

72.   John fell down, was picked up, walked a few steps, was knocked down again, and stayed down this time.

Here there are two passive VPs juxtaposed between three active ones. If one were to generate the active VPs in coordination with the dummy 'placeholder' VPs, one will have to ensure that the dummies are generated in precisely the correct number, and in precisely the right places inbetween the active VPs, in order to get (72). Even if this could somehow be done, there is still a problem, because the source for (72) will be (72a):

72a.   John fell down Δ John walked a few steps Δ John stayed down this time, someone picked John up, and someone knocked John down again.

Here, the Conjunction Substitution rule has to know which VP to replace for which dummy; if e.g. the last VP is substituted for the first dummy, then we get a highly peculiar sequence of events:

72b.   John fell down, was knocked down again, walked a few steps, was picked up, and stayed down this time.

Dougherty makes no mechanisms available that could overcome these difficulties. Given the considerable problems that the Conjunction Substitution faces, and given the fact that these difficulties are clearly figments of the approach rather than difficulties inherent in the structure of coordinated VPs, we must reject the Conjunction Substitution account. As we shall see later on, directionality and linear position, which pose such a problem here for the PS-rule approach, are of crucial importance to any theory of coordination.

The difficulties observed are actually figments of the model, and this can be seen quite readily if we eliminate the Passive transformation.[18] If we do so, and we furthermore eliminate the assumption that major category coordination does not arise exclusively in the base, then we have eliminated the need for a Conjunction Substitution transformation altogether. This runs counter to what Dougherty wants to do, which is to establish that all syntactic and semantic properties of a coordinated node are accounted for by features assigned to that node. It does not, however, detract from one of the generalisations expressed in the PS-rule schema, which is that all major categories can appear as coordinations. If we maintain a rule schema of the sort that Dougherty advocates in addition to one or more coordinate deletion rules, then we can also preserve his account for the observation (Dougherty, 1970:854) that semantic non-singulars (= nondistributive predicates) must occur either with a plural or with a coordination, and we need not appeal to the unlikely deep structures and baroque transformational machinery that a purely transformational account like Tai (1969) requires for sentences like:

73.   John, Bill and Harry are quite similar.
74.   The boys are quite similar.

1.2.3 Summary

If one compares an early fully transformational account (Tai) to an account of coordination which aims to eliminate all deletion rules from the grammar (Dougherty), one must conclude that a combination of direct coordination of categories, and derivation by means of deletion from coordinated grammatical sentences will provide the best description for coordinated structures in English: nonconstituent coordinations cannot be accounted for by base coordination in an *Aspects* model, and non-base constituent coordination (passive and active VPs) also produces some serious problems. The transformational approach finds itself in grave difficulties over the co-occurrence of coordinations and semantic nonsingulars: to derive these coordinations (and, by extension, plurals) from underlying coordinated sentences which themselves do not contain coordinations is a particularly unfruitful enterprise.[19]

But this leaves us with a large overlap where the base-generation account and the transformational account can compete seriously — essentially, the two approaches compete in all those cases of constituent coordination which do not involve semantic nonsingulars. I shall address the balance between base co-ordination and derived coordination in more detail in Chapter 2, where I provide evidence that this balance should be heavy on the side of the deletion rules, and light on the side of PS-rules.

1.2.4 First diversion: respectively-constructions

One question which has played a considerable role in the post-*Aspects* discussion about coordination was that of constructions involving *respectively*. McCawley (1968) observed the following: a plural NP generally refers to a set, so one should be able to perform set-theoretic operations on plural NPs and the indices they bear. In a construction like:

75.   The string quartets of Prokofiev and Ravel.

reference is not to string quartets produced by Prokofiev and Ravel as a team, but to the string quartets by Prokofiev on the one hand, and to the one string quartet by Ravel on the other. Therefore, McCawley (1968) wants to derive (75) from underlying (75a), with as an intermediary stage (75b):

75a.   The string quartets of Prokofiev and the string quartet of Ravel.
75b.   The string quartets and quartet of Prokofiev and Ravel, respectively.

The *respectively*-transformation which is responsible for turning (75a) into (75b) is a type of reordering-cum-deletion-cum-insertion transformation which McCawley does not formalise, but which is intuitively fairly clear. To get from (75b) to (75), the subject NPs have to be collapsed, and *respectively* has to be deleted again. Support for this procedure could be derived from the fact that a sentence like (76) could be paraphrased as (76a); the *respectively*-rule here has turned non-constituent coordination into constituent coordination:

76.   John kissed Mary and Bill Ø Sue.
76a.   John and Bill kissed Mary and Sue, respectively.

There is, therefore, some support for the procedure that turns (75a) into (75b). No such support exists for the rule that turns (75b) into (75); I have already criticised a similar derivation of plurals by means of a *respectively*-rule of some sort in the discussion of Tai (1969) in section 1.2.1. *Respectively*-constructions, however, featured prominently in the discussion about coordination in the late sixties and early seventies, and they have recently begun to make a hesitant comeback in the literature (see e.g. Goodall's (1984) treatment of Gapping). Dougherty (1970) also discusses *respectively*-constructions, and his discussion reflects two things quite neatly: another shortcoming of the approach to coordination which seeks to maximise the role of base-generation, and the role of *respectively* in coordination.

Dougherty proposes to have a rule which rewrites every topmost S-node as [± respectively]; this feature is then percolated down to all lower nodes. For a sentence like (76), this would give us the following structure:

76b.   John [+res] Δ [+res] past[+res] kiss[+res] Mary[+res] Δ
[+res] and Bill[+res] past [+res] kiss[+res] Sue[+res]

A *Respectively-Substitution* transformation then inserts *Bill* and
Sue for the coordinated dummy NP nodes in the manner outlined in section 1.2.3, and inserts *respectively*. This approach,
inelegant through its massive use of features, and involving
surreptitious deletion of the identical verb *kiss*, also has some
very specific shortcomings which are of special interest to us.
Consider sentence (77):

77.   John was hunting lions, but Mary was scared of big game.

Respectively here yields the totally unacceptable:

78.   *John but Mary were hunting lions but scared of big
game, respectively.

Obviously, *respectively* cannot be allowed freely in the
manner that Dougherty suggests. Secondly, the 'dummy node'
proposal gives us no obvious way of relating sentences to their
respectively-paraphrases — sentence (76), for example, is a
sentence coordination, without dummy nodes, while (76a) is
derived from an NP-coordination involving dummy nodes,
which leaves unanswered the question of why we interpret (76)
in the same way as (76a).
    These objections also weigh heavily against e.g. Hudson's
(1976:549) proposal which intends to derive (76) from a structure similar to (76a), by means of a rule which Hudson calls
Conjunct Postposing; this movement rule takes everything but
the leftmost member of a coordination, and right-sister-adjoins
it to the clause in which the conjunct occurs[20] (Hudson,
1976:547). In this way, (79) is derived from (79a) by means of
obligatory conjunct postposing:

79.   You drink too much and you talk too loud.
79a.   *You and you drink and talk too much and too loud.

Hudson's proposal runs into serious difficulties if Conjunct
Postposing is allowed to apply as freely as he suggests; consider
for example sentence (80):

27

80.   My wife and I have given up fatty foods and alcohol.

There is nothing to stop Conjunct Postposing from turning this into (80a), which has a completely different interpretation:

80a.   My wife has given up fatty foods and I, alcohol.

It is difficult to see how Conjunct Postposing could be prevented from simply extraposing *any* coordination into a Gapping-type structure; even non-S-paraphrasable coordinations could be postposed by this rule as Hudson outlines it. It is interesting to see that Hudson's account, which bases itself on base generation of coordinated constituents, and subsequent postposing, is almost the exact reverse of Tai's (1969) account, and runs into almost exactly the reverse of the problems which we have observed for this account. Note also that the observed problems here revolve crucially around the rule which rearranges linear order within the coordination.

Hudson's proposal, in addition to suffering from the inadequacies observed above, is furthermore somewhat unrealistic in view of the processing difficulties hearers experience when they interpret *respectively*-sentences. There can be no doubt that McCawley's, Dougherty's and Hudson's observations about what *respectively* requires are correct: what it requires (if we view the matter from the interpretation angle) is that a constituent, either a plural or a coordination, should be broken up into two or more parts, and these parts should be paired, in the linear order of the original coordination (if coordination is involved, that is: the problem gets rather more complicated if plurals are involved) with parts of constituents similarly broken up. This is an operation which is relatively easy to carry out if a hearer is informed beforehand that this is what is required of him, and only two pairs of constituents (the minimum number) are involved. However, *respectively* occurs at the *end* of a sentence, and *respectively*-sentences do not have special intonational characteristics to alert the hearer to the fact that they will have to perform a processing operation which will require them to remember the entire sentence *verbatim*, in its exact linear order, and that parsing can only start after the word *respectively* has occurred: this is why hearers are almost systematically unable to answer a simple question like: 'Who seemed to be trying to kiss Mary?' after hearing (81):

81. John, Bill, Harry and Paul seemed to be trying to kiss
     Harriet, Selina, Mary and Sue respectively.

The answer to such a question is easy enough to work out if one
has pen and paper to hand, but not if one only hears the
sentence once. For that reason, *respectively*-sentences are
extremely rare in spontaneous speech, and are usually restricted
to conjoined pairs of constituents. If Hudson's proposal is to be
interpreted, in any sense, as reflecting some sort of underlying
psychological reality, then one has to conclude that what speakers and hearers do all the time is to carry out this extremely
complex *respectively*-operation. This is an unlikely state of
affairs, and one which leaves us with no explanation of why it is
so difficult to interpret *respectively*-constructions when they
occur in spontaneous speech. One can conclude, therefore, that
Hudson's proposal to derive Gapping-type sentences which
crucially involves some kind of respectively-type reordering
within conjuncts, is not viable.

   The criticism of 'lack of psychological appeal' can also be
applied to Dougherty's proposal for *respectively*-sentences:
since he marks all sentences as [+respectively] or [−respect-
ively], there is no reason why hearers shouldn't interpret a
sentence with a coordination or a plural as ambiguous between
[+respectively] and [−respectively] until the point where they
hear, or fail to hear, the disambiguating word *respectively* itself,
and that again means that *respectively*-sentences should be as
readily interpretable as 'normal' sentences, which they clearly
are not.

   Having criticised various approaches to *respectively*, I will
offer no real alternative. The statement of a rule like *respectively*, which I see as a stylistic optional rule applying to surface
structure, will have to run more or less as follows; this statement, though inadequate the informal, captures most of the
observations about *respectively* given above:

   Interpret the highest[21] two (or more[22]) plurals or sentence-
   paraphrasable[23] coordinate constituents as consisting of two
   (or more[22]) separately identifiable entities, actions or events
   in the same sentence, and in the same linear order, in which
   the plurals and the coordinations occurred.

This rule will 'undo' McCawley's or Tai's *respectively*-

collapsing rule. From the formulation it will be clear that it is not of central importance to coordination or deletion under identity. Furthermore, it is a stylistic operation which can be quite difficult to process without pen and paper, is only very rarely found in spontaneous speech, and will cause speaker judgments to go 'fuzzy' almost at once. For these reasons, I shall not involve a detailed account of *respectively*-constructions in the discussion of coordination.[24]

1.2.5 Second diversion: Dik's functional approach

Dik's (1968) book *Coordination* should, on the face of it, be of considerable importance to us here. The reason why I have chosen to discuss it under a heading 'second diversion' (with all its connotations of marginality) is that Dik's book is as much an attack on Standard Theory Transformational Generative Grammar as it is an account of coordination. A considerable portion of the discussion in the book is not of central relevance to what concerns us here. I shall not discuss it in full, but restrict myself to Dik's functional approach to coordinated structures. For a very insightful and detailed discussion of the whole of Dik's book, the reader is referred to Matthews (1969).

Dik (1968:71) rejects what he calls the 'reduction postulate', which derives constituent coordination from underlying co-ordination of sentences for three reasons. He cannot agree with the derived constituent structure that results from the application of coordinate reduction rules, he notes problems with the notion of identity implicit in the reduction postulate, and he notes the by now familiar non-availability of a coordinated sentence source for constructions like (82):

82. John and Mary collided.

Dik's first objection, which involves derived structure, is based mainly on the fact that if we derive a sentence like:

83. John and Mary, Roger and Helen, and Bill and Sue went to the show.

from an underlying coordination of six simple sentences not

containing coordinations, we cannot account for the fact that, given proper intonation, there can be an interpretation in which there are three pairs of coordinations, rather than one coordination containing six members. This is rather a disingenuous objection: a rule which recursively coordinates S can achieve the correct pairing of NPs by first introducing S three times, and then twice for each of the three Ss thus coordinated. The appropriate deletion rules and pruning rules (Tai's (1969) proposal will work quite adequately in this case) will achieve the desired structure. Quite apart from this, one can also have serious doubts about the strength of arguments of this type, since it is extremely difficult to argue about the correctness or incorrectness of derived constituent structures in the absence of rules which *require* a *specific* constituent structure for the purposes of interpretation. Arguments of the type advanced by Dik are usually of an emotional kind: constituent structures are 'felt' to be correct or incorrect. Yet there are also some non-emotional arguments for specific derived constituent structures which relate to intonation patterns (see e.g. Ross (1967)); for a brief discussion, see note 28 of this chapter.

Dik's second objection is a much more serious one. In the period in which Dik's book appeared, the notion of identity required for the purposes of deletion was not given much thought: it was simply assumed that identity is a notion which is easy enough to define. Dik observed that referential identity must be what is needed for the subject in a sentence like (84) if we wish to derive it in accordance with the reduction postulate. This makes a theory of reference a necessary prerequisite for a theory of coordination (Dik, 1968:81).

84.   The man was old, tall, tired, and friendly.

Such a sentence cannot be interpreted as referring to four different men, which Dik claims would be a possible interpretation for a sentence consisting of four separate coordinated sentences: therefore, under the reduction postulate, there is a potential difference in interpretation between source sentences and derived sentences which may be difficult to resolve.

One may have reason to question Dik's intuitions about sentence (84): it is quite possible for the source sentence for (84) under the reduction postulate to have exactly the same interpretation as (84) itself. Examples (85/86) demonstrate quite clearly that referential identity is not a necessary prerequisite for coordinate deletion:

85.   Many people went to Greece and Spain this summer.
86.   I hit, and Bill kicked someone.

In (85) the same people that went to Greece did not necessarily also go to Spain, and in (86), the person that I hit is not necessarily the same person whom Bill hits. Nevertheless, Dik's point here is well taken: the notion of identity is of central importance to a theory of deletion under identity. Furthermore, it seems that there is a quite definite problem here: at least in initial position in the sentence, one can find cases where one might perhaps wish to argue that sameness of intended reference is needed for coordinate deletion to apply to existentially quantified expressions:

87. Someone bought a box of cigars and a bottle of gin.

Here, the preferred interpretation is where the person buying the box of cigars is also the one buying the bottle of gin. This interpretation is *not* preferred or necessary for the S-coordinated sentence which, under the reduction postulate, is the source for (87):

88.   Someone bought a box of cigars and someone bought a
      bottle of gin.

The reduction postulate faces a potential problem here which we shall return to in considerable detail in Chapter 3.

Dik's third objection is one which we have already encountered in section 1.1.3. Dik documents this counterargument very carefully and in great detail; however, he does not accept Lakoff and Peters' (1969) proposal to have both phrasal and sentential coordination. Instead, he employs rule schemata of two essentially different types: one schema conjoining *categories* (e.g. plural NP =====> Member ....&+Member$_n$), and another conjoining syntactic *functions*; subjects, for instance, are conjoined by a rule: (Sentence======> subject(+......subject$_n$) predicator + adjunct). This allows Dik to account for the difference between (89) and (90):

89. John and Harry embrace frequently.
90. John and Mary sleep separately.

In (89), we have a coordination functioning as the sole subject of a Predicator, while in (90) we have a coordination of which the members each function separately as subjects. This correlates with the [±joint] interpretation of coordinate NPs which we have discussed in section 1.1.3. Dik's proposal has the advantage of not being subject to the objections we have raised against Lakoff and Peters (1969), and accounts quite well for the difference in interpretation of coordinated subject NPs in (89,90).

However, Dik's account faces serious problems in those cases where non-category coordination or non-function coordination is involved: rules like Gapping and Right-node Raising produce results which can clearly not be accounted for by the rule schemata outlined above. This means that for sentences like (91,92), we will still need a deletion rule:

91. John caught a rabbit, and Peter Ø a fox.
92. John killed Ø and Peter cooked the rabbit.

Also in later work (Dik, 1980), we find that the functional account remains restricted to coordination of single categories: Nonconstituent coordination remains intractable for Dik's approach, as it did for Dougherty's. Therefore, Dik's attack on transformational generative grammar as inadequate for constructions like coordination loses much, if not all of its force, since nonconstituent coordination is precisely the area which provides the most powerful evidence for the need for deletion transformations.

1.3 GAPPING AND RELATED RULES

1.3.1 Gapping

One of the most important papers written about deletion in coordinated structures is undoubtedly Ross's (1970)[25] paper entitled 'Gapping and the Order of Constituents'. This paper is not primarily concerned with finding a precise formulation for the rule of Gapping,[26] but with a method of establishing whether a sentence has SOV or SVO word order in underlying representations (Ross, 1970:250). However, in addition to drawing attention to the fact that Gapping is a phenomenon which is pretty widespread in the world's languages, it also proposes a hypothesis which has turned out to be extremely important in the literature on coordinate deletions:

> The order in which GAPPING operates depends on the order of elements at the time that the rule applies; if the identical elements are on left branches, GAPPING operates forward; if they are on right branches, it operates backwards. (Ross, 1970:251)

I have already referred to this constraint as the Directionality Constraint (DC); it allowed Ross to account for e.g. the fact that Japanese, which is verb-final, has the Gapping pattern SO+SOV, while English, which is verb-medial, has the Gapping pattern SVO+SO:

93. Watakusi-wa sakana- o Ø, Biru-wa gohan- o tabeta.
     I   (prt. fish (prt.) Ø Bill (prt.) rice (prt.) ate
94. I ate fish, and Bill Ø rice.

The DC has been extended to cover all deletions under identity in coordinated structures (see Tai, 1969), and it has, in its formulation as a 'mirror-image' rule, been subjected to considerable criticism (see e.g. Maling (1972), Hankamer (1972)) which we shall not discuss in detail here. The rule of Gapping itself, as well as other rules which delete under identity in coordinated structures, have been the subject of a highly interesting and stimulating discussion which still continues.

1.3.2 Jackendoff

A very lively exchange of ideas took place after the publication of Jackendoff's (1972) paper 'Gapping and Related Rules'. In this paper, Jackendoff made a few very important observations about Gapping, especially in English. First of all, he observed that Gapping is a rule which is restricted to coordinated structures:

95.   *Sam played tuba whenever Max Ø sax.

A logical consequence of this is, of course, that the conjunction in between the gapped clause and its antecedent must be a co-ordinating conjunction: *and, or,* or *but.*[27] Secondly, Jackendoff observed that Gapping crucially involves verbs: NPs deleted from the middle of a coordinated clause systematically give rise to unacceptable sentences (1972:21):

96.   Dolores gave incriminating evidence about Harry to the FBI, and Frank sent Ø to his mother-in-law.

This, for Jackendoff, is an important reason to distinguish between Gapping, which deletes from the middle of a clause, and Conjunction Reduction, which deletes from the end of a clause (1972:21):

97.   Vera sent a baby alligator to Max and Ø Ø a leather dinosaur to Bill.

Jackendoff also considers VP-deletion: a rule which, as the name suggests, deletes VPs, as a rule which is essentially different from Gapping. VPD always leaves behind a finite auxiliary, and this type of structure also occurs outside co-ordination (1972:27):

98.   Charlie will leave town if his mother-in-law doesn't Ø.

Having thus isolated Gapping as a rule which deletes verbs, plus possibly something else, from the middle of coordinated clauses, Jackendoff gives us a number of important observations on Gapping: observations which have as yet not received adequate attention in the literature.

Gapping cannot take place with unlike auxiliaries (though see Levin (1978) on what she calls Pseudogapping):

99.   *John has written the words, and Paul will Ø the music.

Gapping (at least in American English) does not tolerate unlike adverbs before the verb:

100. *Simon quickly dropped the gold, and Jack suddenly Ø the diamonds.

Like auxiliaries will gap along with the verb, and sometimes adverbs will gap along with the verb as well:

101. John has written the words, and Paul (*has) Ø the music.
102. Simon quickly dropped the gold, and Jack Ø Ø the diamonds.

In (102), the gap is *quickly dropped,* and not just *dropped.*[28] Jackendoff also cites Ross's observation that a negation attached to an auxiliary cannot gap, unless the conjunction is changed from *and* to *nor*:

103. I didn't eat fish and Bill didn't eat rice.
104. *I didn't eat fish and Bill Ø rice.
105. I didn't eat fish, nor Bill rice.

Identical NPs or PPs next to the verb can gap, if followed by another constituent:

106. John writes poetry in the garden, and Max Ø Ø in the bathroom.

Jackendoff then proceeds to give a demonstration that NPs also allow deletion 'from the middle':

107. Either Ted's gin from New Jersey or Bill's Ø from Iowa will satisfy the uneducated palates of our guests.

He also notes that peripheral nouns may be deleted:

108. I like Bill's yellow shirt, but not Max's.

He then proposes to collapse the four rules which could be held to be responsible for the example sentences cited above: Gapping, Ñ-Gapping, Ñ-deletion, and VP-deletion, into two: X̄-deletion and X̄-Gapping. The latter deletes the head of a phrase, all the material to the left of the head, and all but one constituent to the right of the head. The former, X̄-deletion, deletes the head of a phrase and everything to the right of it. I shall not discuss this proposal in any great detail, but merely cite some evidence that the generalisation which Jackendoff proposes is suspect.

First of all, Ross (1970) demonstrates that Gapping is a process which occurs in a number of languages. Ñ-Gapping, however, does not: while there are acceptable cases of Ñ-Gapping in English,[29] there are none in Dutch and German, although these two languages are closely related to English, and are very similar to it in main-clause Gapping:

109. John eats fish, and Bill Ø rice.
110. John isst Fish, und Bill Ø Reis.
111. John eet vis, en Bill Ø rijst.
112. My   wine from France   and yours Ø from
                              California are excellent.
113. *Mein Wein aus Frankreich und dein Ø aus
                              Kalifornien sind ausgezeichnet.
114. *Mijn wijn uit Frankrijk en jouw Ø uit
                              Californië zijn uitstekend.

It is possible not to use the noun *Wein* in German, or *wijn* in Dutch, but what then remains is certainly not something from which just the head NP is missing: *dein* changes to *deiner* in German and in Dutch *jouw* changes to *jouwe* (there is a similar change to nominal status in English, a fact which Jackendoff fails to account for), and in Dutch, the remnant (if it is a remnant rather than a pro-form) has to take a determiner *de*:

115. Mein Wein aus Frankreich und deiner aus Kalifornien sind ausgezeichnet.
116. Mijn wijn uit Frankrijk en de jouwe uit Californië zijn uitstekend.

Secondly, VP-deletion and Ñ-deletion are different in that Ñ-deletion is 'bidirectional' in coordinations: it may delete either forwards or backwards. VPD may only delete forwards in cordinated structures:

117. Is that your second glass, or your third Ø?
118. Is that your second Ø or your third glass?
119. Bill likes red wine, and Harry does Ø too.
120. *Bill does Ø, and Harry likes red wine too.

Thirdly, although Dutch and German both exhibit what Jackendoff calls N̄-deletion, they do not have VPD: as a matter of fact, English is probably the only language that *does* have VPD. The Dutch and German translations of (117) and (119), with the finite auxiliaries at the deletion site, are ungrammatical:

121. Ist das dein zweites Glas, oder dein drittes Ø?
122. Is dat je tweede glas, of je derde Ø?
123. *Bill mag Rotwein, und Harry macht Ø auch.
124. *Bill houdt van rode wijn, en Harry doet Ø ook.

Jackendoff's intended generalisations are not terribly promising, and have not been followed up in the literature. Nevertheless, he has made some crucial and challenging observations, observations which will play an important role in our discussion of coordinated structures.

1.3.3 Recoverability of deletion: Hankamer

Hankamer (1973) proposes a number of strong restrictions on coordinate deletions which he intends to be part of a larger restriction on the recoverability of deletions and movement, which he construes as 'the ability of a hearer to recover the underlying representation of a sentence which may have undergone various processes of ellipsis or rearrangement in the course of its derivation' (Hankamer, 1973:17). The motivation for such a constraint on recoverability will be clear: in a model of grammar where semantic interpretation is done on deep structure alone, the hearer must be able to find the deep structure on the basis of the surface structure that he is confronted with — in other words, he will have to 'undo' the derivation, which, in the case of deletions, involves recovering the material that has been lost in surface structure as a result of such rules as ellipsis and deletion. Recoverability of deletion is therefore not a constraint that ensures correct syntactic patterning of sentences, but one which helps to ensure an unequivocal relation between surface structure and interpretation of a sentence.

Hankamer's precise hypothesis is that structural ambiguity cannot arise as a result of deletion rules involving variables; the condition preventing such ambiguity (which in this case applies specifically to Gapping) is the no-ambiguity condition (NAC) which states that:

> Any application of Gapping which would yield an output structure identical to a structure derivable by Gapping from another source, but with the 'gap' at the left extremity, is disallowed. (Hankamer, 1973:29)

This rule is a rather more general statement of a pretty *ad hoc* rule in Jackendoff (1972) which was proposed to account for the fact that a sentence like (125):

125. Jack wants Mike to wash himself, and Arnie to shave himself.

is not ambiguous between a reading where Arnie is expected to go and shave himself, and one where Arnie expects Mike to shave himself. Hankamer added to Jackendoff's original observation the facts that (126) and (127) show the same type of non-ambiguity:

126. Max seemed to want Alice to get lost, and Susan to stay.
127. Max persuaded Jim to come to the party, and Alex to bring Susan.

This non-ambiguity is catered for quite neatly by the NAC. The NAC as a constraint on Gapping, however, has some serious shortcomings. First of all, it is quite restricted in its application. It is a constraint on recoverability, and not on acceptable or unacceptable syntactic patterns. It cannot account for those cases noted by Jackendoff where there are unlike auxiliaries or adverbs preceding the verb: cases in which Gapping yields unacceptable results. The NAC, in other words, will have to be supplemented to account for facts of this nature. Secondly, Hankamer himself notes that there are a few uncomfortable exceptions to the NAC in Jackendoff (1972): (128-130) are unambiguous violations of the NAC, since they have non-leftmost gaps, and cannot be interpreted as having leftmost gaps:

128. Massachusetts elected McCormack Congressman, and Pennsylvania Schweiker.

129. Max writes plays in the bedroom, and Harvey in the basement.
130. Paul Schachter has informed me that the basic order in Tagalog and related languages is VOS, Ives Goddard that the unmarked order in Algonkian is OVS; and Guy Carden that the basic order in Aleut is OSV. (cf. Ross:1970).

Hankamer suggests no alternative formulations of the NAC to remedy these shortcomings.[30]
   A third problem is the observational inadequacy of the NAC. Hankamer suggests that (131) is blocked if the gap is *wanted to put the eggplant*: according to the NAC, the gap should be *Max wanted to put* (Hankamer, 1973:31). This is a rather doubtful interpretation of the facts, and would certainly be incorrect for a sentence like (132):

131. Max wanted to put the eggplant on the table, and Harvey in the sink.
132. Drinking gives you cirrhosis, and smoking cancer.

Sentence (132) could not possibly be interpreted as having a leftmost gap: drinking does not give smoking cancer. Undoubtedly, sentence (131) is slightly different from such a clear-cut case as (132). It is of a type that may make readers smile, or raise their eyebrows or something — not because the sentence is unambiguous about Max wanting to put Harvey in the sink, but precisely because it is ambiguous (contrary to what the NAC claims) between a leftmost-gap reading, and a non-leftmost gap reading. Other sentences of this sort are (133-135):

133. David ties up his parcels with string, and his wife with ribbons.
134. Penny put the clothes in the drier, and Paul through the mangle.
135. Harry had steak for breakfast, and his secretary for dinner.

What happens in the interpretation of such sentences is not unlike what we saw in the interpretation of *respectively*-sentences in section 1.2.4: there, *respectively* required the reader to have remembered the sentence he had just heard *verbatim*, with all the constituents in their exact linear order.

However, the hearer was not informed that he should have done this until the end of the sentence, when he hears the word *respectively*. This is what makes it so difficult to process *respectively*-sentences with more than two coordinations of two constituents each. In 'gapped' sentences, a similar operation has to take place: In order to make sense of the structure that is formed by the remnant constituents of the gapped clause, the hearer has to pair the remaining constituents of the gapped clause with constituents from the antecedent[31] non-gapped clause. This means that the preceding clause has to be remembered *verbatim*, in its original linear order, and the hearer will not be aware that this is what is required of him until he hears the subsequent clause which contains the gap. Naturally, the more material there is to be remembered, the more difficult it will be to pair constituents: this may be one of the reasons why gapped clauses with three remnants are generally considered to be more awkward than those with two.[32] Hankamer's NAC serves to put the 'gap' as far to the left as possible in its clause, meaning that the constituents with which the remnants have to be paired will be as close to the remnants as possible, and this in turn means that there will be a minimum of material which has to be remembered *verbatim* in processing the gapped clause: there is minimal distance between the constituents in a gapped clause and their structural counterparts in the antecedent clause. In sentences (133-136), the hearer will follow an NAC-type strategy which requires the least amount of material to be stored *verbatim*, but this strategy of minimum effort in processing immediately highlights the 'funny' interpretation, and will cause hearers to look for an interpretation which violates the NAC. Such a reading will put the gap further to the right, and will therefore require the hearer to have remembered more of the clause antecedent to the gapped clause.

It will be clear that the NAC as an absolute constraint on syntactic configurations is incorrect. The problems raised by the NAC, to which we shall return briefly in Chapter 3, are attributable to processing facts rather than to universal constraints on grammatical rules. Sentences (133-135) are genuinely ambiguous, and even strikingly so,[33] while (132) is a clear and unambiguous violation of the NAC. Sentences of this type are serious counterexamples to the NAC, as are ambiguous sentences like:

41

136. Inflation will cause dissatisfaction today, and unemployment tomorrow.

One can also raise some theoretical objections at this point. A fourth objection is that the NAC, formulated specifically to prevent ambiguity as a result of Gapping, is an extremely powerful constraint: it makes simultaneous reference to the linear ordering of constituents in the surface structure of a sentence, plus the linear order of any other sentence containing the same lexical items, plus again the derivation of that sentence.[34] This power, given that its only legitimate use is to rule out the non-leftmost gapped readings of (125-127) — and remember that we have found the NAC to be too strict for the other examples discussed in this paragraph — is excessive. We can furthermore observe that (125-127), in their 'illegitimate' reading, require that Gapping should be allowed to 'eat into' a subordinate clause: this is something which Jackendoff (1972) had already observed is not allowed. The good effects of the NAC can quite easily be captured by the observation that Gapping only applies to coordinated clauses, and does not eat into subordinate clauses.

A fifth objection is that the general constraint against structural ambiguity of which the NAC forms part, the *Structural Recoverability Hypothesis* (SRH), is suspect. This hypothesis runs as follows:

Deletion rules involving variables are universally subject to a transderivational condition which prevents them from applying in such a way as to introduce structural ambiguity. (Hankamer, 1973:40)

Comparative Deletion and VP-deletion, both of which fall under the SRH, will clearly produce ambiguous sentences:

137. John likes horses more than Sue.
138. I am suggesting that you are wrong, and the others are, too.

Here the ambiguity is again, as with the counterexamples to the NAC, between a reading involving a leftmost deletion site, and one not involving a leftmost deletion site.

1.3.4 Peripherality: Langendoen

Although the NAC can be rejected as a condition on Gapping for various reasons, it does spell out one quite important characteristic: it refers to the linear surface order of constituents, and to the peripheral position of the deletion site in that linear order. These notions of surface linear order and peripherality were taken up by Langendoen in his 1975 paper entitled: 'Acceptable Conclusions from Unacceptable Ambiguity'. Langendoen rejects Hankamer's hypotheses, both on empirical grounds and because transderivational constraints like the SRH and NAC fitted badly in the standard TG framework that was then current, and failed to limit the generative capacity of grammars. The empirical objections Langendoen raises against the NAC are of interest here. Unfortunately, Langendoen's paper is concerned primarily with rejecting Hankamer's NAC and only one alternative which he provides to the NAC merits serious consideration. Langendoen notes that the NAC will have to be supplemented in some way, and he does so on the basis of sentences like:

139. Max wanted Ted to persuade Alex to see Mary, and Walt Ira

Here there are a number of deletion options involving the leftmost material *Max wanted*, but only one deletion is allowed, namely where the deletion site is [-----and *Max wanted Ted to persuade* Walt *to see* Ira]. To account for this, Langendoen proposed the *Non-left Peripheral NP Constraint* (NLPNPC), which claims that no coordinate deletion rule can apply so as to delete non-leftperipheral strings that contain NP (Langendoen, 1975:112). This constraint has the same effect as does Hankamer's NAC, and derives further support from sentences like (140-142):

140. *Jackendoff despises bassoonists and McCawley admires Ø.
141. *Show Rafael that you love him and tell Ø that he's wonderful.
142. *Leave the car in the garage and put the bus Ø.

In order for Langendoen's argument to go through, he first of all has to reject e.g. Tai's unitary proposal, or, for that matter, any unitary proposal employing a notion of directionality of deletion: NLPNPC will obviously not hold for backwards deletions like Right-node Raising. These are peripheral, and will, in most cases, contain NP. NLPNPC, which refers specifically to leftperipheral strings, could not be generalised to all deletions, or even to all peripheral deletions:

143. Jackendoff despises, and McCawley admires bassoonists.

Secondly, Langendoen has to ignore (as indeed he does) Jackendoff's (1972) observation that NPs immediately adjacent to the verb gap along with the verb, as for instance in (106) cited earlier:

106. Max writes poetry in the garden, and Max Ø Ø in the bathroom.

Given that the string here is not peripheral, it will be clear that NLPNPC should apply to it, and since (106) is acceptable, NLPNPC cannot be correct for Gapping.

Thirdly, VP-deletion could never be constrained by NLPNPC, since VPD will obviously violate both the 'peripherality' part and the 'leftmost' part of NLPNPC:

144. Molly Malone likes shellfish, and Bill does too.

Fourthly, the sentences we have cited as counterexamples to Hankamer's NAC also constitute clear counterexamples to the NLPNPC under the reading where the 'gap' is not leftmost, and (132) only has the reading which violates the NLPNPC:

(132) Drinking gives you cirrhosis, and smoking cancer.
(133) David ties up his parcels with string, and his wife with ribbon.
(134) Penny put the clothes through the drier, and Paul through the mangle.
(135) Harry had steak for breakfast, and his secretary for dinner.

Although NLPNPC is inadequate and clearly too limited in scope, Langendoen has to be credited with singling out a factor that is of considerable importance in the coordinate deletion discussion, namely that it is precisely because the NP in a sentence like (141) is not in a leftperipheral position that it cannot be deleted. As soon as the NP in (145) moves to leftmost position, deletion can apply:

145. Rafael was shown that he was loved and Ø told that he was wonderful.

We shall return to sentences of the type (141,145) in considerable detail in Chapter 2.

1.3.5 Functional constraints: Kuno

On the basis of Hankamer's (1973) and Langendoen's (1975) papers, Kuno (1976) presents a rather different approach to Gapping: a functional approach.[35] Kuno wishes to demonstrate that Gapping is a rather more complicated process than Hankamer and Langendoen originally had suggested: Gapping must be subject to perceptual, discourse-based, and semantic conditions.

Kuno first of all notes a few quite strong counterexamples to the NAC and NLPNPC: sentence (146), for instance, which is a counterexample to the NAC because it is clearly structurally ambiguous, and which, like the unambiguous (147-148), is also a clear counterexample to the NLPNPC (Kuno, 1976:306-7):

146. My brother visited Japan in 1960, and my sister [visited Japan] in 1961.
146a. My brother visited Japan in 1960, and [my brother visited] my sister in 1961.
147. Tom told this story to his mother, and Harry [told this story] to his father.
148. Two days ago, John took Mary out to dinner, and this afternoon, [John took Mary out] to the movies.[36]

These are strong counterexamples not only to the NAC and NLPNPC, but also to Kuno's own *Minimal Distance Principle* (MDP); a principle which he claims to be a perception-oriented restatement of the NLPNPC and NAC. The principle is stated as follows:

The two constituents left behind by Gapping can be most readily coupled with the constituents (of the same structures) in the first conjunct that were processed last of all. (Kuno, 1976:310)

Because of the existence of such counterexamples, the MDP will have to be supplemented with other principles — Kuno has three further ones that are of immediate relevance to Gapping, namely the *Functional Sentence Perspective* principle of Gapping, the *Tendency for Subject-Predicate Interpretation*, and the *Requirement for Simplex-Sentential Relationship*.

The FSP requires constituents which are to be deleted by Gapping to be contextually known, while constituents left behind necessarily represent new information. Generally speaking, it will be the case that the closer a given constituent is to sentence-final position, the newer the information it represents (Kuno, 1976:310). The Tendency for Subject-Predicate Interpretation (1976:311) states that there will be a preference for subject-predicate interpretation if the remnants of Gapping are an NP and a VP. The Requirement for Simplex-Sentential Relationship (1976:314) states that the constituents left behind by Gapping[37] are most readily interpreted as entering into a simplex-sentential relationship, and difficult to interpret otherwise.

Kuno's principles and tendencies (and note the quite important fact that these are principles and tendencies on the *interpretation* of Gapping rather than constraints on the syntactic patterning which Gapping produces: they therefore leave unaffected the requirement for constraints on Gapping which will differentiate between admissable applications of Gapping and inadmissable applications of Gapping) seem to me to be not precise enough, *ad hoc*, and unhelpful, although the observations underlying these principles and tendencies are very often quite correct and valid. Since there is, among certain linguists, a tendency to dismiss Gapping phenomena (or even all co-ordinate reduction rules resulting in non-constituent coordination) as 'stylistic' or 'discourse' rules which a sentence grammar need not concern itself with openly (see e.g. Sag *et al.*, 1958-160; Steedman, 1985:544), since such dismissals are not supported by anything even remotely approaching sound argumentation, and since Kuno's is the only 'extragrammatical' approach to Gapping which comprises a clear set of hypotheses which transcend the level of sentence grammatical constraints, I shall discuss Kuno's proposal in some detail, and critically so. The conclusion of this discussion will be that to treat Gapping, or any other deletion rule operating under identity in co-ordinated structures as a stylistic rule, or as something not governed by the rules of sentence grammar, is an ineffective move: formulating the stylistic rules or processing rules, or any other type of extragrammatical rules that account for the syntactic patterning of coordinations is an exercise which demands (not surprisingly) the same type of rigour and explicitness which the formulation of 'rules of grammar' requires, and it is furthermore an exercise which concerns itself with the same primary empirical question, namely that of finding an elegant, non-*ad hoc* statement for why certain types of coordination are acceptable, and others aren't.

My criticism of Kuno's four nonsyntactic constraints does not entail the conclusion that Gapping is therefore necessarily a rule of sentence syntax, but it will leave us with the conclusion that Gapping phenomena receive a much less successful treatment as *non*syntactic phenomena than that they receive as syntactic facts, which is why I shall continue to treat Gapping, together with other coordinate deletion rules, as a rule of sentence syntax.

The first thing we can observe about Kuno's four principles is that they may be in conflict — they are tendencies, not absolute rules. Kuno notes sentences which *violate* one or more principles, but which are nevertheless acceptable because they *satisfy* one or more principles: and these are principles which may in turn be violated by other sentences (Kuno, 1976:314). In other words, it will be quite difficult to assess the linguistic consequences of the individual principles which Kuno proposes. Fortunately, this does not preclude a critical examination of the individual tendencies and principles.

Kuno's MDP speaks of two constituents being left behind by Gapping — but Gapping can leave more than two constituents behind:

149. John left for Canada last week and Peter Ø for New York a few days after.
150. Peter has to repaint the window-sills of the Smiths before the end of the week, and Harry Ø the garden shed of the Joneses before the month is out.

47

It may be the case that sentences with three remnants are some-times harder to interpret than two-remnant sentences: they involve a greater strain on processing abilities and memory (three constituents have to be paired, and a much longer sentence has to be remembered *verbatim* for this pairing to take place) but there is no doubt about the acceptability[38] of sentences like (149-150) which have three remnants. Hermann (1985) even cities acceptable examples from Russian where four remnants are left behind by Gapping. Given this fact, one could wonder about the content of the MDP, since the 'distance' referred to in the MDP may be the same in a three-remnant gapped sentence obeying the MDP and a two-remnant sentence obeying the MDP: if one remnant is the first consti-tuent, this first remnant constituent will indeed be paired with the constituent of the same structure in the first conjunct that was processed *last* of all, but this same constituent was also the constituent that was processed *first* of all, since it is the first constituent of the entire sentence. Although the 'distance' in terms of number of constituents between remnants of Gapping and their antecedents is obviously greater in the case of three-remnant sentences than it is in two-remnant sentences the MDP will fail to distinguish between the two. The MDP is therefore not concerned with 'distance', but simply says something like: 'proceed from left to right in pairing constituents', and even this can be reduced to some sort of principle of least effort, since skipping one or more constituents in the pairing process requires more memory-storage of constituents and the linear order in which they occur. A mirror-image pairing in which the first constituent is paired with the last remnant, and so on, would require storage of the entire sentence, while pairing of first constituent with first remnant does not. Furthermore, the mirror-image pairing would require the hearer to be aware of the left-to-right linear order of constituents as well as of the right-to-left order, which makes for more complicated process-ing. As a matter of fact, *any* pairing which is not left-to-right will serve to complicate processing; it is presumably this which underlies such constraints as the 'parallelism constraint' of Goodall (1984:52 ff.). In an ambiguous sentence like:

151. You met an Englishman in Nepal, and your sister in Tierra del Fuego.

The interpretation of the gap as *you met* requires that *an Englishman in Nepal* be stored for pairing, while a gap *met an Englishman* will require storage of the entire sentence for pairing of constituents. This may be why the 'preferred' interpretation for (151) is with a leftmost gap; see also 1.3.2 for discussion of this problem. Kuno's observation is interesting and correct, but it is not adequately accounted for by the MDP.

A second objection to the MDP is that it is demonstrably incorrect for backwards gappings. Ross (1970) had already observed that German[39] in subordinate clause allows both forward and backward Gapping:

152a. Ich glaube, dass Johann Fisch isst, und Willi Reis Ø.
152b. Ich glaube, dass Johann Fisch Ø,   und Willi Reis isst.
       (I   believe that John   fish   and Bill rice eats)

The MDP is obeyed in (152a), but it has to be totally reversed for (152b), which is as common and unexceptional a gapped sentence as (152a) is. Here, the two constituents left behind by Gapping need to be coupled with the constituents of the same structure in the *last* conjunct (so not the first) that were processed *last* of all (so not first of all). This objection cannot be eliminated by rejecting the 'mirror-image' formulation of Gapping proposed in Ross (1970), since the MDP is a perception-oriented constraint, and therefore says something about the linguistic perception of a hearer rather than about a specific rule in a specific grammar of an individual language. To claim that a German speaker will use one principle of perception for (152a), and will then effortlessly reverse his perceptual strategy for (152b) is totally unwarranted, and extremely unlikely at best. Nor is this type of argument restricted to Gapping in German: English presents its problems as well, since Right-node Raising also requires a mirror-image operation of the MDP. In other words, in spite of the many similarities between Gapping and Right-node Raising (which has caused a number of linguists, e.g. Tai (1969) to'collapse the two), the MDP claims that there could hardly be a phenomenon that is more different from Gapping than RNR, since they require opposite perceptual strategies. This is obviously undesirable.

Kuno's second extragrammatical principle, the Functional Sentence Perspective of Gapping (FSP), fares little better. This

requires the constituent deleted by Gapping to be old information, while what is left behind by Gapping must be new
information. In one sense, this is a type of constraint on the
recoverability of deletions (see 1.3.3): since Gapping deletes
identical material (this is a *syntactic* constraint on Gapping), the
claim that the material deleted may represent old, contextually
known information could undoubtedly be correct, but it adds
little to our understanding of the Gapping rule. But for other
processes than Gapping in English it is manifestly incorrect:
here again Right-node Raising and 'bidirectional' Gapping in
German and Dutch subordinate clauses provide conclusive
evidence against FSP. The material deleted here is *not* contextually known material, because it is the *antecedent* occurrence of
the identical material which is deleted, and not the *subsequent*
occurrence — so the deleted material is *new* information, and
what is left behind is old. The same objection as raised against
the MDP applies: speakers have to be conjectured to use dia-
metrically opposed functional principles in Kuno's approach,
when they deal with Gapping and RNR in English, or with
'bidirectional' Gapping in Dutch and German. This is highly
unlikely, and not supported by any arguments.

Nor is it the case that old information can always be deleted.
If we take the three sentences (153-155), we find that the
second constituent in all three cases represents old information
— yet only in (153) can the old information be deleted:

153. John ate fish and Bill Ø rice.
154. *Am I ill and must sleep?
155. *Show your mother your term report and tell Ø what
      you're planning to do about it.

Sentences like these make it quite clear that something besides
functional principles must be responsible for the acceptability of
deletions. The FSP will not differentiate between (153-155).

Kuno's third principle, the Tendency for Subject-Predicate
Interpretation, and the fourth principle, the Requirement for
Simplex-Sentential Relationship, are odd ones. Kuno calls them
nonsyntactic constraints (1976:315), yet they make crucial
reference to syntactic notions like 'constituting a *sentential*
pattern' (1976:311), and 'entering into a simplex-*sentential*
relationship' (1976:316). It seems, therefore, that these two are
ill-disguised syntactic constraints, a suspicion which is

confirmed when we read that these constraints are needed to explain the *grammaticality* of sentences, rather than to explain, for instance, certain preferred or non-preferred interpretations (1976:314,317). Given these observations, it will clearly be difficult to subject these two principles to any rigorous empirical tests: they are principles which freely allow counterexamples, which may be in conflict, and which make no definite predictions. One should observe that a sentence like (156a) (= Kuno, 1976:55d):

156a. *John hugged his sister to please his mother, and [*John hugged] his wife [to please] his father.

which Kuno (correctly) rules out as ungrammatical, becomes grammatical if we do not delete *to please*:

156b. John hugged his sister to please his mother, and his wife to please his father.

Kuno calls (156a) ungrammatical because it violates the Requirement for Simplex-Sentential Relationship, but it obeys the MDP and FSP. Sentence (156b) still obeys MDP and FSP, but violates both the Tendency for Subject-Predicate Interpretation, and the Simplex-Sentential Relationship Requirement. Nevertheless, we cannot see (156b) as a clear counterexample to any of the tendencies and principles discussed in this paragraph, since it is not stipulated which set of constraints, principles or tendencies has to be obeyed for a sentence to be grammatical; nor is it stipulated which violations or conflicts between principles will result in ungrammaticality. The Tendency for Subject-Predicate Interpretation claims to be a semantic constraint (although it makes crucial reference to syntactic notions), but we are not given any reference to a theory of semantics that it might belong to. Likewise, the Requirement for Simplex-Sentential Relationship claims to be a perceptually motivated constraint (although it again makes crucial reference .to notions of syntax), but we are again not given the theory of perception that it could fit into. This makes Kuno's constraints and principles entirely untestable.

Kuno's proposals are clearly unsuccessful. It needs to be said, however, that although they do not stand up to scrutiny, they are the only serious proposals for a set of nonsyntactic constraints on

Gapping in existence. What this means is that those researchers who consider Gapping to be outside the realm of syntax proper, a stylistic rule, some sort of phonological mapping rule, or some sort of discourse rule, still face the same task that Kuno faced, namely to demonstrate that Gapping cannot be a rule of sentence grammar, and then to give a clearly nonsyntactic account of Gapping which is an actual improvement on earlier syntactic accounts of this phenomenon. Until this is done, all claims about the syntactic or nonsyntactic nature of Gapping are clearly vacuous, and syntactic accounts of coordination which do not involve Gapping because they deem it to be 'discourse' clearly lack a necessary part of their empirical basis. I shall therefore continue to treat Gapping as a syntactic process, subject to syntactic constraints. We shall return to the place that coordination occupies in the grammar in Chapter 3.

1.3.6 Deep structure factorisation: Williams

Williams' (1978) paper entitled 'Across-the-Board Rule Application', although it ignores Gapping and the proposal is incapable of dealing with Gapping, is of considerable interest to the study of coordinate deletions for a number of reasons. What Williams attempts to do is to formalise Ross's (1967) notion of across-the-board rule application, and to provide an alternative to the conjunction-reduction derivation of sentences like:

157. The man who John saw and Bill hit was tiny.

The Conjunction Reduction (CR) approach derives this sentence by deleting the second occurrence of *who* from (157a):

157a. The man who John saw and who Bill hit was tiny.

Williams, in his across-the-board (ATB) approach, derives (157) from (157a) by means of WH-Movement, which puts *who* in the complementiser and simultaneously deletes the other occurrences of *who*. WH-movement is restricted so as to move and delete identical factors[40] in this case, and identity should be seen as follows: the conjuncts of a coordinate structure are written on top of each other, and then split by means of factor lines. If a factor then contains an identical part in each conjunct (i.e. is what Williams calls a *simultaneous factor F*, which consists of a number of factors $F_1...F_n$), then it can be subjected to movement and deletion. A factor, in Williams' proposal for coordination, is any substring of a well-formed labelled bracketing that does not begin with a right bracket or end with a left bracket, and if one conjunct is split by factor lines, then all conjuncts must be split. If they are split, all left conjunct brackets must belong to the same factor: in other words, all conjuncts are neatly aligned on top of each other. Coordinated sentences are generated in deep structure in ATB format, and factorisation takes place at deep structure level. A sentence like:

158. The man who opened the door and left was my brother.

will have had the underlying structure as in (158a):

158a. $\text{COMP} \begin{bmatrix} [\text{who} & [\text{opened the door}]\text{S} \\ [\text{who} & [\text{left}]_\text{S} \end{bmatrix}_\text{S}$

158b. *The man who who opened the door and left was my brother.

who is moved into COMP, and the two occurrences of *who* to the left of the factor line are deleted.

Williams' proposal, which we shall return to in some detail in Chapter 3 in the discussion of recoverability of deletion, comprises a few important claims about coordinate deletions. The first is that either all the factors which form part of a simultaneous factor go at once, or not at all, and the second is that factorisation for coordinate deletion must take place in deep structure. Neither of these claims is correct for coordination. First of all, not all simultaneous factors need to be deleted at once: a sentence like (159) has, as possible reduced variants (159a,b,c):

159. John gave the books to Mary, and John gave the records to Sue, but John gave the diamonds to his boyfriend.
159a. John gave the books to Mary and the records to Sue, but John gave the diamonds to his boyfriend.
159b. John gave the books to Mary and John gave the records to Sue, but the diamonds to his boyfriend.

159c. John gave the books to Mary and the records to Sue, but the diamonds to his boyfriend.

As a matter of fact, Williams' proposal as it stands cannot produce any of the reductions (159a-c), but only the unacceptable:

159d. *Gave the books to Mary and the records to Sue, but the diamonds to his boyfriend.

There is a clear difference between (158) and (159): in (158), the entire simultaneous factor *must delete*, otherwise we end up with one *who* which has been moved into COMP and one *who* which remains in S, which is unacceptable, as will be clear from (*158b). In (159), at least one factor contained in the simultaneous factor *must remain*; if we delete all simultaneous factors, we end up with unacceptable (*159d). Furthermore, CR can take place in any single pair or series of adjacent conjuncts that can be appropriately factorised, and Williams' proposal will have to be adapted to take such facts into account.

Let us assume that the shortcomings mentioned above can be remedied somehow. We are then left with the claim that, since ATB format and factorisation are deep structure processes, coordinate deletion must be a phenomenon ruled by deep structure configurations and factorisations. This claim is clearly wrong: CD is a surface structure phenomenon. Consider the following Dutch sentence:

160. Jan koopt het schilderij van Klaas en Jan geeft het
                                              schilderij aan Marie.
    (Jan buys   the   painting   from Klaas and Jan gives   the
                                              painting to   Marie)

In Dutch, which is verb-second in main clauses, any constituent may be topicalised: the verb will retain second position in the surface S. (The precise analysis of this process is not crucial here: let us assume that the topicalised constituent moves into a TOPIC position, and the verb then moves into COMP.) If, in (160), we front the direct object, we get:

160a. Het schilderij koopt Jan van Klaas, en het schilderij geeft Jan aan Marie.

In (160), we can apply deletion to the identical subject *Jan*, which will give us:

160b. Jan koopt het schilderij van Klaas en Ø geeft het schilderij aan Marie.

Let us assume the appropriate amendments so that Williams' proposal can account for this sentence. To (160a), we can also apply CD, which will give us:

160c. Het schilderij koopt Jan van Klaas en Ø geeft Jan aan Marie.

Such a sentence could only be accounted for by allowing the type of derivation Williams used for (158) above: let us assume a rule that moves *het schilderij* into TOPIC position and deletes all subsequent occurrences. But now we find that if we combine the derivations of (160b) and (160c), we get the totally unacceptable (160d):

160d. *Het schilderij koopt Jan van Klaas en Ø geeft Ø aan Marie.

What is wrong with (160d) is that deletion has applied to a *non-leftmost surface* factorisation: only if a constituent is leftmost in the *surface* can we apply deletion in the case of (160,160a). We cannot delete the nonleftmost object in (160), or the nonleftmost subject in (160a):

160e. *Jan koopt het schilderij van Klaas en Jan geeft Ø aan Marie.
160f. *Het schilderij koopt Jan van Klaas en het schilderij geeft Ø aan Marie.

There are appropriate simultaneous deep structure factorisations available, in Williams' approach, for (160b-f), and we therefore expect all deletions to be grammatical, which they clearly are not: a simultaneous factor (for this restricted body of data) has to be *leftmost in the surface* in order to be a candidate for deletion. This demonstrates quite clearly that *deep structure* factorisation is not the appropriate notion for coordinate deletion: the best results will be obtained from a suitably

restricted version CD operating on *surface structure* factorisation. I conclude that Coordinate Deletion is a surface structure phenomenon.

A third objection one might raise against Williams' approach,
although it is only tangentially connected with the issues
addressed in this section, is that he does not extend it[41] to parallel types of ATB rules like Gapping and Right-node Raising,
rules which, like Coordinate Deletion, apply across-the-board in
coordinated structures. I shall return in some detail to Williams'
proposal in Chapter 3; for the moment, let us observe that at
deep structure, simultaneous factorisation is not a fruitful notion
for coordinate deletions.[42]

1.3.7 Gapping: Neijt

The most comprehensive single study of Gapping is undoubtedly Neijt (1979). Neijt's account, which is based on data from
English and Dutch, is furthermore one of the few explicit
attempts to link the theory of Gapping with the question of
learnability of language.[43] This connection is made in the
following passage in which the rule of Gapping is formulated:

> *Gapping* (final version): 'DELETE'.
> The rule is similar to Chomsky's 'Move' for movement rules
> (Chomsky 1978:4) ... From a learnability point of view, the
> rule is quite attractive: the child only needs to learn whether
> or not the language displays (this rule). Therefore, in the
> present context it holds as a point of method that (this rule)
> should not be cluttered up with rule-specific conditions or
> notational devices. (Neijt, 1979:95-6)

Whether one should agree or disagree with this approach is a
matter which I shall not discuss here;[44] I shall concern myself
only with the empirical consequences of this formulation. The
first and most important consequence is of course that such a
rule will overgenerate wildly, and will have to be restricted in a
number of ways. In spite of the methodological preliminaries,
however, Neijt does not restrict the rule 'delete', but only the
rule of Gapping: she claims that rules like Right-node Raising,
Forward and Backward Conjunction Reduction, and VP-
deletion are essentially different from Gapping.[45] The burden of

proof rests with Neijt, who assumes a difference between Gapping and other rules (who, in other words, assumes a lack of generality within deletions in coordinated structures). She sets out to demonstrate that Gapping must necessarily be different from other rules that effect deletion in coordinated structures in Dutch and English. A brief discussion of Neijt's arguments will reveal whether it is indeed impossible to collapse Gapping and other coordinate deletion rules.

First of all, let us take the relation between Gapping and Forward Conjunction Reduction, which is responsible for sentences like (161), taken from Ross (1967):

161. The University's students are intelligent and committed to freedom.

Neijt argues that Forward Conjunction Reduction does not introduce strings that are not one constituent: forward CR is therefore superfluous and can be replaced by a set of PS-rules (1979:51). She also rejects Sag's (1976) rule of Left-peripheral Deletion, which deletes leftmost strings in coordinated structures, and is responsible for sentences like (162), which were also noticed in Williams (1978):

162. John gave a book to Mary and a bunch of flowers to Sue.

This sentence cannot readily be accounted for as a base co-ordination of VPs, but, as Neijt argues, has been derived from a base coordination of VPs through Gapping, which has deleted the identical verbs. A part of Neijt's observations about Forward Conjunction Reduction is correct — in the formulation of Ross (1967:220), forward CR deletes constituents from the extreme left of a coordination, and this will result, in English, in a coordination of VPs if the extreme left constituent (the subject) is deleted from a coordination of Ss; compare:

162a. John gave a book to Mary and Ø gave a bunch of flowers to Sue.

There is, however, nothing to stop forward CR from applying to the verb in (162a) to yield (162); this is essentially also what Neijt's Gapping rule does. It is also what what Sag's Left-peripheral Deletion rule does: the three rules are therefore equivalent with respect to sentences like (162), with the proviso that Gapping crucially involves verbs in the deletion target, and therefore requires that sentences like (162a) are generated as base coordinations of VPs.

But now note how this gives rise to the following anomalous situation. Consider yes-no questions in Dutch, or imperatives in Dutch and English. Dutch forms yes-no questions by putting the finite verb in sentence-initial position; in imperatives, both in Dutch and in English, the verb will occupy initial position. These initial verbs may be deleted by Forward CR, Left-peripheral Deletion, or Gapping, and in none of these cases will a constituent coordination result:

163. Wil   jij   een ijsje   en Ø Marietje limonade?
     (want you an ice-cream and Ø Marietje lemonade)
164. Geef het boek aan Jan en   Ø de plaat   aan Piet.
165. Give the book to   Jan and Ø the record to   Piet.

Gapping, like Left-peripheral Deletion and Forward CR, must be able to apply to initial constituents. Neijt's hypothesis could be maintained if we were to stipulate that Gapping targets must always have a verb in them: then we could claim that it was actually Gapping which is responsible for (162-165), and Forward CR and Left-peripheral Deletion are superfluous. Gapping could then delete either S-initial or S-medial constituents (or strings of constituents, where necessary), provided that these have a verb in them somewhere. But now consider sentence (160c), discussed in the previous section:

160c. Het schilderij koopt Jan van Klaas en   Ø geeft hij
                                                    aan Marie.
      (the painting buys Jan from Klaas and Ø gives he
                                               to   Marie)

Here, the object NP *het schilderij* has been deleted, and the remnant of the deletion is the subject, the transitive verb, and the PP. Although it is possible to base-generate such co-ordinated structures in Generalised Phrase Structure Grammar (see Gazdar (1981), discussed later in this chapter), it could not have been base-generated in the model of grammar which Neijt assumes. Therefore, we have to say that either there is a need for a forward-deleting rule like Ross's Forward CR, or Sag's

Left-peripheral Deletion, or we are committed, if Gapping is the only forward-deleting rule operating in coordinated structures, to allow Gapping to apply to non-verbs, or strings of constituents not containing a verb. I follow Neijt's approach, who has a marked preference for a single forward deletion rule (1979:50), but observe that this forward deletion rule is probably not Gapping, since Gapping traditionally involves deletion of identical verbs, and the deletion in (160) does not involve verbs. A distinction between Gapping and some other forward deletion rule like Forward CR or Left-peripheral Deletion seems to me artificial[46] in the light of the data presented so far in this chapter.

Ross (1967) formulates his Conjunction Reduction rule as a mirror-image rule. Above, I have followed Neijt in questioning the distinction between the various possible forward deletion rules. One could now wonder whether there is a distinction between Gapping (or any other type of forward deletion rule operating in coordinated structures) and Backward Conjunction Reduction (also known, I believe as a result of Postal's (1974) raising-cum-deletion analysis, as Right-node Raising (RNR), a term which I shall use in this book). Neijt is quite explicit in her opinion that Right-node Raising is different from Gapping: she claims that Gapping, but not RNR, leaves major constituents behind, deletes variables rather than a single final constituent, may delete discontinuously, and applies to a specific domain rather than to all sorts of constituents. Neijt observations, however, are not always correct, and the arguments on this point are therefore inconclusive.[47]

First of all, about the major constituency of remnants. Hankamer (1973) proposed that the remnants of Gapping should all be major constituents. That is, they should all be dominated by S_0 or immediately dominated by VP which is dominated by S_0. Such a constraint on remnants, it has to be observed, can be readily reversed in the following manner: Given that all constituents left behind by Gapping must be major constituents, Gapping cannot be a true variable deletion rule in the sense in which Neijt intends. It must itself also delete major constituents: either single major constituents or (possibly discontinuous) strings of major constituents. If Gapping did not delete major constituents, then it would 'eat into' a major constituent and thus not leave only major constituent remnants. Only if rules like RNR or VP-deletion do not delete major constituents will the Major Constituent Condition differentiate between Gapping on the one hand, and VP-deletion and RNR on the other. Given that VPD deletes VPs, which are major constituents by the definition of Hankamer, and that RNR deletes a rightmost constituent which will be immediately dominated either by S_0 (in e.g. the case of sentence adverbs) or VP dominated by S_0 (in the case of e.g. direct objects and indirect objects, all of which are major constituents, we cannot use the Major Constituent Condition to differentiate between Gapping and backward deletion rules like RNR, or forward deletion rules like VPD.[48] Furthermore, if Gapping is not, as we observed above, a true variable deletion rule in that it cannot apply to leave non-major constituents behind and must therefore be a rule which itself deletes either major constituents or strings of major constituents, then the one crucial difference between Gapping and RNR that remains is that the latter deletes S-final single constituents, while Gapping can delete strings of constituents. However, either this is false, or some rule other than RNR must be held responsible for (166):

166. John gave Ø Ø, and Peter sold a book to Mary.

Variable deletion vs. single constituent deletion will therefore not differentiate between Gapping and RNR. That it is difficult to find a principled distinction between Gapping and RNR will also be clear from the fact that Gapping and RNR in the Dutch and German subordinate clauses (167-170)[49] have the same effect. The only difference is that RNR deletes antecedent constituents, while Gapping deletes subsequent constituents. There are no clear stylistic or grammatical differences between these sentences: all are equally frequent and acceptable sentences of Dutch and German.

167. Ich glaube, dass Peter dem Hund Fleisch gibt, und Susan
der Katze Ø Ø.
168. Ik geloof dat Peter de hond vlees geeft, en Susan
de kat Ø Ø.
169. Ich glaube, dass Peter dem Hund Ø Ø, und Susan der
Katze Fleisch gibt.
170. Ik geloof dat Peter de hond Ø Ø, en Susan de
kat vlees geeft.
(I believe that Peter the dog Ø Ø and Susan the
cat meat gives)

Whatever process is responsible for antecedent deletions (RNR, Backwards Gapping, or Backwards CR), it will be clear that this process does not just delete final constituents.

Neijt observes that Gapping may delete discontinuous strings, which RNR may not do. This observation is correct, but consider (171-172), where in both cases the deletion target is a discontinuous verb. This deletion target may delete forwards discontinuously, by means of Gapping, or the past participle may delete backwards, by means of RNR, while the auxiliary deletes forward, through Gapping:

171. Jan heeft de hond geslagen en Piet Ø de kat Ø.
172. Jan heeft de hond Ø, en Piet Ø de kat geslagen.
     (Jan has   the dog Ø, and Piet Ø the cat hit)

Although RNR does not delete discontinuous strings (which would indeed be difficult to achieve, given that RNR is explicitly formulated to apply to rightmost nodes (or strings)), it is applicable to rightmost parts of discontinuous strings, and if those rightmost parts are also included in a Gapping target, then Gapping and RNR apply at least partly to the same strings — again a clear indication that the distinction between Gapping and RNR is not all that clear-cut.

Lastly, Neijt suggests that RNR applies to different sorts of domains, which Gapping does not. She suggests, as domains for RNR, VPs, NPs and PPs:

173. I am confident of Ø and dependent on a successful outing at the track.
174. John interviewed people who like Ø and people who dislike potatoes.
175. John jumped over three Ø or over four gates.

There is certainly some backwards deletion rule that is responsible for these deletions — but there is an equivalent forward deletion rule that can also delete from VPs, NPs and PPs:[50]

176. John gave a book to Mary and Ø Ø a record to Sue.
177. I'll have the red wine, and my girlfriend the white Ø.
178. John jumped over three gates, and not over four Ø.

The differences between a forward-deleting rule like

Gapping, and a backward-deleting rule like RNR are, if they exist, quite difficult to isolate: none of the major differences which Neijt lists will differentiate unequivocally between the two rules.[51]

Neijt's attitude towards VP-deletion, another forward-deleting rule which can operate in coordinated structures, is curious: although she maintains that Gapping is the only forward-deleting rule which operates in coordinated structures (1979:50), she notes that VP-deletion, which in English deletes identical VPs in both coordinate and subordinate structures (see e.g. Sag (1976)), is not available for Dutch (Neijt, 1979:20). This means that English has at least *two* forward-deleting rules which operate in coordinated structures, if Gapping is distinct from VPD. Furthermore, there are Dutch counterparts for English VPD-sentences:

179. I drink wine, but John doesn't.
180. Ik drink wijn, maar Jan niet.
    (I drink wine, but Jan not)

All coordinate instances of VPD-equivalent sentences in Dutch will therefore have to be catered for by some variety of Gapping, and this immediately makes the distinction between Gapping and VPD suspect for English; certainly if we expect (following Ross (1970)) that Gapping is a general phenomenon rather than something which is restricted to a few scattered languages. I shall return to this point in section 1.3.8 of this chapter, and not discuss it any further here.

Neijt has to be commended for undertaking one of the very few serious attempts to isolate a rule of Gapping which is distinct from other coordinate deletion rules. Nevertheless, this attempt has not provided conclusive proof: Gapping, Forward Conjunction Reduction, and Left-Peripheral Deletion (the latter two of which Neijt mistakenly argues are superfluous) can be shown to be part of the same rule: a rule which, since it also applies to sentence-initial constituents, is not Gapping in any familiar formulation of that rule. Secondly, the characteristics which Neijt gives as differentiating between Gapping and RNR do not warrant a distinction between these two rules, and at least for Dutch there cannot be a difference between Gapping and VPD in coordinated structures: a point we shall return to also in Chapter 3. For these reasons, the most plausible assumption about coordinate deletions is still the most general one, namely that there is only one (mirror-image) rule effecting deletion in coordinated structures. Although Neijt's book contains more material that is of interest to us than can be discussed in this section,[52] I shall adhere to this assumption and, after an intermediate conclusion, move on to VP-deletion.

1.3.8 Conclusion

The rule of Gapping, once it had been identified by Ross, led a bit of a peculiar life: from a mirror-image formulation intended to account for the directionality of deletion across languages, it was quickly transformed into a rule which accounted for forward deletions of the verb in English. Jackendoff (1972) observed some crucial facts about the applicability and non-applicability of Gapping: facts which, rather surprisingly, have not played the role in the discussion of Gapping that they should have played.[53] Hankamer (1973) explored the notion of recoverability of deletions: this notion has, in various forms, played a considerable role in the discussion about deletions under identity, and we shall return to this issue in some detail in Chapter 3. Hankamer's attempt to link the notion of recoverability of deletion to an injunction against the introduction of ambiguity has turned out to be unsuccessful. Langendoen's (1975) sharp reaction to Hankamer is inadequate as an account of coordinated deletions, but it did produce the notion of peripherality of deletion target sites. As we shall see in Chapter 2, this is a crucial notion. Kuno's functional approach, the only serious attempt to find a non-syntactic solution for some of the problems facing the Gapping rule, has been shown to be seriously inadequate. Williams' (1978) proposal for the formalisation of across-the-board rule application has been shown to be mistaken in at least one principle: Williams' approach bases itself on deep structure factorisation, and coordinate deletion is clearly a surface structure phenomenon.[54] Neijt's (1979) detailed proposal to single out Gapping as distinct from other coordinate deletion rules has been shown to be inconclusive. This leaves us with the following state of affairs for Coordinate deletions: no reason can be found not to make the simplest possible assumption, namely that all deletion under identity in coordinated structures is one single unitary rule. This rule is clearly a syntactic rule, and it operates at surface structure. Its effect must be recoverable in some sense, and the notion of peripherality of deletion target site will play an important role. But the most important conclusion is that there remains a host of highly interesting unresolved problems.

1.3.9 VP-deletion: Sag

Sag's (1976) Ph.D. thesis entitled 'Deletion and Logical Form' is not only concerned with the proper formulation of the rule of VP-deletion (VPD), a rule which was first formulated by Bouton (1970) (though see Gleitman (1965) on what she calls 'conjoined tags), but also with Gapping, and with recoverability of deletions. For a critical discussion of Sag's Gapping proposals, see Neijt (1979); we shall return in some detail to the subject of recoverability of deletion in Chapter 3. Our only concern in this section will be with Sag's formulation of VP-deletion as distinct from other deletion rules which can delete material under identity in coordinated structures: Sag considers VPD to be different from Gapping, Left-peripheral Deletion, Coordination Reduction, and Right-node Raising, VPD, in Sag's analysis, is a sort of post-auxiliary ellipsis (1976:35). Sag provides the following (overgenerating) formulation of VPD as a variable deletion rule (1976:32):

181.　　$W_1 - X - W_2 - Aux - X - W_3$
　　SD: 1　　2　　3　　4　　5　　6
　　SC: 1　　2　　3　　4　　Ø　　6

Sag suggests two conditions for this rule: First of all, $2 = 5$,[55] and secondly, VPD seems to be restricted to the material commanded by AUX.

What is obvious from this formulation of VPD is that it is, like Neijt's Gapping, a rule which deletes forwards under identity. Two obvious superficial differences between VPD and Gapping are that VPD leaves AUX behind, which Gapping doesn't, and that for VPD the clause connector is left unspecified, while for Gapping the clause connector must be a coordinating conjunction.

There are a number of objections one can raise against a rule of VPD as distinct from Gapping, RNR, and Coordinate Deletion. First of all, it has to be observed that VPD is a specifically English rule. Languages like Dutch, German and French, which are geographically and historically quite close to English, do not have such a post-auxiliary deletion rule in coordinated structures: the auxiliary has to delete as well. In subordinated structures, there is no deletion rule like VPD available at all, but some sort of pronominalisation has to take place:[56] compare, for instance, the Dutch translations of (182-183), and their English transliterations:

182. John eats fish, but Bill doesn't Ø.
183. I will leave when you do Ø.
184. John eet vis, maar Bill Ø niet Ø.
    (John eats fish, but Bill Ø not Ø)
185. Ik ga weg als jij dat doet.
    (I go away if you that do)

VPD, which might arguably merit a place somewhere as a rule of English syntax, is, as we have already observed earlier, probably quite restricted across languages: Neijt (1979) remarks that Dutch does not have VPD; nor does German. But even as a rule of English syntax, it faces some significant problems. VPD, in spite of the formalisation cited in (181), is not a variable deletion rule, but a rule which applies to VPs. It is restricted by a condition on recoverability of the deletion that has applied: in Sag's account, a deletion has to be recoverable at the level of logical form. At LF, the representation of the deletion target VP and the antecedent VP have to be identical in a specifically construed sense; for a fuller discussion of identity, see Chapter 3. Furthermore, a VP-deletion has to be maximal: given an AUX, all the material under VP commanded by that AUX has to go. This latter point makes it immediately necessary to have a recursive category VP,[57] since there is no 'fixed' constituent VP to which VPD can apply. Place adverbials and time adverbials, for instance, can and must be deleted by VPD if they are identical, but they may not be deleted if they are not identical. This requires that the grammar contains a rule of the type VP======> VP ADV; this makes it possible for sentences (186-189) to be accounted for:[58]

186. John saw Mary in Paris, and Peter did Ø too. (Ø=saw Mary in Paris)
187. John kissed Mary in Paris, and Peter did Ø in Rome (Ø=kissed Mary)
188. John will see Mary today, and Peter will Ø as well (Ø=see Mary today)
189. John will kiss Mary today, and Peter will Ø tomorrow (Ø=kiss Mary)

The idea of variable constituency thus introduced for VPD with respect to adverbs is strongly reminiscent of Jackendoff's (1972) observation that like adverbs preceding the auxiliary must gap along with the verb. VPD must have the same effect: like adverbs preceding the AUX delete along with the verb, and unlike adverbs don't:

190. John sometimes washes his hands, and Peter always does Ø (Ø=wash his hands)
191. John carefully cleaned his teeth, and Peter did Ø as well (Ø=carefully clean his teeth)

The same type of phenomenon observed for (191) can be observed for Gapping in (192):

192. Peter carefully washed the glass, and Mary Ø the china cups (Ø=carefully washed)

It is in fact quite difficult to see how Gapping could be prevented from applying to (191) to yield the unacceptable (191a):

191a. *John carefully cleaned his teeth, and Peter Ø his teeth as well.

Sentence (191) is a problem for Sag's account of VPD anyway, since the formulation in (181) of VPD as post-auxiliary deletion does not permit VPD (unlike Gapping) to delete discontinuous material; nevertheless, in (191), material *preceding* and material *following* the AUX has been deleted. VPD must therefore be able, like Gapping, to delete discontinuous material.

A further similarity between Gapping and VPD, if they are separate rules, is that for both the remnants will have to be constrained — but where it could be said for Gapping that there is, as a rule of thumb, one remnant preceding the gap, and one or two following the gap, the remnants for VPD are much harder to specify. Yet a specification of remnants will be necessary: a sentence like (193), which meets all the conditions for VPD, results in unacceptable (194) if VPD is applied:

193. John went home and Peter went home.
194. *John went home and Peter did Ø.

If we add an additive adjunct,[59] or an adverb to (194), the application of VPD is legitimate again:

195. First John went home, and then Peter did Ø.
196. John went home, and Peter did Ø too.

Sag makes extensive use of additive adjuncts like *too, as well, also* in his discussion of VPD without referring to the crucial role these play for the acceptability of his example sentences: a crucial role which had already been observed by Gleitman (1965); see also section 1.1.1 in this chapter. This weakens his account seriously: most of the sentences with additive adjuncts which he uses as examples would be unacceptable without them. This in turn means that there will have to be some sort of constraint on the remnants of VPD. However, it is not easy to see how the possible remnants of VPD could be specified: one cannot (as has been done for Gapping; see Neijt (1979)) specify that there should be at least two remnants, or that there should be an additive adjunct somewhere, since there is no additive adjunct remnant in (197), and only a single remnant in (198):

197. John went home, but Bill didn't Ø.
198. John didn't go home, but Bill did Ø.

Yet another problem for VPD emerges in sentences with identical subjects — a sentence like (199) should not be subject to VPD (although there is nothing in Sag's account to block VPD in this case; see the discussion relating to examples (186-189)), but it should only be subjected to Coordination Reduction: (200) is unacceptable, (201) is not. If we turn (199) on to a question, we find the same type of situation, in spite of the fact that that the AUX now both precedes and commands both the subject and the VP:

199. Peter loved Betsy in Paris, and Peter loved Betsy in Rome, too.
200. *Peter loved Betsy in Paris, and Peter did Ø in Rome, too.
201. Peter loved Betsy in Paris, and Ø in Rome, too.
202. *Did Peter love Betsy in Paris, and did Peter Ø in Rome, too?
203. Did Peter love Betsy in Paris, and Ø in Rome, too?

It seems to be extremely difficult to define the domain of VPD; and defining the relation between VPD and other coordinate deletion rules like Gapping and Coordinate Deletion is especially problematic.

It also needs to be observed that VPD, as Sag formulates it, is not restricted to VPs in coordinated Ss; it also applies to VPs in subordinate Ss:

204. My wife goes home whenever I do Ø.

There are, however, some important differences between VPD in coordinate clauses and VPD in subordinate clauses, and at least one similarity. The similarity is that also in subordinate clauses, VPD will have to delete identical pre-AUX adverbs along with the verb, as in (205):

205. When you gradually increase the pressure, I will Ø, too.
     (Ø=gradually increase the pressure)

The first difference between coordinate VPD and subordinate VPD is that the problem observed for sentences (193-198) disappears for subordinate VPD: subordinate VPD seems not to require a remnant constraint:

206. I will go home if you will Ø.

Secondly, no reduction or ellipsis whatsoever is possible for VPs not preceded by an unlike subject in subordinate clauses, unlike (199-203):[60]

207. *Whenever Peter loved Betsy in Paris, Ø (did) in Rome, too.
208. *Did Peter love Betsy in Paris if (did) Ø in Rome?

Lastly, subordinate VPD need not only delete subsequent occurrences of identical VPs, but it may also delete antecedent occurrences:

209. If you can Ø, please bring me some cheese from the market.
210. Please bring me some cheese from the market if you can Ø.
211. If you can bring me some cheese from the market, please do Ø.

Undoubtedly VPD could be refined in such a way that these differences between coordinate VPD and subordinate VPD can be accounted for. What remains, however, is a clear indication that it will be extremely difficult (if not impossible) to disentangle coordinate VPD from other deletion rules such as Gapping and Coordinate Deletion, which also apply in coordinated structures, and which have domains of application which largely overlap with that of VPD. Given this fact, and given the fact that there are unmistakable differences between subordinate VPD and coordinate VPD, one can raise the question of whether VPD is indeed one single phenomenon: it may very well turn out to be the case that VPD in coordinated structures is part of the same type of coordinate deletion rule that also includes Gapping and Coordination Reduction, while VPD in subordinated structures is a different process again. This hypothesis is supported by the fact that languages like Dutch and German, which are closely related to English, have a coordinated deletion type roughly equivalent to VPD, but have nothing resembling subordinate VPD: there, pro-form substitution of some sort is required. We shall return to the notion of a unitary coordinate deletion rule which includes coordinate VPD but which does not affect subordinate VPD in considerable detail in Chapter 2, and we shall return to the question of VPD and constraints on VPD in Chapter 3.

1.3.10 GPSG — Gazdar

Generalised Phrase Structure Grammar (henceforth GPSG) has, in the last few years, attracted considerable attention, not least because of the original approach it presents to coordinate structures. In this section, I shall discuss Gazdar's (1981) influential paper 'Unbounded Dependencies and Coordinated Structure', as well as subsequent work which addresses the type of issue raised here: Schachter and Mordechay (1983) and Sag *et al.* (1985).

The one important aspect in which the GPSG account of coordination differs from other approaches outlined in this chapter (barring Dik's (1968) functional approach) is that GPSG does not allow transformations at all, and therefore also does not allow deletion transformations. The basis for the GPSG account is a set of PS-rules which are in principle not unlike those used by Dougherty (1970); the rule schema outlined in (212):

212. $a ======> a_1$ ....and/or a_n, where a = any syntactic category

is referred to by Gazdar as: '... nothing new. They data back at least as far as Dougherty (1970), and can be found in many more recent works.' (Gazdar, 1981:157)

Gazdar is quick to point out two disadvantages of such schemata: first of all, as we have already seen in section 1.2.2, in a model of grammar which incorporates a Passive transformation as well as a rule schema of this type, sentences like:

213. The Dodgers beat the Red Sox and were beaten by the Giants.

cannot be accounted for without resorting to a deletion rule of some sort. But since GPSG has no transformations, and therefore no Passive transformation, this problem simply disappears. A second disadvantage is that there is no semantics available for such rule schemata, but this will have to be devised separately. Given that propositional logic makes available a semantics for sentential coordination, there is no need for a separate semantics of non-sentential coordination if one simply avoids rule schemata of the type (212) and treats all coordination as derived from sentence coordination by means of deletion rules.[61] We shall return to this semantic problem briefly in Chapter 3, and restrict ourselves here to the syntax of coordination in GPSG.

The first thing to observe is that adherence to rule schemata like (212) causes problems of description whose existence has been known for at least 20 years — Gleitman (1965) had already observed sentences like (9-11) as counter-examples to Chomsky's (1957) suggestion that coordination is always constituent coordination:

(10) I gave the girl a nickel and the boy a dime.
(11) He took John home and Mary to the station.
(12) The man was haggard and the girl sick with exhaustion.

These sentences are clear examples of non-category coordination. Other instances are cases of what we have earlier described under the name of Gapping: if Gapping leaves one remnant before the gapped verb, and one or more after it, then these remnants will not form a category which is coordinated with a category of the same type in the way suggested in rule schema (212). Gazdar (1981) does not address these questions: he assumes that a solution for these problems is to be found in the proper formulation of the rule of Gapping.[62] But even if these problems are somehow solved, there is at least one interesting type of problem which remains for the PS-rule approach suggested by Gazdar which casts serious doubt on the validity of a rule schema like (212) even for constituent coordination: this problem was pointed out by Rögnvaldsson (1982). The problem concerns impersonal verbs in Icelandic; these are verbs which, irrespective of the person and number of the subject, always take a 3rd person singular form if the subject is in an oblique case, i.e. accusative, dative, or genitive (Rögnvaldsson, 1982:558):

214. Mig   vantar   bókina.
     Me (acc) needs (3sg) the book (= I need the book)
215. Mér   likar   þetta.
     Me (dat) likes (3sg) this (= I like this)

These verbs take 3rd person singular form as a result of the oblique-case subject: there are also verbs which usually take a nominative subject (which triggers normal subject-verb agreement), but which may also take an oblique subject: with the oblique subject, the verb will again be 3rd person singular.

216. Við   hlokkum (1pl) til jólanna.
      *Við   hlakkar   (3sg) til jólanna.
      We (nom) look   forward to Christmas.
217. *Okkur   hlokkum (1pl) til jólanna.
      Okkur   hlakkar   (3sg) til jólanna.
      Us (acc/dat) look   forward to Christmas.

The reverse is also possible: verbs which are usually impersonal will, if the subject is in the nominative case, agree with this subject, and not take the 3rd person singular form (Rögnvaldsson, 1982:559). 'Normal' verbs taking nominative subjects can be coordinated with impersonal verbs; in this case, or in the case in which coordinated VPs in which a 'normal' verb occurs in one VP, and an impersonal verb occurs in another VP, the subject will be nominative if the first verb is 'normal', and oblique if the first verb is impersonal. The impersonal verb in such a coordination will be 3rd person singular, irrespective of whether there is an oblique subject overtly present or not:

218. * þeir sjá   stúlkuna og finnast (3pl) hún álitleg.
          þeir   sjá   stúlkuna og finnst (3sg) hún álitleg.
       They (nom) see (3pl) the girl   and find   her attractive.
219. * þeim   likar   maturinn og   borðar (3sg) mikið.
          þeim   likar   maturinn og   borða (3pl) mikið.
       Them (dat) likes (3sg) the food and   eat   much.

This poses a considerable problem for constituent coordination: although it is clear that we have constituent coordination in these cases (VP *and* VP), we need to refer to an oblique subject in (218), and to a nominative subject in (219) in order to get the correct verb form. However, the overt subjects are nominative in (218), and dative in (219). In a deletion account, it will be easy enough to assign the correct verb forms in the subsequent coordinated VPs in (218-219) if we derive them from sentence-coordinations by means of deletion of the oblique and nominative subjects, respectively. It is however quite difficult to see how a GPSG model, which does not allow such deletions,

would handle these facts in a non-*ad hoc* way: to my knowledge, no account has been suggested so far. The Icelandic data
provide strong evidence that even in some cases of constituent
coordination, some sort of coordinate deletion rule will be
preferable to a 'pure' PS-account.

Ken Hale (personal communication) has alerted me to the
following facts from Hopi, which pose a slightly different
problem for GPSG-type constituent coordinations. In Hopi,
conjoined coordinations have the conjunction *niq* in subject
position, but *nit* in non-subject position:

220. Ni' 'it   taavot   nit   'it   sowit   niina.
    (I   this-acc cottontail-acc and this-acc jackrabbit
                                          kill nonpl. obj)
    I killed this cottontail and this jackrabbit.

221. 'Ima totimho 'yam niq 'itana   taataptiy   qᵘöqya.
    (these boys-pl   and our father cottontail-pl-acc kill-pl
                                                    -obj)
    These boys and our father killed cottontails.

In order to account for such facts, GPSG would have to invoke
a rule generating conjoined subjects, or conjoined sentences
with different subjects, and another (using a different coordinating conjunction) generating conjoined sentences with same
subjects or conjoined NPs which are not subjects, in the appropriate places. But here, non-optimal use is being made of the
notions 'different' and 'the same'. Within a deletion approach,
we can make better use of these notions. In order to account for
deletion, we need to be able to refer to constituents or strings
being identical or nonidentical. In order to account for switch-
reference facts, this requirement becomes only slightly more
specific: we only need to be able to identify subjects as being
'different' or 'same'. This option will be needed in the grammar
anyway (see e.g. Comrie's (1986b) review of Finer (1985)).
The Hopi data can thus readily be treated as a case of switch-
reference where 'same subject' and 'different subject' are
marked on the coordinating conjunction rather than on the
verb, and same-subject and same-object deletion then apply in
regular fashion. Such an analysis is quite plausible, especially
since subject-verb number agreement in Hopi is with the last
member of the coordination rather than with the 'whole' subject

NP. We shall return to agreement in more detail in Chapter 3.

A very interesting suggestion in Gazdar (1981) is the treatment of Right-node Raised constituents.[63] Gazdar, in order to account for unbounded dependencies, gives an elegant extension of the notion of constituent: given a set of rules expanding *basic* categories, it is possible to define a set of rules expanding *derived* categories in the same way in which the corresponding basic rules would have expanded the basic categories: the derived categories, however, will differ from the basic categories in one or more features.[64] The feature which is relevant to us here is SLASH, to be interpreted as: as constituent with a phrase missing from it. Thus *S/NP* is to be interpreted as: an *S* with an *NP* missing from it somewhere. Given a set of rules expanding *S*, the derived set of rules will give the same expansion, with the difference that all expansions are */NP* (SLASH NP) if that is the feature in which the derived rule set is designed to differ from the basic rule set. This extension of the traditional notion of category for instance allows Gazdar to account for sentences which are traditionally thought of as involving deletion rules like RNR or Backward Conjunction Reduction as simple cases of derived category coordination. A sentence like (222), of which the RNR variant is (223) have as corresponding structures (222a) and (223a) in GPSG:

222.   Harry caught the rabid dog, and Mary killed the rabid dog.
223.   Harry caught, and Mary killed the rabid dog.
222a.

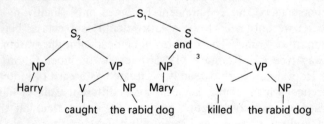

223a.

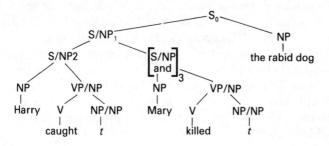

There is a derivational relation between (222a) and (223a) in the following sense: GPSG has a set of rules which derive categories from basic categories, and rules (called *metarules*)[65] which derive (context-free PS) rules from other CFPS rules. Such a metarule establishes the relation between (222a) and (223a) as follows (very informally stated): if there is a set of PS-rules generating a certain sentence structure, then there is a set of rules that will give you that same structure, but with an NP missing from S_1 which is present as an immediate rightmost daughter of the higher S_0.

Gazdar's proposal allows him to maintain Chomsky's (1957) suggestion that all coordination can be seen as coordination of same constituents for RNR-type structures: structures which, before Gazdar (1981), had always been treated as coordinations which are derived transformationally from sentence-coordinations. This makes Gazdar's account a welcome and striking innovation. But it is too restricted as an account of RNR-type constructions,[66] since it restricts them to single rightmost constituents, which is clearly wrong: Gleitman (1965) cites a number of cases where we have two constituents in the 'raised' position (repeated in this section as examples 10-12), as does Williams (1978). Secondly, because the coordination schema expands categories into coordinations of same categories, it cannot account for coordinations of unlike categories as in, for instance, (224), where we have a coordination of an adverb and a prepositional phrase:

224. She walked slowly and with great care.

Thirdly, it ignores the fact that 'right-node raisings' may also be bidirectional. Rightmost verbs in Dutch and German subordinate clauses may delete either in the antecedent clause, or in the subsequent clause: this fact was first observed for German in Ross (1970).[67] While both (225) and (226) are equally good and common sentences of Dutch, and neither is stylistically marked, Gazdar's (1981) account predicts that (225) is fine (a case of an RNR-type construction), but that (226) is essentially different, and cannot be accounted for as a grammatical coordination: Gazdar's syntax of coordination predicts that (226) should not exist.

225. Ik geloof   dat Jan vis Ø, en Piet kaas eet.
226. Ik geloof   dat Jan vis eet, en Piet kaas Ø.
    (I believe that Jan fish eats, and Piet cheese Ø)

The first problem for the analysis in Gazdar (1981) noted above is discussed in Schachter and Mordechay (1983), and the second problem is discussed in Sag *et al.* (1985), and in Gazdar *et al.* (1985). Steedman (1985) also presents an interesting solution to some of the problems presented here, but this will be discussed in a separate paragraph, because Steedman's solution is couched in terms of categorial grammar and not in terms of GPSG.

The first problem, namely that RNR constructions are not limited to single rightmost constituents, is taken up in Schachter and Mordechay (1983). Noting sentences of the sort also observed e.g. in Gleitman (1965), and in van Oirsouw (1981, 1983a), they question the validity of Gazdar's (1981) general schema for rightward dependencies,[68] and propose to divorce RNR from other rightward displacements. The sentences in question are of the following type:

227. John gave Ø Ø, and Peter sold some records to Mary.

From such sentences they conclude that what is usually called RNR must be allowed to apply to a sequence of phrasal categories as well as to single phrasal categories (Schachter and Mordechay, 1983:265).[69] They also note sentences like:

228. John gave the books to Mary and Ø Ø the records to Sue.

where they conclude that not only rightmost sequences can be 'raised', but also leftmost sequences (although it must be observed that (228) can also be seen as a 'raised' leftmost verb in a coordination of V/VPs). They propose the following two rule schemata for Right-node Raising and Left-node Raising (1983:265-7):

229. RNR $[\alpha/\beta^R [+crd] \beta]$
$\quad \alpha$

> where crd. = coordination; R = rightmost; α, β = any category or sequence of categories

230. LNR $[\beta [+crd] \alpha/\beta^L]$
$\quad \alpha$

> where crd. = coordination; L = leftmost; α, β = any category or sequence of categories

These rules have the effect of introducing 'raised' categories or sequences of categories to the left or to the right of a coordination of SLASH categories or sequences of categories. This preserves the generalisation that only same categories can be conjoined, but also extends it to sequences of categories. The feature [+crd] ensures that rightmost and leftmost dependencies of the sort exemplified in (227-228) occur only in co-ordinated structures. Now given that rules (229-230) are near-mirror-images of each other, Schachter and Mordechay propose to collapse these two into one as follows:

231. $[\alpha/\beta^P [+crd] \beta]$
$\quad \alpha$

> where P = peripheral; crd = coordination; α, β = any category or sequence of categories

They thus seek to capture Ross's (1970) 'mirror-image' formulation of coordination, a formulation which was worked out in an early transformational model as the type of deletion rule found e.g. in Tai (1969).[70] Schachter and Mordechay's rule (231) states that a construction belonging to. a category can have, as its constituents, a set of conjuncts belonging to the category α — with-a-peripheral-β -hole in it (1983:271).[71] This proposal is interesting for two reasons. First of all, it extends the notion of 'hole' from single constituents to sequences of constituents, thus making the GPSG approach to coordinated structures roughly equivalent to the transformational approach (excluding Gapping): GPSG uses variable holes in coordination, transformational grammar uses variable deletion rules. Secondly, it brings out the importance of the notion of *peripherality*; a deletion target (or, in GPSG terms, a hole) must be peripheral to its construction. This fact was first noted in Langendoen (1975), and later taken up and elaborated in van Oirsouw (1981, 1983a,1984,1985). But a notion like peripherality necessarily refers to the linear order of the constituents of a construction, and that linear order will be surface order. This is implicitly so in Langendoen (1975), and explicitly so in van Oirsouw (1984,1985). It is also explicit in Schachter and Mordechay (1983), since the GPSG framework in which their approach is cast makes a distinction between rules responsible for immediate dominance relations (ID rules), and rules responsible for linear order (LP rules).[72] The rule schema in (231) will create the coordination of SLASH categories and the 'raised' (string of) constituents, and a linearisation rule will assign the hole to the proper (left or right) periphery. The 'raised' (string of) constituents is assigned to the left of a left-peripheral hole, or to the right of a rightperipheral hole. That the 'raised' constituent must be at the same end of the sentence as the hole will be clear from (232,233), where the holes are not preceded or followed by the corresponding 'raised' constituents:

232. *Ø Ø Mary a book, and Peter gave Sue a record.
233. *John gave Mary a book, and Peter sold Ø Ø.

Note, incidentally, that (232,233) are ruled out in GPSG in two ways: by the linearisation rules, and by the fact that a rule schema as in (231) conjoins same categories (or sequences) only: in (232,233) the 'raised' constituent intervenes in between the coordinated SLASH categories, which makes it impossible to fit constructions of this type into a rule schema like (231). The 'raised' category must always immediately precede or follow its hole; any linearisation which fails to do this will automatically violate (231).

However, this iron-clad prediction that a *right*most hole will have a *right*most raised constituent to the *right* of it, and leftmost for a leftmost hole, is precisely one of the most serious drawbacks of the GPSG account of coordination. Ross (1970) pointed out that there is a number of languages that allow 'bidirectional' Gapping; these are typically verb-final languages. Dutch and German are cases in point. These two languages allow bidirectional Gapping of verbs in subordinate clauses, which have SOV word-order. A direct object can also gap along with the verb, either in the antecedent clause, or in the subsequent clause:

234. Ich glaube, dass Johann Bier trinkt, und Peter Wein Ø.
     Ik geloof dat Johann bier drinkt, en Peter wijn Ø.
     (I believe that Johann beer drinks, and Peter wine Ø)
235. Ich glaube, dass Johann Bier Ø und Peter Wein trinkt.
     Ik geloof, dat Johann bier Ø en Peter wijn drinkt.
236. Ich glaube, dass Johann Maria eine Schallplatte schenkt,
                                    und Peter Susan Ø Ø.
     Ik geloof dat Johann Maria een plaat   geeft,
                                    en Peter Susan Ø Ø.
     (I believe that Johann Maria a   record   gives,
                                    and Peter Susan Ø Ø)
237. Ich glaube, dass Johann Maria Ø Ø, und Peter Susan eine
                                    Schallplatte schenkt.
     Ik geloof dat Johann Maria Ø Ø, en Peter Susan een
                                    plaat   geeft.

Sentence (235) can readily be accounted for by both Gazdar (1981) and Schachter and Mordechay (1983) as simple cases of rightmost constituent raising (V in this case). Sentences (237) are a problem for Gazdar (1981) since they involve the raising of a rightmost string of constituents, but they can be accounted for by Schachter and Mordechay (1983), either by means of rule (229) or (231). But sentences (234) and (236) cannot be accounted for as a coordination of SLASH categories in either proposal, since here the non-SLASH category S is coordinated with SLASH categories S/V and $S/V,NP$. Sentences like (234) and (236) are by no means exceptional in Dutch or German: they are as normal and frequent as their counterparts (235) and (237). They therefore constitute strong evidence against the GPSG approach to coordination, or rather, to any approach to coordination which relies crucially on coordination of same constituents[73] and prohibits deletion.

As noted earlier, it is also possible to coordinate unlike categories. Gazdar *et al.* (1985) and Sag *et al.* (1985) offer an elegant solution to the problem posed by sentence (224) cited earlier. In this sentence, as in sentence (238), unlike single constituents have been coordinated:

224. She walked slowly and with great care.
238. His father was well known to the police and a devout catholic.

Given that categories can be seen as bundles of feature specifications, one can observe that e.g. the copular verb *be* in (238) can select any predicative $\bar{\bar{X}}$; a further feature specification for *BE* is not necessary. If selection can be done on partial feature specification, there is no reason why coordination could not be done on partial feature specification as well. It is possible to coordinate categories which differ in their *full* feature specifications, provided that there is a *partial* feature specification which corresponds to the feature specification on the node immediately dominating the members of the coordination. In the case of (238), the complement of *BE* may be a coordination of partially specified constituents, provided that the specification is compatible with that of *BE*. The full feature specification of these nodes is then of no further relevance to the coordination rule.

This problem is again one which arises specifically in a GPSG-type approach: in a deletion-based account (224,238) would be derived from grammatical clause-coordinations, and, given a proper formulation of the deletion rule, it would follow that a grammatical clause-coordination will always result in a grammatical non-clausal coordination.

Bidirectional deletions of the sort observed in Ross (1970) remain a problem for GPSG — as does all of Gapping. GPSG cannot account for gapped structures like the classic:

239. John ate fish and Bill Ø rice.

since it necessarily involves coordination of unlike categories. Sag *et al.* (1985) wish to relegate rules like Gapping, for which there is no solution forthcoming in GPSG, to some domain outside the grammar. Their basis for this move is that Gapping can occur across speakers in discourse, and the example is (240):

240. Speaker A: I shall miss you.
     Speaker B: And I Ø you.

That Gapping can occur across speakers in discourse is a correct observation — but constituent coordination can also occur across speakers in discourse:

241. Speaker A: I will do the shopping.
     Speaker B: And I will wash the car.

242. Speaker A: You mean Peter went home.
     Speaker B: And did not breathe a word about it to you.
                  Yes, quite.

243. Speaker A: I never suspected that you
     Speaker B: And your own dear wife would start an
                  affair. No, we know. We counted on that.

In (241), we have coordination of clauses across speakers, in (242), we have coordination of VP across speakers, and in (243), we have coordination of NP across speakers. In all these cases we have the shift in deixis which, for Sag *et al.* (1985:160) is a clear indication that we do not have an instance of two speakers collaborating on a single sentence. Category coordination and Gapping are therefore not distinct with respect to their ability to occur across speakers in discourse: Sag *et al.*'s suggestion that Gapping is not a rule of sentence grammar, but a rule of discourse grammar, while category coordination is clearly in the domain of sentence grammar, is therefore unfounded at best.[74]

Sag *et al.* do, however, provide a telling hint as to how the process of Gapping might be constrained. They observe that:

> Gapped structures ... obey a substitutional generalisation. If the result of substituting the remnant for the corresponding element in the preceding conjunct is well-formed, then the gapping structure is well-formed as well. (Sag *et al.*, 1985:160)

Apart from the fact that this substitutional generalisation applies only to forward Gapping and thus ignores the 'bidirectional' type of Gapping first observed in Ross (1970), this substitutional procedure is quite obviously a reversed deletion rule, and is incompatible with the fundamental tenets of GPSG. What it says is roughly: copy the preceding verb into the subsequent corresponding gap, and if the result is well-formed, then the Gapping structure is well-formed as well. This is clearly equivalent to saying: delete the subsequent second occurrence of the same verb: the result will be grammatical. As a deletion rule, this is a gross oversimplification; as a substitution procedure, it is an equally gross oversimplification. It ignores, for instance, Jackendoff's (1972) important observations discussed in section 1.3.2 of this chapter that Gapping does not take place with unlike adverbs preceding the verb. In these cases the non-gapped sentences will be well-formed, and the gapped sentences are not. The substitutional criterion, however, would incorrectly predict that the gapped sentences must be well-formed because the non-gapped sentences are grammatical: the substitutional criterion therefore predicts that Gapping is allowed with unlike adverbs preceding the verbs, or with unlike auxiliaries. As a matter of fact, this substitutional criterion will allow all sorts of illegitimate gappings, since it says that if one 'undoes' the illegitimate gapping, and the result of this is a well-formed sentence, then the gapping cannot have been illegitimate. This is clearly wrong.[75]

Let us sum up the arguments in this section. GPSG, which relies crucially on coordination of same categories (although these categories may have only partial feature specifications), is capable of accounting for a wide range of constituent coordinations, and for the cases of what deletion-type approaches have called Right-node Raising or Backward Conjunction Reduction. Some cases of constituent coordination (notably verbs in Icelandic) are resistant to the GPSG treatment and require a deletion rule of some sort. GPSG is in principle unable to account for 'bidirectional' coordinate deletions, and for Gapping. These will necessarily have to be accounted for by some sort of deletion rule (*pace* Stump, 1975, Goodall, 1983,1984). GPSG has not provided any basis for the hypothesis that Gapping is not a rule of sentence grammar, or indeed for the hypothesis that Gapping is different from other coordinate deletion rules. GPSG seems to be necessarily limited to accounting for a subset of what we shall call leftmost and right-most coordinate deletions in Chapter 2.

1.3.11 Categorial grammar: Steedman

One final interesting and novel approach to coordination is presented in Steedman (1985). Steedman's proposal is couched in terms of categorial grammar: it aims to achieve a more adequate statement of the relation between coordination and unbounded dependencies first formalised in Gazdar (1981), and to account for some notorious cases of intersecting dependencies in Dutch infinitival complements.[76] I shall limit myself to coordination here, and the brief and very informal outline of categorial grammar below will only encompass the notions which are crucial to Steedman's discussion of coordination. For a very good and much more detailed critical discussion of Steedman's work, with special reference to Dutch, see Seuren (1985:86-97).

Steedman's categorial grammar consists of two components: a categorial lexicon, in which each entry includes a 'category' defining the kind of constituent with which the word in question may combine, and the types of constituents that result from this combination. A category may be e.g. simply NP (*dog, cat, I*), or it may be, as in the case of intransitive verbs, seen as: 'something which combines with an object to become VP' (written *VP/NP*, not to be confused with the *slash* notation used in GPSG), or, in the case of ditransitive verbs, as 'something which, if it combines with an NP, will combine with yet another NP to become VP' (written (*VP/NP)NP*). The second component is a set of PS-rules (called 'combination rules'); these are responsible for the linear order of constituents. Categories of the form X/Y are seen as functions over Y; transitive verbs, for instance, are seen as functions from VPs into NPs. One example of a combination rule would be the *Forward Combination Rule*, where a function. combines with an argument to its right[77] (Steedman, 1985:527):

244. X/Y Y ======> X

The variable in this rule may be either basic categories, like *NP*, or functors, like NP/VP. In order to deal with a topicalised sentence like:

245. Apples, he likes.

where there is a discontinous VP, one needs to be able to combine a subject and an object into a function which combines with the verb to yield an S. What is needed is the following device: if there is a forward-combining category X/Y which is followed by a category Y/Z which is not followed by a Z, then a subtree X may be set up that inherits the requirement that a Z be found somewhere to make up the X; this subtree gets the labelling X/Z. This requirement for a Z to be found may be inherited further if the next combination rule does not eliminate it. Steedman calls this device *Forward Partial Combination*, and proposes a Forward Partial Combination rule which has the following generalised form:

246. $X/Y \; X \; \$/Z ===== > X \; \$/Z$

(246) is a schema for a set of PS-rules which should be read as follows:

> ... if X is the atomic category S, then X\$ is some member of the set including S, S/NP, (S/NP)NP, etc. If Y is the atomic category VP, and if X\$ is S, then Y\$ is VP; if X\$ is S/NP, then Y\$ is VP/NP; if X\$ is (S/NP)NP, then Y\$ is (VP/NP)NP etc. (Steedman, 1985:533)

This Forward Partial Combination Rule combines with the following rule schema:

247. X^+ CONJ X ===== > X where X = any category
    + = one or more

This rule schema embodies in essence the same type of constituent coordination as encountered in Dougherty (1970) or Gazdar (1981); (246) and (247) together are capable of producing constituent coordinations of either basic categories (NP etc.) or functor categories ((VP/NP)NP etc.). Given that (246) is a forward combination rule, it can, in conjunction with

(247), account for what Gazdar (1981) has called 'rightward dependencies' (Right-node Raising) in coordinated structures. It cannot, however, account for leftward dependencies, since these require a functor to find and argument to the left: (246) has the argument Z to the right of the functor.

Steedman's approach allows him to account for a simple coordination of basic categories (248), RNR-type constructions (249), and also, through iteration of the Forward Partial Combination Rule, for a complex coordination in Dutch like (250), where we have conjunction of two pairs of NPs with different grammatical functions, and a 'raised' object NP + verbs; the Dutch sentence means '... *that Jan saw Marie help the children to swim, and Cecilia saw Henk help the children to swim*':

248. John saw Peter and Mary, (= NP & NP)
249. John caught, and Mary killed the rabid dog. (= S/NP & S/NP)
250. ... dat   Jan Marie en   Cecilia Henk de kinderen zag
                                                  helpen zwemmen.
     (... that Jan Marie and Cecilia Henk the children saw
                                                  help   swim)
     (= $S/NP/((FVP/NP_1)/NP_2)$ & $S/((FVP/NP_1)/NP_2)$),
     where FVP = finite verb phrase

Steedman is thus capable of accounting for 'Raising' of strings of rightmost constituents, and his account is therefore, like Schachter and Mordechay (1983), an empirical improvement on Gazdar (1981). Like Schachter and Mordechay, Steedman accounts for the 'remnants' of such complex 'raising' operations (I use quotation marks here because the terms are taken from a different framework, and have no meaning within the GPSG account or the categorial account) as in (250) as coordinations of categories; SLASH categories for Schachter and Mordechay, functor categories for Steedman.[78] Unlike Schachter and Mordechay, however, Steedman cannot account for sentences like:

251. I gave the books to Mary and the records to Sue.

since sentences of this nature involve a leftward dependency and therefore require an argument to the left of the functor.

Steedman does not provide a backward combination rule that could do this, although there seem to be no *in principle* objections to such a rule. Like Gazdar (1981), Steedman proposes that such sentences should be accounted for by means of some variant of Gapping (1985:fn.20). Unlike Gazdar (1981), he *does* include a brief discussion of Gapping; [79] he assumes that Gapping omits the verb group in a right conjunct, and that it does so leaving one constituent before the gap (1985:560). But this is clearly false: there is no remnant before the gap in (251). Nor is there a pre-gap remnant in a Dutch question like:

252. Eet Jan vis, en Ø Wim rijst?
     (eats Jan fish, and Ø Wim rice?)

What is significant here is that the remnant left behind by Gapping[80] consists of the subject + Object, which could qualify as a single functor (S/FVP/NP) in a coordination of subordinate clauses like:

253. ... dat Jan vis Ø en Piet rijst eet.
     (... that Jan fish Ø and Piet rice eats)

This could easily be accounted for by the Forward Combination rule and the coordination schema in (247). Sentence (252) is the mirror-image of (253), but cannot be accounted for because it involves a leftward dependency. Nor is it the case that Gapping omits just the verb group: a direct object may delete along with the verb, as in the Dutch subordinate clauses in (254):

254. ... dat Jan Marie een zoen gegeven heeft, en Piet Sofie Ø
                                                              Ø.
     (... that Jan Marie a   kiss given   has, and Piet Sofie Ø
                                                              Ø)

The verb plus direct object may also delete backwards, giving us:

255. ...dat Jan Marie Ø Ø, en Piet Sofie een zoen gegeven
                                                    heeft.
     (... that Jan Marie Ø Ø, and Piet Sofie a   kiss given
                                                    has)

The coordination in (255) could easily be accounted for in Steedman's approach as a coordination of single functor categories, but it will be clear that if (254) is not accounted for in some similar manner, then the mirror-image generalisation for Gapping first stated in Ross (1970) will be missed. Where (253) and (255) involve coordination of single (functor) categories with an argument to the right, the same functor categories can conjoin with an argument to the left (252) or with an argument which intervenes in between the coordinated categories (254). That this link between what a transformational approach would call forwards and backwards deletion is missed is a consequence of Steedman's approach:[81] (252) requires some kind of backwards partial Combination rule, while (254) requires that the strict condition of category coordination be lifted — or, to recall an observation which we have made earlier: coordination requires a mirror-image formulation, and not all coordination is category coordination. Steedman provides a very ingenious account of basic category coordinations and RNR-type coordinations, but he does not provide an account of Coordination reduction-type coordinations and Gapping-type coordinations. These two types of coordinations are, in combination with RNR-type constructions, precisely the reason why coordination requires a mirror-image formulation, and why not all coordination is category coordination. These two facts about coordination as a whole keep re-emerging, and they will have to play a crucial role in any adequate account of coordination.

1.4 CONCLUSION

In this chapter, I have traced the main issues that have shaped the discussion about coordination in the last three decades. One central issue is the one adumbrated in Chomsky (1957): given that there is a clear syntactic relation between sentential coordination and constituent coordination, does one attempt to account for all coordination as sentential coordination, or as derived from sentential coordination through deletion of identical material, or does one view coordination as much as possible as base-generated, thus reducing the role of deletion rules to a minimum? As Gleitman (1965) has shown, not all coordination is surface constituent coordination, and as Smith

(1969) has shown, not all surface structure constituent coordination can be paraphrased as sentential coordination. Tai (1969) has provided a fully transformational account of coordination which fails crucially in those cases of coordination which are not sentence-paraphrasable, while Dougherty (1970) provides a strongly PS-oriented account which falls short in cases of non-constituent coordination. From the early transformational discussion, the idea of directionality of deletion emerged (Ross, 1967,1970, and Tai, 1969), and along with it the 'mirror-image' formulation of coordinate deletion rules. This idea has been attacked in a number of publications, and is under discussion still: Neijt (1979) prefers a transformational, unidirectional account of Gapping, Schachter and Mordechay (1983) opt for a mirror-image GPSG-type account, and Gazdar et al. (1985) and Sag et al. (1985) opt for a unidirectional approach within GPSG. Steedman (1985) also opts for a unidirectional account not involving deletion. From this situation it will be clear that the transformational vs. non-transformational debate, initiated in full in Dougherty (1970) and Tai (1969), is not resolved: nor is the debate about the mirror-image nature of coordination. The grammatical models have become vastly more sophisticated, but the problems remain the same: non-transformational accounts cannot deal with obvious non-constituent coordinations which result from e.g. Gapping, while transformational accounts still have trouble with NP-coordinations in combination with synmmetrical predicates like *be similar, be a nice pair*. These controversies are real, and recent attempts to relegate rules like Gapping to some domain outside syntax in order to avoid problems, which mostly base themselves on the work in Kuno (1976) are clearly inadequate and uncalled for. Whether coordination is something unitary, or a process which consists of a number of essentially different rules is also an issue which has been addressed in a number of places in this chapter, but no convincing arguments against a unitary approach have been found. Jackendoff's (1972) account of Gapping gave rise to a lively discussion which produced the idea of peripherality of deletion (Langendoen, 1975). This idea has also recurred in various places in the literature; e.g. in Schachter and Mordechay (1983) and van Oirsouw (1983a, 1984, 1985). A rich and fascinating body of data and observations has emerged, with various suggestions of analysis. In the second chapter of this book, I shall draw these different developments and observations together, and present a unitary account of coordinate deletion which makes minimal use of 'base' coordination, and is heavy on the deletion side.

NOTES

1. For a brief introduction to the treatment of coordination before 1957, see Dik (1968), Chs 3 and 6.

2. In footnote 2 to Chapter 5, Chomsky (1957) observes cases of what later came to be known as Right-node Raising. He considers these cases to be rather unnatural, and marked by the same sorts of phonemic features as are usually associated with ungrammatical sentences. He proposes that the more completely we violate constituent structures by means of conjunction, the less well-formed the outcome will be. This position has, of course, been revised since.

3. This does weaken the original case against PS-grammars considerably, but we shall not concern ourselves with that historical issue here.

4. Dougherty's original work is an unpublished 1968 MIT Ph.D. dissertation. Reference is to the two *Language* articles because they contain the same ideas and are more accessible.

5. Gleitman also suggests, however, that a conjunction of an interrogative and an imperative sentence is unacceptable. Although there may be cases in which such conjunctions are indeed odd, they are not ungrammatical. It may be difficult to contextualise a sentence like:

Please don't disturb me with your questions, and why don't you try to find your own answers for a change?

but it is neither markedly odd nor ungrammatical. Gleitman's observations were taken up in R. Lakoff (1971); for a further discussion, see e.g. van Oirsouw (1983b).

6. See also note 2 of this chapter.

7. Lakoff and Peters observe that this problem is a fairly old one; they cite Curme (1931) as someone who has made similar observations.

8. See e.g. van Oirsouw (1982b) for an objection on this basis to Gazdar (1981).

9. These aren't isolated cases; consider also:

Becker and Curren are well-matched opponents.

which is non-S-paraphrasable and will not allow either NP of the co-ordination to be moved at all.

10. I take the publication of these two books as convenient landmarks in the progress of linguistic theory as a whole. They are not, however, of special significance specifically to the study of coordination.

11. To my knowledge, the first formulation of the recoverability condition in deletion transformations is in Chomsky's (1964) *Current Issues in Linguistic Theory.* See also section 1.3.3 of this chapter, and Chapter 3.

12. See section 3 for more details on this problem.

13. For a more extensive discussion, see van Oirsouw, 1983a.

14. Furthermore, it is descriptively grossly inadequate. Such *ad hoc* rules as Prep-each-other Deletion, for instance, will give us:

∗John and Bill bumped Ø. (Ø = into each other)

but will fail to capture the relation one might surmise between (a) and (b):

(a)   John and Bill shook each other's hand.
(b)   John and Bill shook hands.

15. Tai (1969:117) feels that this is a mere notational problem.

16. It is, for instance, very hard to see how, under any interpretation of the term 'psychological reality', Tai's account could be claimed to be 'psychologically realistic'.

17. We gloss over the various prunings that have taken place here.

18. Just eliminating passive does not rid us of non-deep structure coordinated VPs; other 'derived' VPs can be coordinated as well, as Dougherty (1970:853) observes:

Mary was neither anxious to please nor fun to squeeze.
Mary was fun to tease, easy to please, and known to have fleas.

19. See Dougherty (1970) for additional arguments to this effect.

20. Conjunct Postposing is, of course, a blatant violation of Ross's (1967) Coordinate Structure Constraint; Hudson does not discuss this fact.

21. That *respectively* takes the two highest nodes will be clear from the fact that we can convert (a) into (b) by taking the two highest nodes Subject and VP, but not into (c) by taking the subject NPs and the object NPs:

(a)   Peter hit the dog and John kicked the cat.
(b)   Peter and John hit the dog and kicked the cat, respectively.
(c)   ∗Peter and John hit the dog and the cat and kicked, respectively.

An additional problem in the formulation of *respectively* is that it is not certain that only single constituents are involved in this rule: arguably, we can also convert (a) into (d), where the non-constituents [subject+verb] are involved:

(d)   Peter hit, and John kicked, the dog and the cat respectively.

22. That is, if one insists on making interpretation more difficult for one's audience.

23. See section 1.1.3; I have been unable to find instances of grammatical *respectively*-constructions involving non-S-paraphrasable co-ordinations. For this reason, I conclude that such coordinations, since

they allow neither *respectively* nor explicit reference to order of co-ordination, are essentially unordered, like plurals.

24. For the opposite view, see Stockwell *et al.* (1973).

25. This extremely influential paper was first presented in 1967 at the Tenth International Congress of Linguists in Bucharest. Reference in this book is to the most accessible version of the paper, which appeared in Bierwisch and Heidolph (eds) 1970.

26. The paper assumes that there is a generally acknowledged rule of Gapping. To my knowledge, however, it is the first reference to deletion of identical verbs in coordinated structures as Gapping. What exactly the formulation of Gapping is as a separate and isolated rule is still not clear even today.

27. Although it has to be observed here that some speakers will consider *but*-coordinated gapped sentences less acceptable, *but* is a coordinator which does allow Gapping:

John bought a Porsche, but Mary Ø a Ferrari.

28. Some linguists insist on inserting a comma at the deletion site of Gapping. Jackendoff is not one of these. I follow his example, and extend it to Right-node Raised constructions, where there is a super-fluous, if fairly widespread, habit of inserting a comma before the 'raised' constituent. Such commas (possibly a relic from the remarks in Chomsky, 1957, Ch. 5, fn.2; see also note 2 of this chapter) are intended to reflect pauses or special intonation patterns, and though it is certainly good stylistic practice to have commas reflecting a preceding rising intonation, or a pause in sentences like:

Tom, shut up.

as opposed to:

Just you shut up!

there is no obligatory substantial change in intonation pattern between a sentence that has undergone Gapping, and one that hasn't, or a sentence that has undergone Right-node Raising, and one that hasn't. The normal intonation for the (a) sentences below as well as for the (b) sentences is a rising intonation for the first clause, and a fall for the second:

(a) John ate fish, and Bill ate rice.
(b) John ate fish, and Bill rice.
(a) John hit the cat, and Mary kicked the cat.
(b) John hit and Mary kicked the cat.

There are no clear intonational difference between the (a) and the (b) sentences, except that the reduced clauses in the (b) sentences are more 'compressed', which (as an anonymous reviewer has pointed out to me) suggests that intonation is a property of the pre-deletion structure. This compression will accentuate the original intonation. For that reason, it

91

is unwarranted to draw conclusions about the constituent structure of a reduced coordination (as has been done for e.g. Right-node Raising) on the basis of hypothesised intonation differences.

29. In fact, quite a few of the N-gapping cases Jackendoff cites are marginal even in his own opinion (1972:30).

30. He does, however, argue that two of these aren't 'real' counter-examples: *Congressman* he claims to be not an NP, while (119) could be accounted for, in his opinion, if the pronoun is seen as cliticised to the verb. Neither argument is particularly convincing.

31. For languages which gap backwards (e.g. Japanese, or Dutch and German in subordinate clauses), or for rules like Right-node Raising in English, it will be the antecedent clause, of course. The same argument holds only in this case, the 'incomplete' clause has to be retained, and has to be matched with the subsequent clause.

32. Actually, Jackendoff (1972) considers sentences of this type ungrammatical, which is a rather harsh judgment. Not many people will find:

John gave a record to Sue, and Sue Ø a book to John.

an ungrammatical sentence.

33. For a further discussion of syntactic ambiguity, see van Oirsouw (1986), and references cited therein.

34. It is, in other words, a transderivational constraint. For a discussion of the history of transderivational constraints, see e.g. Newmeyer (1980:157-8). Hankamer (1972,1973) are important papers for the development of transderivational constraints.

35. Kuno's functional approach is very different from Dik's; whereas Dik has, as basic principles of functional grammar, the fact that it should contain no transformations, filters, or abstract lexical decomposition. Kuno at least allows transformations: otherwise he could never formulate constraints on rules like Gapping and VP-deletion.

36. From this example, and from examples (99-102), it will be clear that identical material *preceding* an identical verb will gap along with the verb; a fact which has (apart from Jackendoff, (1972) definitely not received sufficient attention in the literature.

37. Kuno speaks consistently of *two* remnants — however, as can be seen from the example in note 32, three remnants of Gapping are also a possibility.

38. I use the terms 'grammatical', 'acceptable', and 'well-formed' interchangeably to refer to sentences which are not ruled out as 'bad' by native-speaker intuitions. In those cases where this could give rise to confusion, e.g. in cases where I need to refer to sentences which are acceptable to native speakers, but which are not provided for in a particular model of grammar, I shall use circumlocutions like 'not accounted for by the model'. Sentences which are ruled out by native speaker-judgments but which are freely produced by a model of grammar I shall refer to with phrases like 'generated by the model'. It should perhaps be observed here that not all areas of judgment are equally clear where reduced coordinations are concerned: I have, however, on the whole

limited myself to the clear-cut cases in this book, and have steered clear of the shady areas. In those cases where I am aware of differences in native-speaker judgments, I say so.

39. This example could be repeated for Dutch, which also has SOV word order in subordinate clauses, and also has forward as well as backward Gapping in these clauses.

40. One could, of course, raise the same objection to Williams' proposal for movement of *who* that was raised against Dougherty's Conjunction Substitution rule (see section 1.2.2), namely that a rule which calls itself a movement rule (or, in the case of Dougherty, a substitution rule) also deletes things, but I shall not press this point here.

41. See Williams (1978:fn.6), where he explicitly ignores Gapping and Right-node Raising, a rather surprising move in view of the extensive literature on the similarities between Conjunction Reduction, Gapping, and RNR, their across-the-board nature, and their common domain of coordination.

42. For a more theory-oriented critique of Williams, see Gazdar *et al.* (1982). To be fair to Williams, it must be said that his account is the first to concern itself with the question of why it is that some relative pronouns are odd when they are conjoined; e.g.:

? John, who and whose friends you saw, is a fool.

Quite a few native speakers, however, see no ungrammaticality in this sentence: see again Gazdar *et al.* (1982:673).

43. For a further discussion of this issue, see Hornstein and Lightfoot (1981), or Lightfoot (1982). Note that Neijt has as a subtitle for her book 'A Contribution to Sentence Grammar': see sections 1.3.10 and 1.3.11 for a discussion of the opinion that Gapping is not part of sentence grammar.

44. I myself am sceptical about this particular version of this approach, although I subscribe to the overall goal underlying it. Only if one develops a theory of what is innate or should be innate, given a set of empirical facts, and an account of a particular grammatical phenomenon, can one claim things about learning or learnability. In the case of Neijt, for instance, there is no *a priori* reason why the rule 'Delete' should be acquired. It might just as well be innately given, and its conditions for application be acquired through exposure to data. Such an approach would account equally easily for the empirical facts which she describes, and it would even produce a less counterintuitive account of language learning, since (as Neijt observes) there are other deletion rules besides Gapping. If one assumes that the rule 'Delete' is acquired as a result of exposure to primary linguistic data which contains Gapping facts, this exposure should also trigger the acquisition of rules like Coordination Reduction, Right-node Raising, and VP-deletion, which are also deletion rules, and which will therefore also receive the simple statement 'Delete'. Neijt's approach thus commits her to the rather awkward position of claiming that rules like Gapping are essentially distinct from rules like RNR, but that RNR facts can be the triggering experience for the rule 'Delete' (read:Gapping), and vice

versa. For reasons of this sort, I shall avoid claims about the learnability of systems which are made in the absence of theories of learning as purely speculative.

45. This fact of course detracts quite strongly from the general formulation of 'Delete' for Gapping — as a matter of fact, this does little more than reiterate part of the Gapping rule, and has no value as a generalisation.

46. The only possible distinction still seems to be the remnant distinction: CR can be constrained to leave coordinated constituents behind, while Gapping cannot. But this yields the observed awkward outcome that (a) is the result of Gapping, while (b) is the result of CR (or possibly base-generated):

(a) Buy books at Heffer's and records at Andy's!!
(b) Buy books and records!!

See Ch. 2 for a further discussion of this problem.

47. This should not be taken to mean that Neijt's book is without merit — for a further discussion of its merits and demerits, see Kooij (1983), or van Oirsouw (1982a).

48. In relation to the non-major constituent remnancy of RNR, Neijt gives examples of the following sort (1979:40):

John came up with evidence against Ø, and Peter adduced arguments in support of the proposal.

But note that this demonstrates only that there is backwards deletion that does not leave major constituent remnants, and not that RNR does not leave major constituents. There is a forwards deletion rule that does not leave major constituent remnants as well; compare:

John came up with evidence in favour of the proposal, and Peter adduced evidence against Ø.

Also, in NP coordinations for instance, identical nouns can be freely deleted, either forwards or backwards, while identical adjectives cannot:

(a) Would you like the red wine, or the white Ø
(b) Would you like the red Ø or the white wine?
(c) *Would you like the red meat, or the Ø wine? (Ø = red)
(d) *Would you like the Ø meat or the red wine? (Ø = red)

These facts lead me to suspect that such deletions from within NPs or PPs are something which is different from coordinate deletions as discussed in this book — which is why I have chosen to exclude them from my discussion, and to leave them for future research.

49. I assume familiarity with the basic word order facts in Dutch and German: verb-second in main clauses, verb-final in subordinate clauses, and verb-initial in yes-no questions.

50. For the purposes of this illustration only, I accept Neijt's assumption that VPs may be coordinated in the base. See also Chapter

2 on this matter. Note that in (173), Neijt's (99), the deletion is NOT from under VP, but from under PP. It is therefore not an appropriate illustration of the fact that RNR may delete from under VP.

51. There is one very acute observation by Koster (1978) which might be taken to constitute evidence of a distinction between Gapping and Right-node Raising. He notes that Gapping is constrained by the Bounding condition (Koster, 1978:68) in Dutch subordinate clauses, while RNR is not. Thus, (A) is distinctly better than (B) in Dutch:

(a) Ik dacht dat Jan de paper Ø, en Mary Ø dat Klaas het boek schreef.
(b) ?*Ik dacht dat Jan de paper schreef, en Mary Ø dat Klaas het boek Ø.
 (I thought that Jan the paper wrote, and Mary Ø that Klaas the book Ø)

It can be easily shown, however, that other forward deletion rules also obey the Bounding Condition; for instance, forward Conjunction Reduction:

*Ik dacht dat Jan de paper schreef, en Mary dat Ø het boek corrigeerde.
(I thought that Jan the paper wrote, and Mary that Ø the book corrected)

Backward Conjunction Reduction does not obey the Bounding Condition:

Ik zag dat Jan Marie Ø Ø en Piet Ø dat Harry Susan een kus gaf.
(I saw that Jan Marie Ø Ø and Piet Ø that Harry Susan a kiss gave)

This is a tantalising fact which is in need of explanation. For the moment, it should be observed that Boundedness does *not* support the existence of an independent rule of Gapping.

52. Actually, the main aim of Neijt's book is to show a connection between WH-movement and Gapping. She suggests a revised form of Subjacency (which she calls Strict Subjacency) to account for similarities in constraints on these rules. For further discussion, see van Oirsouw (1982a), and Kooij (1983).

53. Neijt (1979) for instance does not provide answers to the questions which Jackendoff has raised, which is surprising given the importance of these incisive observations.

54. An objection of this sort could also be raised against Neijt (1979), although remnant constraints such as the Major Category Condition are clear surface structure constraints, Neijt's Strict Subjacency is not.

55. This, actually, could be seen as a requirement on recoverability of deletions, as Sag also suggests on p. 38. We shall discuss this matter in greater detail in Chapter 2.

56. On p. 35, Sag notes a few German sentences as evidence for

VPD in German. These sentences (whose acceptability is *highly* questionable) involve only deletion of the main verb and can therefore not be evidence for Sag's variable-deletion VPD rule. As a matter of fact, English is probably the only language that has VPD in the form that Sag suggests.

57. I am grateful to an anonymous referee for pointing this fact out to me.

58. Note, incidentally, how this brings VPD closer to Gapping in at least the area of Hankamer's (1973) Major Constituent Condition on Gapping: at least *3* recursive occurrences of VP are needed, with only the lowest VP being deleted, in order for VPD to violate the MCC in coordinated sentences.

59. I follow Quirk *et al.* (1972) in calling such things as *too, as well, also, either* additive adjuncts: mainly for want of a better name.

60. Do-so substitution can systematically take place if the subject remains, though, so that the inapplicability of VPD cannot easily be attributed to the absence of a properly analysable VP (assuming the validity of do-so substitution as a criterion for VP-constituency).

61. This, of course, is an oversimplification — not all coordination is sentence-coordination or derived from sentence-coordination, as will be clear from the discussion in sections 1.2.1 and 1.2.2.

62. Though see Hudson (1982) for some arguments that the rule responsible for (9-11) is not the same rule that is responsible for gapped structures. Note also that Gapping is a deletion transformation in most of its formulations (though see Stump (1978) for an unsuccessful interpretative account), which turns Gazdar's assumption into an assumption that Gapping is outside (GPSG) syntax, since syntax contains no transformations, and therefore no deletion transformations. This (forced) assumption that a properly formulated rule of Gapping is outside syntax is one that recurs with monotonous regularity in accounts that do not allow deletion rules (Gazdar *et al.*, 1985; Sag *et al.*, 1985; Steedman, 1985).

63. The actual term Right-node Raising was, I believe, made popular by Postal (1974-125-6). Postal accounts for sentences like:

Jack may be, and Tony certainly is a werewolf.

by means of an RNR rule which copies and right-sisteradjoins the rightmost constituent of a pair of coordinated Ss to the topmost S, and which deletes all original occurrences of that constituent. It changes (1) into (2):

(1)

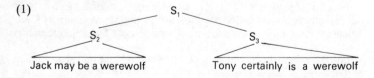

(2)

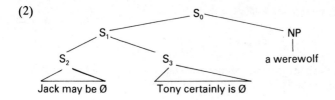

64. In this case, the category-valued feature SLASH which marks constituents with a phrase missing somewhere. For further discussion of the distinction between atom-valued and category-valued features, see Gazdar *et al.* (1985:25 ff).

65. For further discussion, see Gazdar *et al.* (1985), ch. IV.

66. Actually, it is at once too restrictive and too permissive. It will overgenerate structure. A simple sentence like:

John kicked Bill.

will, in a grammar allowing SLASH categories and rightward dependencies of the sort described in Gazdar (1981), make three structures available: the 'normal' structure, as under (a), one where there is a rightward dependency with a 'raised' NP, as in (b) and one where there is a rightward dependency with a 'raised' VP, as in (c).

(a)

(b)

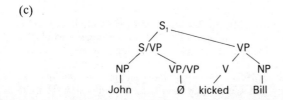

(c)

97

A simple coordination like:

Cows and horses are animals.

will have two structures one 'normal' one, and one with a SLASH VP coordination and a 'raised' VP to the right:

(a)   (b)

This multiplicity of structure is inelegant, and there is no empirical evidence to support it.

67. See van Oirsouw (1982b)

68. The main reason why Schachter and Mordechay question Gazdar's link between RNR and other rightward dependencies is that RNR seems to be much less restricted. The type of schema which Gazdar proposes:

$$\alpha\,[\ \alpha/\beta \quad \beta\,]$$

where α ranges over phrasal categories and β can be any phrasal or clausal category is too restricted for RNR in view of sentences like (a) (= Schachter and Mordechay 14a)

(a)   John gave, and Bill lent, some records to Mary.

α here is a *sequence* of phrasal categories. For sentence (b) (= Schachter & Mordechay 16a), which involves Heavy NP Shift, it is clear that β may *not* be any category; nor may extraposition from NP involve any category, as will be clear from (c) (= Schachter & Mordechay 16b):

(b)   ∗I gave two to John portraits of Bill's first wife.
(c)   ∗Two portraits of were painted Bill's first wife.

In (b), there has been rightward displacement of $\overline{\mathrm{N}}$, while in (c), there has been rightward displacement of $\overline{\overline{\mathrm{N}}}$. Both displacements would be allowed by Gazdar's rule schema. This is therefore too restrictive for RNR, and not restrictive enough for rightward displacements.

69. In Gazdar's (1981) proposal the category containing the SLASH can be any clausal category, and what is in the SLASH itself

can be any phrasal or clausal category. Schachter and Mordechay (1983:265) also question this hypothesis.

70. The actual constructions differ of course in the three proposals.

71. This has as a disadvantage that the inelegance noted for Gazdar (1981) in note 66 of this chapter is extended. A coordinated sentence like:

John gave Mary a book and Peter sold Sue a record.

can now have a 'normal' structure for each of the component clauses, as well as an RNR-type structure with all sorts of 'raised' constituents and strings of constituents (S/NP, S/NP,NP,S/VP). Furthermore, it relaxes the restrictions on what constitutes a constituent to such a degree that it becomes difficult to see what could *not* be a constituent.

72. For a clear and attractive discussion of this separation between Immediate Dominance and Linear Precedence, see Gazdar *et al.* (1985). The linearisation rule here will, of course, have to include Directionality Constraint in some form.

73. Note again the indivisibility of rule schemata of type (231) which conjoin a certain category *n* times in a grammar which differentiates between rules specifying immediate dominance (ID) and linear precedence (LP). The coordination schema is 'transderivational' in some sense: it introduces the (unordered) coordination dominance relations, but it will also be responsible for seeing to it that the daughters of a topmost coordinated node are not scattered throughout the structure by LP rules, since this would probably involve them being moved out from under the topmost coordinated node, entailing a violation of the ID rules. It is questionable whether the ID/LP format has any specific advantages for coordination; the Coordinate Structure Constraint will probably prevent any linearisation which would also be a violation of the ID rules.

74. See also section 1.3.5 for a discussion of a proposal which considers Gapping to be outside sentence grammar. This invalid type of 'cross-sentence/speaker' argument is also adopted by Van Riemsdijk and Williams (1986:185) who wish to eliminate VP-deletion from the grammar.

75. The main discussion in this section does not do full justice to Sag *et al.* (1985), who also address some issues which have not exactly been central to the discussion about coordination in the last few years, namely the distribution of the coordinating morpheme, and verb coordinations of the *go and V* type. In their discussion of the coordinating morpheme, they make heavy use of the argument that there are many logical possibilities of occurrence of coordinating morphemes, but only a few actually occur in English. They do not, however, go into the fact that a coordinating morpheme deletion rule could achieve the same description of the distribution of words like *and*, *or*, and *but*, by simply stipulating that all but the last non-initial coordinating morpheme in English may be optionally deleted. This approach would have the advantage of allowing:

I will neither eat, drink, speak nor write until I have seen my lawyer.

which Sag *et al.* will not allow. Their Iterating Coordination Schema includes a list of *coordinating* conjunctions, and the combination *neither-NIL-nor* is not in their list. Sag *et al.* also fail to refer to Ross's (1967) observation about the German coordinating conjunction *aber* which may also occur *after* the first constituent of the second S, or after the verb in main clauses:

(a) Johann hat eine Frau, aber Willi ist nicht verheiratet.
(b) Johann hat eine Frau; Willi aber ist nicht verheiratet.
(c) Johann hat eine Frau; Willi ist aber nicht verheiratet.
    (Johann has a   wife; Willi is but not   married)

Quechua also has a coordinating conjunction after the first constituent of the second S; see e.g. Pulte (1971), and Dutch has the coordinating conjunction *echter* which may not occur in between two Ss, but must be either before or after the verb in the second S. With respect to constructions like *go and V*, *try and V*, *come and V*, and *run and V*, it needs to be remarked that these are individual and specific cases (I know only of these four), which are subject to highly specific constraints (the order of the verbs, for instance, may not be reversed), whose existence does not decide unequivocally in favour of a PS-analysis of coordination, and against a deletion-based one. Both types of analysis will have to identify these constructions as specifically constrained types of base-coordinated verbs.

76. Steedman (1985) makes no reference to the observations in Schachter and Mordechay (1983) which make Gazdar's (1981) generalisation of rightward dependencies suspect: Steedman's proposal is subject to the same objections that Schachter and Mordechay raised against Gazdar. See note 67 to this chapter for a brief discussion.

77. The directionality of the rule could be reversed: The function then selects an argument to the left as in (a) (Steedman 1985:529):

(a) $Y \ X/Y =====> X$

78. Whether these can be marked as single categories seems doubtful. Seuren (1985:96) points out, quite correctly, that such functor categories are exceptional for instance in that they cannot prepose in Dutch, which is something that basic categories can do. Compare:

(a) Ik gaf de boeken aan Marie en de platen aan Susan.
(b) De boeken gaf ik aan Marie, en de platen aan Susan.
(c) *De boeken aan Marie gaf ik, en de platen aan Susan.
    (The books to Marie gave I, and the records to Susan)

79. Steedman does not provide a full discussion of Gapping: the reason he gives for this is that 'a full analysis of elliptical constructions goes beyond the realm of syntax proper, as shown by Kuno (1976,1981), and will not be attempted here' (Steedman, 1985:544).

100

For Gapping we have seen in section 1.3.5 that Kuno's position (and therefore Steedman's) must be rejected.

80. Steedman's interpretation of 'category' as comprising both basic categories and functor categories comes to grief here. While it is true that in subordinate clauses the remnant of Gapping may be just a single *functor* category preceding the gap (e.g. S/(FVP/NP)), as in (a), it may not be just a single *basic* category (e.g. NP), as in (b):

(a) .... dat Jan vis at, en Piet rijst Ø.
    (.... that Jan fish ate, and Piet rice Ø)
(b) *....dat Jan een auto verkoopt, en Piet Ø Ø.
    (.....that Jan a car sells, and Piet Ø Ø)

81. Steedman actually objects to a backward-operating formulation of Gapping (1985:561-2) on the following basis: while Dutch subordinate clauses allow both forward and backward Gapping, main clauses allow only forward Gapping. The observation is fully correct, but still needs to be accounted for. Ross (1970) attempted to account for exactly the same observation about German: such observations are not in principle objections to a rule of backward Gapping.

2

The Syntax of Coordinate Deletion

2.1 COORDINATE DELETION

In the previous chapter, I have given an outline of how the various approaches to coordination developed, first in transformational generative grammar, and later in other models of grammar such as Functional Grammar, Generalised Phrase Structure Grammar and Categorial Grammar. In this chapter, I have also outlined the various problems which one encounters in dealing with coordination, and I have provided a large body of data which any theory of coordination must be able to handle if it is to be an improvement on earlier accounts. In the present chapter, I shall provide a unitary theory of coordination which accounts for the syntax of coordinated structures in English, Dutch and German by relating a non-S coordination to a co-ordination of two or more coordinated sentences themselves not containing a coordination; in other words, I take the 'reductionist' approach to coordination. Obviously, there are other approaches which one could take: therefore I shall provide arguments why the reductionist or deletion approach is more likely to be fruitful than others. I will also occasionally point out areas in which other approaches than the one that I have adopted may provide viable alternatives. But this chapter is concerned with the syntax of coordination and therefore also with the syntax of rules like Gapping which some linguists would like to relegate to some obscure province of 'style' or 'discourse'. There is no reason to suspect that some aspects of coordination are better treated as stylistic or discourse rules, and there is certainly no account of, for instance, Gapping or VPD as discourse rules available which could account for the observations which will be made in Chapter 2: Coordinate Deletion, Gapping, Right-node Raising and (parts of) VP-deletion all belong to the *syntax* of coordination.[1] I shall also endeavour to maximise simplicity in my account: it is the aim of this chapter to employ as limited a number of theoretical assumptions as possible, and to whittle down the theoretical constructs to a bare minimum. Such assumptions and constructs as I do employ will be amply motivated and illustrated, and they will be notions which will be needed in grammar independently of my account of coordination.

2.1.1 Deletion

The first question we shall have to deal with is: why opt for a deletion account? If one examines sentences (1) to (3), the observations by Gleitman (1965) and Smith (1969) immediately spring to mind: obviously, there are some sentences which one could derive from coordinations of well-formed sentences themselves not containing a coordination, there are sentences which cannot be so derived because there are some well-formed non-S coordinations for which there is no equivalent well-formed coordination of sentences: for sentences of this type, a PS-rule account which coordinates categories would seem more suitable (see e.g. Dougherty, 1970, and Gazdar, 1981), and there are sentences which cannot be accounted for by means of PS-rules because they are not coordinations of categories in any sense. Sentence (3) necessarily requires a deletion account, sentence (2) needs a PS-rule account, and (1) could be accounted for by either — the data, in other words, is split right down the middle:

1. John and Bill live in London.
1a. John lives in London and Bill lives in London.
2. John and Mary are a lovely couple.
2a. *John is a lovely couple and Mary is a lovely couple.
3. John ate fish and Mary rice.
3a. John ate fish and Mary ate rice.

There are, however, some facts which support the deletion approach, and cast doubt upon the PS-account. Consider the sort of generalisation which a very basic type of PS-rule responsible for category coordination like (4) below would make:[2]

4. $X ====== > CONJ\ X_n$

A rule of this type claims that like categories may be coordinated in any number by any coordinating conjunction in any syuntactic environment — the categories may be anything: even any of the 'underspecified' categories found e.g. in Gazdar *et al* (1985). But this is obviously wrong; even if one takes the three coordinating morphemes that are not frequently cited as the coordinating conjunctions of English: AND, OR, and BUT. What we find is that AND may indeed coordinate any number of like categories:

5.   John and Bill and Sue and Harry and Marjorie went fishing.(NP_n)
6.   They ate the food and drank the beer and danced and sang songs and partied.(VP_n)
7.   John kicked and hit and beat and whipped the cat.(V_n)
8.   I want all your books, notepads, diaries, and satchels removed.(N_n)

Likewise, OR may coordinate any number of like categories:

9.   You can call John or Bill or Sue or Harry.
10.   You are allowed to eat or drink or smoke or sing or dance.
11.   You may hit or kick or punch or insult the manager.
12.   Here you can buy books, notepads, diaries, or satchels.

However, BUT may only coordinate *two* like categories:

13.   John ran but fell (*but hurt himself).
14.   You may sing all you like, but close the door (*but after 6 p.m).
15.   You must walk quickly but carefully (*but eagerly) over to me.

Obviously, if we see CONJ in (4) as a coordination variable of some sort, then if we fill in BUT for the variable, we have to add some sort of rider to it that (n=2). Moreover, the variable X

may, if the coordinating conjunction is BUT, not be a noun phrase;[3] compare:

16. *John but Bill went fishing.

And even that will not do, since a coordination of any other category than *NP* will be unacceptable if the only area in which the coordinated constituents *differ* is in an *NP*:

17. *John went fishing but Bill went fishing.
18. *I talked to John but I talked to Bill.

But this means that if we wish to state a PS-schema for co-ordination, we will *have* to make reference not only to the category we are actually coordinating by means of this schema, but also to what the minimal distinction between coordinated categories is — in other words, once we have generated a non-NP BUT-coordination by means of a PS-rule schema, we have to delete all identical material to see if that coordination will be well-formed: the coordination will not be well-formed if, after deletion, an NP-BUT coordination is all that remains. This in turn means that the generalisation expressed in rule (4) is not valid for BUT, and that a 'pure' PS-rule account will have great difficulty in accounting for the grammaticality of BUT-Coordinations. A deletion-type account is much less unlikely for BUT,[4] since the machinery needed to check if a coordination involving BUT is acceptable is readily available.

A similar argument can be set up for the coordinating conjunction FOR; a coordinating conjunction that has hardly featured in the linguistic literature on coordination at all. Let us first of all establish that FOR (plus its Dutch equivalent WANT, and its German equivalent DENN) is indeed a coordinating conjunction.

One clear characteristic which is particular to coordinating conjunctions as contrasted with, say, subordinating conjunctions, is that the former have to occur inbetween the clauses which they coordinate, and the latter need not:

19. John wants to sleep, because he is upset.
20. Because he is upset, John wants to sleep.
21. John wants to sleep, and (but/or/for) he is upset.
22. *And (but/for/or) he is upset, John wants to sleep.

Coordinating conjunctions are mutually exclusive; coordinating conjunctions and subordinating conjunctions are not:

23. John was a crook, and because he stole from me, I fired him.
24. *John was a crook, and but (for/or) he stole from me, I fired him.

A third distinguishing characteristic is word order: in Dutch and German, main clauses (and therefore also coordinated main clauses) have SVO word order, while subordinated clauses have SOV word order:

25. Jan   moet slapen, want hij is ziek.
    Johann muss schlafen, denn er ist krank.
    (John   must sleep,   for   he is ill)
26. Jan   moet slapen omdat hij ziek is.
    Johann muss schlafen weil er   krank ist.
    (John   must sleep   because he   ill is)

We can conclude that FOR, DENN and WANT are coordinating conjunctions — but they are not coordinating conjunctions which obey the generalisation expressed in rule (4), for they can only coordinate two entire clauses — they may not coordinate anything other than S.

27. *John ate fish, for Bill Ø rice.
28. *John ate fish, for Bill did Ø, too.
29. *John hit Ø, for Bill kicked the cat.
30. *John drank the beer for ate the hot chilli.
31. *John for Mary love rice crispies.

This leaves us with one generalisation which (4) seems to capture correctly, namely that AND and OR can coordinate any number of categories any number of times. This approach intends to account for both (1) and (2) above as base-coordinated NPs: incorrectly, however, since it fails to account for the fact that symmetrical predicates *only* take either plural subjects or AND-coordinated subjects, and *never* OR-coordinated subjects:

32. *John or Mary are a lovely couple.
33. *Two or two make four.

A further, and perhaps somewhat unexpected argument why rules like (4) do not express the proper generalisation about coordination lies in the fact that sentences may be started with a coordinating conjunction.[5] Obviously, rule schema (4) cannot account for this, since it will only coordinate like categories, and can therefore at most be held responsible for a coordination of Ss, and not for a sentence beginning with a coordinating conjunction. This could be remedied by allowing rule (4) to insert a coordinating conjunction before a single category: all one would have to do is to allow *n* to be equal to or greater than one. But then the rule schema would make the wrong predictions: only *sentences* can be grammatically introduced by a coordinating conjunction, not *categories*; compare:

34. *And Bill fish.
35. *Or eating the two pieces of cake.
36. *But Harry.
37. *For reluctantly.

A further illustration of why rules like (4) simply do not capture a correct generalisation can be given for *respectively*-sentences: although there are a number of accounts that crucially involve a *respectively*-like stage in the derivation of category or even non-category coordination (a prime example is Hudson, 1976; see Chapter 1, section 1.2.4), *respectively* only occurs either with plurals or with *AND*; to involve *respectively*-like constructions in the derivation of coordinations other than those linked by *AND* will therefore simply make the wrong predictions. Compare the following four sentences:

38. John and Bill kissed Mary and Sue, respectively.
38a. *John or Bill kissed Mary or Sue, respectively.
38b. *John but Bill kissed Mary but Sue, respectively.
38c. *John for Bill kissed Mary for Sue, respectively.

Although we shall not discuss *respectively* in any detail in this book, it will be clear that a rule of type (4) will find it impossible to accommodate these facts; this in spite of the fact that *respectively*-constructions have, in the past, been invoked as support for such rules. We can therefore conclude that the approach which relies crucially on rules like (4) is essentially mistaken in the generalisations which it makes: it is simply not the case that all categories can be coordinated any number of times in any syntactic environment by any type of coordinating conjunction. Each coordinating conjunction has its own specific coordinating characteristics, and these characteristics also vary between languages: a number of languages are quite restricted in the types of coordination they allow. Koutsoudas (1971) gives a list of languages that do not allow coordinations of finite verbs. To give just one illustration: in Mandarin Chinese, we find that e.g. finite VPs may be conjoined, but not finite Vs (Li and Thompson (1978); Sanders and Tai (1972)):

39. Tā xie xiaoshuo mài gudong.
     He writes novels   and sells antiques
40. *Wo dǎle, tile nánháizi
     I hit and kicked the boy

One can readily find other examples: Hilda Koopman (personal communication) has informed me that the Kru languages allow clausal coordination and NP-coordination, but no other coordinations. Such facts are totally unexpected in a theory which bases itself on generalisations of the type expressed in (4).

Observe furthermore how heavy reliance on base generation creates the following problem for auxiliary questions in English, and yes-no questions in Dutch, which are formed by inverting the subject and finite verb form. Declarative sentences allow conjunction of VPs, but the corresponding questions don't:

41. I am ill   and must sleep
     Ik ben ziek en moet slapen.
41a. *Am I ill and must sleep?
     *Ben ik ziek en moet slapen?

The derivation of (41a) from (41) in an approach that base-generates conjoined VPs must be blocked somehow. But if auxiliary questions are derived from their declarative counterparts, this could only be done through some type of purely *ad hoc* filter that blocks the derivation in case there is a conjoined

VP that is affected by the derivation. The alternative would be not to derive questions from their declarative counterparts, but that would mean that the obvious relation that exists between them would then be missed. As will be shown in this chapter, a deletion-based approach has no problems with these facts.

One characteristic which, to my knowledge, all languages share, is that if there is coordination, this will be coordination of at least Ss and NPs: this is why S-coordination and NP-coordination have to be taken as basic. For English, Dutch and German, nearly all coordination can be treated as S-coordination, except for cases involving coordinated NPs which are the subject of symmetrical predicates,[6] possibly *respectively*-coordinations, and possibly some verb coordinations in English.[7] For a further discussion of matters related to the issue of symmetrical predicates, see Chapter 1, 1.1.3. For this approach, the fact that in the Kru languages, the only coordinations that are allowed are either full S-coordinations, or NP-coordinations is not unexpected, but can readily be accounted for by observing that these languages lack the coordinate deletion rule.

Although it will be clear that rule (4) does not provide us with correct generalisations, it is not yet clear that all coordination should be derived from S-coordination — there are a number of approaches which are 'mixed' in the sense that all constituent or category coordination is derived by means of rules similar in nature to (4), while non-constituent coordination is derived by means of Gapping — an example of this approach is e.g. Sag *et al.* (1985), or Gazdar (1981); it is also implicit, or even explicit, in a number of textbooks on linguistics (see e.g. Wekker and Haegeman, 1985). Given that Gapping, in any formulation, crucially involves deletion of verbs, this approach will be incorrect for all those cases of non-category coordination where no verb has been omitted, as will be clear from the following Dutch sentences:

42. Geeft Jan Ø Ø en verkoopt Piet Marie een boek?
     (gives John Ø Ø and sells   Piet Mary a   book?)
43. Ik geloof dat Jan kaas koopt in Nederland   en
                                     ØØ verkoopt in Duitsland.
     (I believe that Jan cheese buys in the Netherlands and
                                     Ø Ø sells   in Germany)

109

In (42), the direct and indirect objects have been deleted in the first clause, leaving a subject + transitive verb, while in (43), subject + direct object have been deleted from the second clause, leaving transitive verb + place adverbial; obviously, these deletions did not involve verbs, so it cannot be Gapping, and they must be accounted for by some sort of deletion rule, since the remnants are not constitutents or categories. Clearly, one could formulate a rule in addition to Gapping that could account for sentences (42/43), but such a rule could very easily produce constituent coordination output: If such a rule can yield a sentence like (43), then it can also produce a sentence containing a straightforward coordination of main verbs like (44), which is the same as (43) except that it does not have the (non-obligatory) place adverbials:

44. Ik geloof dat   Jan kaas koopt en Ø Ø verkoopt.
     (I believe that Jan cheese buys and Ø Ø sells)

It will even prove impossible to prevent properly formulated coordinate deletion rules, which are needed in any grammar, from producing constituent coordinations; the existence of constituent coordination, and the restrictions on it, will simply follow from a proper statement of the coordinate deletion rules. Therefore, there will simply be no need for extensive use of base rules like (4) above, and there will obviously be considerable redundancy in the grammar if we include rules of this sort. For this reason, and because rules like (4) fail to capture any significant generalisations, I shall derive all coordinations at least in English, Dutch and German, both constituent coordination and non-constituent coordination, by means of deletion under identity from coordinated sentences, with one clear exception: coordinated NPs which are the subject of symmetrical predicates.[8]

2.1.2 Unitary deletion

2.1.2.1 One rule

There are, in the literature on coordinate deletions, a number of rules which effect deletion under identity — in Chapter 1, we have encountered Gapping, which deletes medial material, and which must necessarily delete the verb, as in:

45.   John ate fish and Bill Ø rice.

Right-node Raising (RNR), which deletes identical rightmost constituents:

46.   John caught Ø, and Mary killed the rabid dog.

VP-deletion (VPD), which deletes identical verbs;

47.   John sleeps, and Peter does Ø, too

and Conjunction Reduction (CR) which deletes identical rightmost or leftmost material:

48.   John gave Ø Ø, and Peter sold a record to Sue.
49.   John gave a book to Mary and Ø Ø a record to Sue.

There are two obvious reasons for wishing to collapse these four rules, which all delete under identity in coordinated structures, into one: firstly, the desire to remove unnecessary complications from the theory of grammar, and secondly, the need to account adequately for the body of data under examination.

The four rules all serve to reduce the length of a coordination by deleting identical material, and they serve no other purpose.[9] For this reason it would clearly be more elegant and more economical to collapse them into one optional rule, a rule which says: 'delete under identity in coordination'. The second reason for collapsing these four rules into one is one of adequacy: it will be impossible to state these four rules in such a way that they can function independently to produce the desired result. Consider these four rules in English, Dutch and German; first of all Gapping. Gapping deletes medial verbs *unless* the deletion target verb is included in the deletion target for CR, RNR, or VPD: in (50) it is included in the CR target *I saw*, and none of the three languages allows Gapping to take place if the Gapping target is included in a CR target:

50.   *I   see   Mary and I   Ø Sue.
      *Ik   zie   Mary en   ik Ø Sue.
      *Ich sehe Mary und Ich Ø Sue.

In (51), the Gapping target is included in the VPD target *kiss Mary*, and Gapping is disallowed:[10]

51.   *I kissed Mary and John Ø Mary as well.

In (52), it is included in the RNR target *een kus geeft/einen Kuss gibt*,[11] and Gapping is not allowed:

52.   *Ik geloof dat   Jan Marie een   kus   geeft, en Piet
                                      Susan een   kus   Ø
        *Ich glaube, dass Jan Marie einen Kuss gibt, und Piet
                                      Susan einen Kuss Ø,

We can conclude that Gapping cannot take place if the Gapping target is included in the target of any other coordinate deletion rule.

Secondly, consider RNR. RNR may not apply if its target is included in a VPD target, as in:

53.   *John doesn't drink Ø, and Peter does drink beer.

Nor may RNR apply if the RNR target is included in a CR target:

54.   *John sometimes drinks Ø and Peter often drinks beer.

Thirdly, CR. This rule may not apply if the target is included in a VPD target;

55.   *John Ø Ø and Peter drank beer as well.

This situation could be accounted for by stipulating a parochial ordering between these four rules whereby VPD precedes CR precedes RNR precedes Gapping; this would produce the correct results for (50/55). However, it is also possible to demonstrate that the inverse ordering should hold: VPD may not apply if its target is included in a CR target:

56.   *John drank beer and Peter Ø Ø.

Nor may VPD apply if the target also qualifies as a Gapping target:[12]

57. *John lives in Paris and Peter does Ø in Rome.

We now have an ordering problem: VPD has to precede AND follow Gapping and CR. This ordering problem will prove extremely difficult, if not impossible to solve: an appeal to cyclic rule application of some sort, for instance, will be of little use: also, all four rules are commonly considered to be postcyclic rules in models of grammar which allow for a rule cycle. Given that the four-rule approach faces this problem, and since a unitary approach is obviously the more attractive option, I shall make the simplest assumption possible in the rest of this chapter, namely that

THERE IS ONLY ONE OPTIONAL RULE DELETING UNDER IDENTITY IN COORDINATED STRUCTURES

The rule is optional because the grammaticality of a coordination does not depend on the application or non-application of the coordinate deletion rule; the coordinate deletion rules does not 'filter out' ungrammatical strings, but only maps grammatical strings into grammatical strings. This assumption, which is based partly on our earlier rejection of Tai (1969) (see Chapter 1, 1.2.1) who did allow for obligatory coordinate deletion rules, and partly on what has become, either tacitly or overtly (see e.g. Koutsoudas (1971), or Hankamer (1979)) standard practice in the discussion on deletion under identity in coordinated structures, will be evident from all the example sentences. We shall have occasion to return to the notions of identity and coordination, which also play a crucial role in the definition, later on in this book, in Chapter 3, section 3.2. The place of the coordinate deletion rule as a 'late' rule in the grammar will be further discussed in that same chapter, section 3.5.1.

2.1.2.2 Similarities

What the above section has done is to demonstrate that, in coordinated structures, it will be impossible to specify a proper interaction between deletion rules. This problem simply disappears if we collapse all rules which effect deletion in coordinate structures into one, and our goal then becomes finding the ways in which the deletion rule, when it operates in coordinated structures, is constrained. From this it follows that if

Gapping, RNR, the coordinate part of VPD and CR are all part of this same coordinate deletion rule (CD), they should be subject to similar constraints. For English, one could assume a simple structure as in (58):[13]

58.

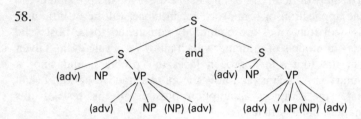

One can then observe that for an identical constituent or string of constituents to be a deletion target, it is necessary for that identical constituent or string of constituents to be *peripheral* to its immediately dominating node; for a brief discussion, see Chapter 1, 1.3.2/1.3.4. Remember that Jackendoff (1972) observed that Gapping cannot take place with unlike adverbs preceding the verb; a sentence like (59) is unacceptable:

59.   *John slowly dropped the gold, and Peter quickly Ø the diamonds.

Like adverbs gap along with the verb; in (60) the gap is *sometimes beats*:

60.   Max sometimes beats his wife and Ted Ø Ø his dog.

A similar observation holds for unlike auxiliaries preceding the verb. To these observations, we can add that if a deletion target verb is preceded by *not* and its antecedent isn't, Gapping may not apply:

61.   *John drinks beer, but Harry doesn't Ø alcohol.

In sentences (59/61), the deletion target verb is not peripheral to its immediately dominating constituent, which is why Gapping is not allowed. Right-node Raising is similar to Gapping in that it cannot apply if the deletion target verb is followed by an unlike adverb: a sentence like (62) is unacceptable:

62. *Mary makes Ø quite regularly, but her husband eats beef casserole only occasionally.

RNR is also similar to Gapping in that like adverbials following a deletion target object, for instance, will delete along with it — in (63) we interpret the gap as *rare books from college libraries*, not just as *rare books* or *from college libraries*:

63. John permanently borrows Ø Ø, and Harry simply steals rare books from college libraries.

Here again, we see that in (62), the deletion target node is not peripheral to its immediately dominating node, while the string in (63) is peripheral: peripherality is a constraint both on Gapping and RNR — and also on VPD; in (64) the deletion target VP string is not peripheral to its immediately dominating node, and deletion is unacceptable:

64. *Clint drew his gun quickly, but Lee didn't Ø Ø with such speed.

Like VPD, Gapping and RNR, CR is also subject to the peripherality constraint: an unlike adverb preceding a like subject will block deletion of that subject, as in (65):

65. *Yesterday John ate a hamburger and the day before Ø had a burrito.

This evidence strengthens the claim that Gapping, VPD, CR and RNR are one and the same rule: they are subject to at least one same constraint. A second set of observations which confirms this is that in those cases where we can move constituents so that we 'free' the deletion target (i.e. make it peripheral to its immediately dominating node), for instance by moving an unlike adverbial, then it will become possible to delete the identical material; compare:

66. John dropped the gold slowly, and Peter Ø the diamonds quickly.
67. Mary regularly makes Ø, but her husband only occasionally eats beef casserole.

68. John ate a hamburger yesterday and Ø had a burrito the day before.

A third thing which these four rules have in common is Ross's (1970) Directionality Constraint (see Chapter 1, section 1.2.1), which states that elements on left branches (verbs, pre-verbal adverbs, and subjects in (57) above will delete forwards, while elements on right branches (adverbs, direct objects, indirect objects) will delete backwards — as can be seen from (59-68), the four rules cited obey the Directionality Constraint: elements on right branches have their antecedent identical occurrence deleted, while elements on left branches have their subsequent identical occurrence deleted.

2.2 MORE COORDINATED SENTENCES

Although a number of facts can be accounted for by referring to constraints on peripherality and directionality in a structure like (58), such an account has at least one serious drawback. It relies crucially on a structure which deviates from what is common linguistic practice (e.g. the constituent structure specified by any of the current versions of X̄-theory): (58) is underspecified, and if it were more specified, or involved fewer branches and greater depth of branching, the account would no longer work. Further-more, although it might be easy enough to specify directionality of branching if branching were always binary, it is quite difficult to establish, in a non-circular fashion, what the directionality of branching is in a flat and many-branching structure. This problem can be solved quite easily: one simply abandons the structure as under (58).

This is what I shall do: In the rest of this chapter I shall not refer to constituent STRUCTURES, but to constituent SEQUENCES — in other words, I shall not use the structural relations between constituents to define constraints on, but only the linear sequence in which constituents occur in a surface structure coordination.[14] This has a number of advantages: first of all, it rids us of the problems observed above. Secondly, we no longer need to worry about what the STRUCTURE of a coordination is like after deletion has applied: whether there are empty branches, traces, null anaphors, or some sort of restruc-tured tree is immaterial to the coordinate deletion rule. This does not mean that there will be no structure in a coordination before or after deletion; only that coordinate deletion provides no EVIDENCE about the structure of a coordinated sentence before or after deletion; only that coordinate deletion provides ible with quite a few theories of grammar, while eliminating quite a few others, which is a desirable result.[16] It will be compatible with any theory of grammar which allows deletion rules and recognises a surface level for sentences, and will disallow any theory of grammar which does not allow deletion rules (a prominent example of such a theory that springs to mind is Generalised Phrase Structure Grammar; see e.g. Gazdar *et al.*, 1985). As the account of coordination progresses, other requirements will emerge: a theory of grammar, in order to be compatible with the facts of coordination, will have to incorporate a notion of verb, a notion of beginning and end of sentence, and a notion of first constituent in a sentence — all uncontroversial requirements, and the last one of these, which is perhaps somewhat novel, will be motivated in some detail below.

Although I will not make direct use of the structural relations that hold between constituents in the account of coordination in this book, and will therefore call my approach 'linear' or 'non-structural', it should be pointed out, in order to forestall possible confusion, that the account makes indirect use of such structurally defined notions as 'well-formed sentence' and 'constituent'. The account takes these notions as primitives, and defines, on the basis thereof, what a well-formed coordinated structure is: if it is known what the well-formed sentences of English, Dutch and German are (excluding those that involve coordination), and what their constituents are (or rather where their constituents begin and end), then one can define what their well-formed coordinations are. Obviously, it is well outside the scope of this book to define the notions *well-formed sentence* and *constituent*; the definition of these two is one of the major and most important tasks of any grammar of a language, and we are concerned only with coordination here. The account of coordination is 'non-structural' in the sense that it does not need to refer to the internal structure of either a well-formed sentence or of a well-formed constituent for the definition of its constraints (and, as will become clearer as the argument progresses, works so well precisely because it does not do so). We shall return to the matter of structure in some detail in Chapter 3, sections 3.4.2 and 3.4.3, under the heading of recoverability of deletion.

A serious empirical objection that can be raised against most previous accounts of coordination is that they are not adequate descriptions of coordination facts that have been known in the literature for quite some time, and that they do not serve to bring into focus new bodies of data that can shed new light on old problems. The greater part of the literature on coordination has been concerned with English: even theories which purport to account for other languages (Neyt, 1979 is a case in point) will often focus on English and the similarities between English and the other language(s) under examination (to the detriment of the account provided for the facts from the other language) rather than on providing adequate and mutually compatible accounts of the coordination facts of the languages in question. If one takes English, Dutch and German, languages which have a strong historical connection, it will be clear that there are some similarities between Dutch, English and German with respect to coordination: in main clauses, medial verbs delete under identity, as do initial subjects, and final indirect and direct objects. Verbs and subjects delete forwards, and direct and indirect objects will delete backwards:

69. John eats meat, and Bill Ø rice.
    John eet vlees, en Bill Ø rijst.
    John isst Fleisch, und Bill Ø Reis.
70. John eats meat and Ø drinks beer.
    John eet vlees en Ø drinkt bier.
    John isst Fleisch und Ø trinkt Bier.
71. John buys Ø, and Peter sells cheese.
    John koopt Ø, en Peter verkoopt kaas.
    John kauft Ø, und Peter verkauft Käse
72. John gave Ø Ø, and Peter sold a record to Mary.
    John gaf Ø Ø, en Peter verkocht een plaat aan Mary.
    John gab Ø Ø, und Peter verkaufte eine Schallplatte
    an Mary.

There are also a number of facts in Dutch and German which are remarkably unlike English — as we have already seen in Chapter 1, 1.3.9, Dutch has no equivalent of VPD; nor does German. A VP consisting of a verb + direct object, for instance, will delete without leaving a finite verb form behind:

73. John eet kaas,   en   Peter Ø ook Ø.
    John isst Käse,   und Peter Ø auch Ø.
    (John eats cheese, and Peter Ø too   Ø)

Secondly, consider the following: Dutch and German have a
verb-second rule which demands that the verb is the second
constituent from the left in main clauses, irrespective of what
the first constituent is.[17] In a sentence like (74):

74. Ik verkoop nooit   kaas   aan die   kluns.
    Ich verkaufe niemals Käse   an diesen Trottel.
    (I sell   never   cheese to this   nerd)

we can have adverbial, direct object, or indirect object in initial
position, giving us:

74a. Nooit   verkoop ik kaas aan die   kluns.
     Niemals verkaufe ich Käse an diesen Trottel.
74b. Kaas verkoop ik nooit   aan die   kluns.
     Käse verkaufe ich niemals an   diesen Trottel.
74c. Aan die   kluns   verkoop ik nooit   kaas.
     An diesen Trottel verkaufe ich niemals Käse.

In such sentences, it is still possible to delete identical verbs and
identical objects, but once a like subject has ended up in third
position as a result of the fronting of, say, an adverbial, then it
will be impossible to delete it:

75. Soms   eet Jan vlees en   Ø Ø Peter rijst.
    Manchmal   isst Jan Fleisch und Ø Ø Peter Reis.
    (Sometimes eats Jan meat   and Ø Ø Peter rice)
76. Vaak koopt Jan Ø en   Ø verkoopt Peter kaas.
    Oft   kauft Jan Ø und Ø verkauft Peter Käse.
    (often buys Jan Ø and Ø sells   Peter cheese)
77. *Soms   eet Jan vlees en   Ø drinkt Ø bier.
    *Manchmal isst Jan Fleisch und Ø trinkt Ø Bier.
    (Sometimes eats Jan meat   and Ø drinks Ø beer)

A third fact which makes Dutch and German coordination
different from English is that if a past participle or infinitive is
rightmost to the sentence, then either the first or the subsequent
occurrence may be deleted, as in (78); both (78a) and (78b) are

equally common and acceptable reduced variants of (78):

78. Jan heeft kaas gekocht, en Piet heeft vlees   gekocht.
     Jan hat   Käse gekauft, und Piet hat   Fleisch gekauft.
     (Jan has   cheese bought, and Piet has   meat   bought)
78a. Jan heeft kaas Ø, en   Piet Ø vlees gekocht.
     Jan hat   Käse Ø, und Piet hat Fleisch gekauft.
78b. Jan heeft kaas gekocht, en Piet Ø vlees Ø.
     Jan hat Käse gekauft, und Piet Ø Fleisch Ø.

An indirect object preceding the rightmost past participle or
infinitive may delete, together with the past participle or infinitive it is immediately adjacent to, also either in the first or in the
subsequent coordinated clause, as in (79a/b):

79a. Jan heeft een boek aan Marie gegeven, en Peter Ø een
     plaat Ø Ø.
     Jan hat ein Buch an Marie gegeben, und Peter Ø eine
     Schallplatte Ø Ø.
     (Jan has a book to Marie given, and Peter Ø a record Ø
     Ø)
79b. Jan heeft een boek Ø Ø, en Piet Ø een plaat aan Marie
     gegeven.
     Jan hat ein Buch Ø Ø, und Piet Ø eine Schallplatte an
     Marie gegeben.

In subordinate clauses the differences between English on the
one hand and German and Dutch on the other are equally striking. Dutch and German have SOV wordorder in subordinate
clauses; in subordinate clauses, subjects may delete:

80. Ik geloof dat Jan vlees eet en Ø bier drinkt.
     Ich glaube, dass Jan Fleisch isst und Ø Bier trinkt.
     (I believe that Jan meat eats and Ø beer drinks)

The deletion occurs in the second coordinated clause and may
not occur in the first. One unusual fact about direct objects in
subordinated clauses in Dutch and German is that they can
never be deleted under identity, neither in the first nor in the
second clause.[18]

81a. *Ik geloof dat Jan Ø schopt en Peter de hond slaat.
    *Ich glaube, dass Jan Ø tritt und Peter den Hund schlägt
    (I believe that Jan Ø kicks and Peter the dog hits)
81b. *Ik geloof dat Jan de hond schopt en Peter Ø slaat.
    *Ich glaube, dass Jan den Hund tritt und Peter Ø schlägt.

Objects may delete, but only if they delete along with an identical verb, or with an identical subject, as in:

82. Ik geloof dat mannen Ø Ø en vrouwen make-up gebruiken.
    Ich glaube, dass Männer Ø Ø und Frauen Make-up gebrauchen.
    (I believe that men Ø Ø and women make-up use)
83. Ik geloof dat autohandelaren auto's kopen en Ø Ø verkopen.
    Ich glaube, dass Autohändler Autos kaufen und Ø Ø verkaufen.
    (I believe that car-dealers cars buy and Ø Ø sell)

Identical verbs in subordinate clauses may delete either in the antecedent clause or in the subsequent clause:[19]

84. Ik geloof dat Jan kaas koopt, en Peter vlees Ø.
    Ich glaube, dass Jan Käse kauft, und Peter Fleisch Ø.
    (I believe that Jan cheese buys, and Peter meat Ø)
    Ik geloof dat Jan kaas Ø en Peter vlees koopt.
    Ich glaube, dass Jan Käse Ø und Peter Fleisch kauft.

If there is for instance a like direct object preceding the like verbs, this will delete along with the verb, either forward or backward:

85. Ik geloof dat Jan een boek Ø Ø, en Piet een plaat aan Marie geeft.
    Ich glaube, dass Jan ein Buch Ø Ø, und Piet eine Schallplatte an Marie gibt.
    Ik geloof dat Jan een boek aan Marie geeft, en Piet een plaat Ø Ø.
    Ich glaube, dass Jan ein Buch an Marie gibt, und Piet eine Schallplatte Ø Ø.
    (I believe that Jan a book to Marie gives, and Piet a record Ø Ø)

121

However, if there is only one unlike constituent in the coordination of subordinate clauses, deletion may not leave that constituent as the rightmost constituent of the matrix S. A sentence like (86a) may not be reduced to (86b):

86a. Ik geloof dat mannen make-up gebruiken en vrouwen make-up gebruiken.
Ich glaube, dass Männer Make-up gebrauchen und Frauen Make-up gebrauchen.
(I believe that men make-up use and women make-up use)
86b. *Ik geloof dat mannen make-up gebruiken, en Ø Ø vrouwen.
*Ich glaube, dass Männer Make-up gebrauchen, und Ø Ø Frauen.

Data of this sort will play a crucial role in the discussion of coordinate deletion in this chapter. Although I will restrict myself mainly to Dutch, German and English, I shall occasionally cite data from other languages that show parallel constructions: data that strongly suggest that the approach advocated here can be extended relatively straightforwardly to deal with more than just coordination in the three languages analysed here. Russian, for instance, shows behaviour which is quite similar to what we have seen in Dutch and German. It allows both SVO and SOV main clause wordorder, and in SOV clauses Gapping can be either forward or backward (Hermann, 1985:111):

87. Ja čitaju naučnuju statju, a on Ø detektiv.
(I read a scientific article, and he Ø a detective novel)

87a. Ja naučnuju statju čitaju, a on detektiv Ø.
87b. Ja naučnuju statju Ø a on detektiv čitaet.

I will, however, mostly restrict myself to Dutch, German and English: these three languages provide a wealth of data, much of which has not yet been observed or adequately discussed in the literature.

2.2.1 Deletion target sites

In an approach like the present, which derives well-formed non-S coordinations from well-formed S-coordinations by means of deletion, the crucial question is of course what can be deleted under which circumstances, in other words, what the *possible deletion targets sites* are. The data from Dutch, German and English we have examined so far can be divided up into three main deletion target sites: leftmost sites, rightmost sites, and verb sites. Examples of leftmost sites we have encountered are: deletion of identical subject, subject + verb, subject + pre-verbal adverb in English, and in Dutch and German main clauses, and deletion of subject + direct object in Dutch and German main clauses. Rightmost deletion target sites have included direct objects, verb + direct object, direct object + indirect object in English and in Dutch and German main clauses, and indirect object + verb in Dutch and German subordinate clauses. The third class consists of medial deletions: pre-verbal adverb + verb, verb + indirect object, verb + direct object. I have called sites of this sort verb sites because they always involve deletion of a verb: verb-sites will cater for all the data that earlier accounts have relegated to a rule of Gapping, a rule which also always involves deletion of at least a verb under identity.

The deletions are subject to a version of Ross's (1970) Directionality constraint: leftmost sites delete forward (i.e. the subsequent occurrence of the identical material disappears), rightmost sites delete backwards (i.e. the antecedent occurrence of the identical material disappears) and verb sites delete forwards again. They are also subject to a version of what was called the Peripherality Constraint in van Oirsouw (1983a): for an informal discussion, see section 2.1.2.2. The Peripherality constraint can now be construed as follows: for a deletion target site to be accessible to deletion, it must be peripheral, i.e. immediately left-adjacent or right-adjacent to its S-boundary. This can be represented schematically as follows for leftmost sites:

88. $_S$ [....... (X X) X]$_S$ *CONJ* $_S$[......... (X X) X]$_S$

For rightmost sites:

89. $_S$ [X (X X) ......]$_S$ *CONJ* $_S$ [X (X X) ....]$_S$

For verb sites:

90. $_S[0 \ldots \text{-V-} \ldots(\text{X X})]_S \; CONJ \;_S[0 \ldots \text{-V-} \ldots (\text{X X})]_S$

This should be interpreted as follows: X is any unlike constituent,[20] O is an ignored constituent, ... is identical material, *CONJ* is the conjunction, *-V-* is a verb which occurs somewhere in the deletion target site, *[ ]* indicates S-boundaries, *( )* indicates optionality; i.e. an (X) is a constituent position which need not necessarily be filled.

Our notion of *(O)*, the ignored constituent, needs some explanation: this constituent will always be the first constituent of the S, and will be ignored (or rather, not 'seen') in English, Dutch and German if the deletion target site includes a verb. I shall not attempt to provide a motivation for *(O)* here, but leave that until section 2.5 in this chapter. For the time being, it suffices to observe that this allows us to preserve the Peripherality constraint for Gapping-type sentences: if the first constituent (in English, usually just the subject) is ignored in determining peripherality, then the verb will be immediately adjacent to the leftmost S-boundary and thus be accessible to deletion. As we shall see later on, the ignored constituent *(O)* also occurs in other languages, for instance Russian and Egyptian Arabic.

Given this characterisation of accessible deletion sites, it follows that we will be left with a number of impossibilities for deletion sites. First of all, one inaccessible site (91):

91. $_S[(0) \text{ X} \ldots\ldots \text{X}]_S \; CONJ \;_S[(0) \text{ X} \ldots\ldots \text{X}]_S$

If a site is inaccessible, deletion will be disallowed: in (91), the deletion target *(.......)* is 'hemmed in' on either side by non-identical material, thus screening it from access by the deletion rule. We shall have ample occasion to return to the notion of inaccessible site; for the moment we can observe that it accounts for the impossibility of e.g. deleting the indirect object in a sentence like (92), where it is 'hemmed in' on either side by unlike material:

92. *John gave Ø to the pretty girl, and Peter handed his money to the burly bouncer. (Ø= his money)

In addition to the one inaccessible site, we also have the following non-sites: non-sites are simply not possible deletion sites, either because they do not contain identical material, or because they consist only of identical material. Non-sites are the following:

93. $_S[\,X\,X\,X\,X\,X\,]_S\ CONJ\ _S[\,X\,X\,X\,X\,X\,]_S$

94. $_S[\,0\,X\,X\,X\,X\,]_S\ CONJ_S\ [\,0\,X\,X\,X\,X\,]_S$

95. $_S[............]_S\ CONJ\ _S[............]_S$

96. $_S[.0\,........\,]_S\ CONJ\ _S[0\,........\,]_S$

We shall return briefly to the matter of non-sites in the discussion of recoverability of deletion, and in our discussion of site overlap; note, for the time being, that the difference between (93) and (95) on the one hand and (94) and (96) on the other is that there is an ignored ('unseen') first constituent in the latter, but not in the former. These non-sites can be seen as constraints blocking deletion from applying both to fully identical coordinations and to fully non-identical coordinations. This may have the following consequences: (93) will never give rise to deletion, while (94), if the ignored first constituent in the first clause is identical to that in the second clause, MAY give rise to left-peripheral deletion. Likewise, (95) contains no unlike material at all, whereas (96) MAY contain at least one unlike constituent, namely the first constituent. What that means is that a site that can be recognised as a rightperipheral site (see (89) above) and can at the same time be recognised as a non-verb site. And this in turn means that, in a sentence like (97), we can apply deletion as for rightmost sites, but not for verb sites: (97a) is acceptable, since rightmost deletion will *not* block, but (97b) is not, since verb-site deletion *will* block:

97.   John ate fish and Bill ate fish.
97a. John Ø Ø and Bill ate fish.
97b. *John ate fish and Bill Ø Ø.

We shall now test the predictions which the coordinate deletion rule makes when we apply it to accessible sites in English, Dutch and German.

2.2.2 Leftperipheral sites

For the three languages under consideration, or predictions for leftperipheral sites are as follows: in English, and in non-topicalised Dutch and German main clauses, the subject will be leftmost and will therefore be deletable under identity:

98. John ate a hamburger and Ø drank a beer.
     John at een hamburger en Ø dronk een biertje.
     John ass einen Hamburger und Ø trank ein Bier.

Backwards deletion will be disallowed, which is correct:

98a. * Ø Ate a hamburger and John drank a beer.
      * Ø At een hamburger en John dronk een biertje.
      * Ø Ass einen Hamburger und John trank einen Bier.

Given that the deletion target site does not contain a verb in the stretch of identical material, and given that if one ignores the first constituent, all material will be unlike, the deletion site fails to qualify as a verb site on two counts. If there are no unlike adverbs preceding a like verb in English, then identical subject + identical verb will qualify as a leftperipheral site. In Dutch and German, if no topicalisation has taken place, the subject will occupy initial position, and the verb in main clauses will always be second, so that deletion will operate in the same way as for English:[21]

99. John gave Mary a book and Ø Ø Sue a record.
     John gaf Mary een boek en Ø Ø Sue een plaat.
     John gab Mary ein Buch und Ø Ø Sue einen Schallplatte.

A further prediction is that if, in English, the subject occupies second position because there is an unlike adverbial preceding the subject, an identical subject will no longer be deletable: it is not peripheral, and because the deletion target site does not contain a verb, it will not be possible to ignore the first constituent. This prediction is correct:

100. *Yesterday John ate like a pig but the day before Ø was very modest.

Such sentence-initial adverbs as in (100) can be moved to the end of their clause. If we do so, the subject once again is the leftperipheral constituent of the sentence, and deletion will be possible again:

100a. John ate like a pig yesterday but Ø was very modest the day before.

If there is an identical adverb preceding the subject, this will delete along with the subject, since they now form a left-peripheral site together:[22]

101. Yesterday John ate like a pig and Ø Ø got blind drunk.

A further prediction is as follows: in Dutch or in German, the subject will take up third position if there is a sentence-initial adverb, since the verb in main clauses will always take up second position in the linear order of constituents. If adverb and verb are unlike, we get the same situation as in English (100) the like subject cannot be deleted since it is not peripheral.

102. *Gisteren liep Jan erg snel, maar vandaag was Ø erg langzaam.
     *Gestern lief Jan sehr schnell, aber heute war Ø sehr langsam.
     (yesterday ran Jan very fast, but today was Ø very slow)

For Dutch and German subordinate clauses, we predict that the subjects, which take up initial position in the clause, will delete forwards:

103. Ik geloof dat Jenny een hamburger eet en Ø een biertje drinkt.
     Ich glaube, dass Jenny einen Hamburger isst und Ø ein Bier trinkt.
     (I believe that Jenny a hamburger eats and Ø a beer drinks)

We also predict that in subordinate clauses in Dutch and German, subject+indirect object will delete forwards:

127

104. Ik geloof dat Jan Marie een boek geeft en Ø Ø een
                                              plaat   leent.
    Ich glaube, dass Jan Marie ein Buch gibt und Ø Ø eine
                                              Schallplatte leiht.
    (I believe that Jan Marie a   book gives and Ø Ø a
                                              record   lends)

We also predict that, as has been observed earlier, direct objects
in Dutch and German subordinate clauses cannot delete under
identity; they are neither leftmost nor rightmost in the sentence,
and they are not verbs, so they will not be accessible: they can
only delete along with a peripheral constituent, e.g. a subject,
together with which they can form an accessible string:

105. *Ik geloof dat Jan de hond schopt en Peter Ø slaat.
     *Ich glaube, dass Jan den Hund tritt und Peter Ø schlägt.
     (I believe that Jan the dog kicks and Peter Ø hits)
106. Ik geloof dat Jan de hond schopt en Ø Ø slaat.
     Ich glaube, dass Jan den Hund tritt und Ø Ø schlägt.

Note also that this statement of peripherality as a constraint on
deletion target sites copes quite elegantly and naturally with
Langendoen's (1975) unacceptable sentence (107) (also cited
as (141) in Chapter 1):

107. *Show Rafael that you love him and tell Ø that he's
     wonderful.

The indirect object here is not peripheral, and is therefore not
accessible to deletion. Indirect objects in comparable Dutch and
German imperative clauses will not be deletable either:

108. Bel je moeder op en maak Ø blij.
     *Ruf deine Mutti an und mach Ø froh.
     *Call your mother up and make Ø glad.

The predictions of the deletion rule under the constraint of
peripherality are obviously correct for English, Dutch and
German, and account for familiar data (deletion of identical
subjects) as easily as for observations which have not been made
before in the literature (e.g. the unacceptability of deletion of
identical subjects when they are preceded by unlike material).
We shall now examine the predictions for rightperipheral sites.

2.2.3 Rightperipheral sites

To take the familiar RNR-type cases first, we predict for right-peripheral sites that if we have a like direct object, a like direct object + indirect object, or verb + direct object, for instance, these will all delete backwards in English and in Dutch and German main clauses:

109. Udo catches Ø and Ilse kills the rabid dog.
     Udo vangt Ø en Ilse doodt de dolle hond.
     Udo fängt Ø und Ilse tötet den tollwütigen Hund.
110. John gave Ø Ø and Peter sold a book to Mary.
     John gaf Ø Ø en Peter verkocht een boek aan Mary.
     John gab Ø Ø und Peter verkaufte ein Buch an Mary.
111. Peter Ø Ø and Harry drink red wine.
     Peter Ø Ø en Harry drinken rode wijn.
     Peter Ø Ø und Harry trinken Rotwein.

A further prediction is that if, in English,[23] there is an unlike adverb following the deletion target site, deletion will be impossible, since the deletion site is not peripheral:

112. *Mary makes Ø frequently, but her husband eats roast potatoes only occasionally.

If we move the adverb to pre-verbal position, the direct object becomes a rightperipheral site again, and deletion will be possible:

112a.Mary frequently makes Ø, but her husband only occasionally eats beef casserole.

For all three languages we also predict that if we have a sequence of Direct Object+Indirect Object, and the indirect objects are identical, deletion should be possible, but not if the order is the reverse:

113. John gave a book Ø, and Peter sold a record
     John gaf een boek Ø, en Peter verkocht een plaat
     John gab ein Buch Ø, und Peter verkaufte eine Schallplatte
     to the girl in the red sweater.
     aan het meisje in de rode trui.
     an das Mädchen in dem roten Pulli.

114. *John gave Ø a   book, and Peter sold
     *John gaf Ø een boek, en   Peter verkocht
     *John gab Ø ein Buch, und Peter verkaufte
     the   girl   in the red sweater a record.
     het   meisje   in de   rode trui een plaat.
     das   Mädchen in dem roten Pulli eine Schallplatte.

In Dutch and German subordinate clauses, the clause-final
verbs should delete backwards, which indeed they do:

115. Ik geloof dat Johann Maria Ø, en Peter Sophie kust.
     Ich glaube, dass Johann Maria Ø, und Peter Sophie küsst.

If the direct object preceding the verb is also identical, it forms
part of the rightmost site and will therefore also delete backwards:

116. Ik geloof dat Johann Maria Ø Ø, en Klaus Susan een boek
     geeft.
     Ich glaube, dass Johann Maria Ø Ø, und Klaus Susan ein
     Buch gibt.

But if we change the order of indirect object and direct object,
the deletion site will no longer be rightmost, but be 'hemmed in'
by unlike material, and will therefore no longer be deletable:

116a. *Ik geloof dat Johann Ø Ø aan Maria, en Klaus een
      boek geeft aan Susan.
      *Ich glaube, dass Johann Ø Ø an Maria, und Klaus ein
      Buch gibt an Susan.

In Dutch and German, past participles and infinitives may be
rightmost in main clauses. If they are rightmost, they may delete
backwards; identical constituents immediately preceding the
past participle or infinitive will then delete along with it:

117. Hans mag   Ø en Jan moet komen.
     Hans darf   Ø und Jan muss kommen.
     (Hans is allowed Ø und Jan has to come)
118. Hans mag   Ø Ø en Peter moet Marie zoenen.
     Hans darf   Ø Ø und Peter muss Marie küssen.
     (Hans is allowed Ø Ø und Peter has to Mary kiss)

This concludes our discussion of rightperipheral sites.

2.2.4 Verb sites

Verbs may delete under identity in English — sentences of the type:

119. John eats fish, and Bill Ø rice.

have featured prominently in the linguistic literature of the last 20 years. This, according to the definition of verb-string deletion, is allowed: a verb string has to be accessible, i.e. leftmost or rightmost to its S, in order to be accessible to deletion, but will it always ignore the first constituent of its S. If there is in addition to the first constituent, a second constituent preceding the V-string, this constituent then cannot be ignored, and if there is then also unlike material following the V-string, it will be inaccessible to deletion. Jackendoff's (1972) observations on Gapping are a clear illustration of this; sentence (120) is unacceptable:[24]

120. *John always eats fish, and Bill very rarely Ø rice.

A like constituent preceding the verb will gap along with the verb, since such constituents are, according to our definition of the V-string, part of the deletion target site:

121. John sometimes eats fish, and Bill Ø Ø rice.

The 'gap' here is interpreted as *sometimes eats*, and not just as *sometimes* or *eats*. A like constituent following the verb will also be part of the V-string, and will therefore also delete forwards, as in:

122. John spends his money on   horses,   and Peter Ø Ø
                                                 on   women.
     John geeft   zijn geld uit aan paarden, en Peter Ø Ø
                                                 aan vrouwen.
     John gibt   sein Geld aus an Pferde, und Peter Ø Ø
                                                 an   Frauen.

These observations also hold for Dutch and German subordinate clauses: in the subordinate version of (122) the
deletion target string also qualifies as a verb string: there is only
one constituent intervening between the deletion target string
and the nearest left S-bracket:

123. Ik geloof dat John zijin geld uitgeeft aan paarden, en Peter
Ø Ø aan vrouwen.
Ich glaube, dass John sein Geld ausgibt an Pferde, und
Peter Ø Ø an Frauen.
(I believe that John his money spends on horses, and Peter
Ø Ø on women)

Given that V-string deletion operates both in subordinate
clauses and in main clauses, we now have a very elegant explanation for the hitherto unexplained observation why what is
traditionally called Gapping (although it needs to be observed
that Ross (1970), who was the first to call attention to the facts
from German in the transformational literature, referred to the
deletion of identical verbs only: as will be obvious from the
examples we have cited so far, this is too restricted) in the
linguistic literature operates both forward and backward in
Dutch and German: if the deletion targets are rightmost, they
may delete backwards as rightperipheral sites, and if they
contain a verb, then they are verb sites, and since they are rightperipheral, they are accessible verb sites and are as such allowed
to delete forwards. It is worth repeating that there is no difference in style or markedness between forward-deleted and
backward-deleted coordinations in these two languages: both
types of deletion are equally common and equally acceptable. A
few examples:

124. Ik geloof dat Johann bier drinkt, en Peter wijn Ø.
Ich glaube, dass Johann Bier trinkt, und Peter Wein Ø.
124a. Ik geloof dat Johann bier Ø, en Peter wijn drinkt.
Ich glaube, dass Johann Bier Ø, und Peter Wein trinkt.
(I believe that Johann beer Ø, and Peter wine drinks)
125. Ik geloof dat Jan Marie een plaat   geeft, en
Piet Susan Ø Ø.
Ich glaube, dass Jan Marie eine Schallplatte gibt, und
Piet Susan Ø Ø.

125a. Ik geloof dat Jan Marie Ø Ø, en Piet Susan een plaat
geeft.
Ich glaube, dass Jan Marie Ø Ø, und Piet Susan eine
Schallplatte gibt.
(I believe that Jan Marie Ø Ø, and Piet Susan a record
gives)

Note that for sentence (124), we predict that the forward-deleted
version is the only possible one, since the deletion target site
there is accessible as a verb site, but not as a rightperipheral
site: this prediction is correct, as we can see if we change the
directionality of deletion in (123):

123a. *Ik geloof dat Jan Ø Ø aan paarden, en Peter zijn geld
uitgeeft aan vrouwen.
*Ich glaube, dass Jan Ø Ø an Pferde, und Peter sein
Geld ausgibt an Frauen.

These observations are by no means restricted to English,
Dutch and German. Egyptian Arabic presents a parallel case;
for relevant further discussion, see Wise (1975). It allows both
leftmost and rightmost deletion in coordinated structures; (126)
can be reduced to (126b) (Wise, 1975:158):

126. Makanʃ ʕaayiz yiddiini ḥaaga wi makanʃ ʕaayiz
yisallifni ḥaaga
He didn't want to give me anything and he didn't want to
lend me anything.
126b. Makanʃ ʕaayiz yiddiini Ø wala Ø yisallifni ḥaaga.
He didn't want to give me Ø or Ø lend me anything.

It also allows Gapping of either single verbs or strings including
a verb. (Wise, 1975:157):

127. Ana kalt bamya   wi huwwa kal ruzz.
I   ate ladies' fingers and he   ate rice.
127b. Ana kalt bamya wi huwwa Ø ruzz.
128. Ilʕabb kaan zaʕlaan min ilwalad wi ʕummu kaanit
zaʕlaana min ilxaddaama
The father was angry with the boy and his mother was angry
with the servant

128b. Il ͡ abb kaan za ʕ laan min ilwalad wi ʕ ummu Ø Ø min
ilxaddaama.

Like auxiliaries, as in English, Dutch and German, must gap
along with the verb; (128c) is unacceptable.

128c.*Il ͡ abb kaan za ʕ laan min ilwalad wi ʕ ummu kaanit Ø
min ilxaddaama.

We shall now test some further predictions that the theory of
accessible deletion sites as outlined above makes in the next few
sections, but before we do so, let us consider a rather different
case, namely Japanese. As Ross (1970) had already observed,
Japanese deletes verbs only backwards. The only Gapping
pattern that Japanese (which is a verb-final language) allows is
(126): unlike in Dutch and German subordinate clauses, which
also have SOV word order, (127) is not allowed.

129. John-ga raisu-o Ø Bill-ga sushi-o tabeta.
    (John   rice   Ø Bill   sushi ate)
130. John-ga raisu-o tabete, Bill-ga sushi-o Ø.
    (John   rice   ate   Bill   sushi Ø)

The easiest way of account for this fact is to assume that
Japanese simply does not have verb sites as possible deletion
sites: in other words, Japanese will not delete verbs forwards as
in verb sites, but according to whether they are left- or rightperipheral. Given that they are rightperipheral, they delete
backwards. This assumption accounts quite neatly for Ross's
observation and actually preserves most of his original account.
It would also seem to be rather trivial and of no great interest to
our present discussion: note however, that the assumption that
Japanese does not have deletion of verb sites leaves the other
two accessible deletion sites, rightmost and leftmost sites, unaffected, and they should behave in the same way that rightmost
and leftmost sites behave in English, Dutch and German. This
turns out to be so; we have already observed, in note 18 to this
chapter, that identical direct objects in Japanese cannot delete,
in the same way that identical direct objects in German and
Dutch subordinate clauses cannot delete under identity.
Japanese main clauses, however, have an option available which

is not available in Dutch and German subordinate clauses, namely that of Scrambling: provided that the verb remains final, there is considerable freedom in ordering subjects and direct and indirect objects. The following example is from Saito (1984:4):

131. Mary-ga John-ni sono hon-o watasita
     Sono hon-o John-ni Mary-ga watasita
     John-ni sono hon-o Mary-ga watasita
     (John-to that book-acc Mary-nom handed)
     Mary handed that book to John.

If we scramble the identical direct object in Japanese, so that it becomes sentence-initial, it should then delete forward as a leftmost site. This turns out to be the case:

132. *John-ga raisu-o katte,   Bill-ga Ø tabeta.
      (John   rice   bought, Bill   Ø ate)
132a. Raisu-o John-ga katte,   Ø Bill-ga tabeta.
      (rice   John   bought Ø Bill   ate)

It therefore also follows that if we have an identical subject in Japanese, this should delete forwards, but it should be inaccessible to deletion if we topicalise the direct object. This is also correct:

133. John-ga raisu-o katte,   Ø sushi-o tabeta.
      (John   rice   bought, Ø sushi   ate)
133a. *Raisu-o John-ga katte,   sushi-o Ø tabeta.
      (rice   John   bought sushi   Ø ate)

Deletion of an identical subject is also impossible if that identical subject is preceded by a non-identical adverb, as in:

134. *Tokyo-de John-ga raisu-o tabeta shi, London-de Ø
                                              biiru-o nonda.
     (Tokyo in John   rice   ate   and London in Ø
                                              beer   drank)

If the unlike adverb does not precede the subject, it will be accessible to deletion, as in:

134a. John-ga Tokyo-de raisu-o tabeta shi, Ø London-de
                                                    biiru-o nonda.
   (John Tokyo-in rice ate and Ø London-in
                                                    beer drank)

The case of Japanese, although it is different in one aspect from the three languages we have examined in detail so far, conforms in principle to the present framework,[25] and thus lends further support to it.

2.2.5 Diversion: first constituent

In the preceding sections, I have assumed that the first constituent of a sentence may simply be ignored for the purposes of establishing peripherality of deletion target strings, and this assumption needs to be spelled out in some more detail. As it now stands, it is an extremely convenient assumption in that it allows us to preserve the peripherality constraint, and thus to account very elegantly for Gapping-type constructions, but it is seemingly *ad hoc*: there is no clear formal reason why it should be the *first* constituent that is ignored. We might just as well ignore, say, the fifth constituent, or the third constituent to the left of the coordinating conjunction, if this were to give us the same insights into coordinate deletions that ignoring the first constituent gave us.

Although the main reason for assuming that it is the first constituent that can be ignored rather than any other constituent resides precisely in the very revealing account of coordinate deletions that emerges if we incorporate this assumption, it is also independently quite plausible. One parallel that immediately springs to mind between 'first constituent' and 'rest of the sentence' is that of topic and comment, theme and rheme, and old and new information. It can not be demonstrated to the exclusion of all possible counterexamples that the ignored constituent is the topic, theme, or old information, and the rest of the sentence is the comment, theme, or new information. For one thing, this would involve a detailed discussion of an extensive literature that is not always equally clear on crucial points, or uncontroversial in its assumptions, and such a discussion is outside the scope of this book. For a number of very insightful comments on the matter of sentence topics, see Reinhart (1981). But it is possible to point to a number of interesting facts and correlations that suggest very strongly that it is indeed only the first constituent position, rather than some other constituent position, that is special in a sense that makes it much more 'ignorable' than other constituent positions.

First of all, a large number of very diverse languages topicalise by taking a constituent and placing it precisely in first position in the sentence: English, Dutch and German are familiar examples. Other, totally unrelated, languages do the same thing. To mention just two instances: Diyari (an Australian language; Austin, 1981:150) topicalises by placing a definite NP in sentence-initial position, and so does Luo, a Nilo-Saharan language (Creider, 1981). Such a topicalised constituent will typically represent *old* information; although Reinhart (1981:73) observes correctly that topichood cannot be *defined* as 'being old information', topics very strongly tend to be old, familiar information. New topics are typically introduced in discourse by referential-indefinite nouns. Givón (1979:26) reports on a number of languages where there is a categorial constraint against precisely referential-indefinite nouns in initial position, in other words, the (topic) position that we have called 'ignorable'. Generally speaking, new information may not be in the 'ignorable' position. Givón (1979:27-8) also notes that 90 per cent of English subjects (the initial position) are definite (old information), while referential-indefinite subjects amount to only 10 per cent. Indefinite nouns (new topics) are typically introduced in object (non-initial) position in English: Givón (1979:52-3) gives 82 per cent new indefinite nouns in object position. Reinhart (1981:62) also observes that there is a strong tendency to interpret the NP in subject position as the topic. She furthermore notes that there is a structurally marked topic position at the beginning of a sentence for topicalisation and left-dislocation. Halliday (1967), using different terminology, identifies the *theme* with the first expression in the sentence. In other words: the material that occupies initial constituent position is generally 'known'.

If material is known (is a topic) it may be absent from the sentence under certain circumstances. The most striking case of this that I know is in Dyirbal; the following passage is from Dixon's description of this phenomenon. Although Dixon (1979) speaks of pivot rather than topic, I shall, for ease of exposition, call it 'topic-drop'. Nothing hinges on terminology here: Ross (1982) refers to a similar process as 'pro-zap'.

> We can consider any text (conversation, monologue etc.) in Dyirbal to be underlain by a sequence of simple sentences. If a number of consecutive sentences in such a sequence have a common NP, with common referent, then they will form a topic chain: this entails each sentence being transformed into a form in which the common NP is topic NP (i.e. is in nominative case). This NP may only be stated once, at the beginning of the topic chain: optionally all or part of it may be deleted later in the chain. (Commonly, just the noun marker may be repeated). Thus it is quite usual to encounter a chain of a dozen sentences all 'commenting' on a single topic occurrence. Two topic chains may run through a text in 'leapfrog' fashion. (Dixon 1972:71)

Dixon has since changed his terminology on this point, and he now refers to the omitted constituent as depending on a pivot rather than on a topic (see Dixon, 1979). But the omissibility remains, and if we now combine the two observations that the first constituent position in a sentence is the most obvious position to contain familiar material, and that familiar material may be 'dropped' under certain conditions, then we are led to suspect that if it is at all possible in languages like German, Dutch and English, to 'drop' familiar material more or less in the way in which Dyirbal does, then the most likely place from which it will be dropped is going to be the first constituent position in a sentence: that is the position which is specifically reserved for 'old' information. If we do find such instances where the first constituent is simply absent, this provides strong support for the hypothesis that that first constituent can indeed be 'ignored' in the production and processing of sentences, which makes it no longer strange that it should also be 'ignored' by the coordinate deletion rule when it establishes the accessibility of a deletion target site.

One of the possible tests for topichood is to look at the behaviour of constituents questions. If X is in both the question and the answer to the question, then it is very likely that X is a topic (see also Reinhart, 1981:56). In answering yes-no questions in spoken English (e.g. 135), we see that two things are repeated: *John* and the addressee/speaker. Of those two consti-

tuents which are singled out as potential topics by the question-
answer test, we can only 'drop' the first. There is nothing odd
about question-answer pairs like (135-136), and indeed one
hears them quite frequently:

135. Q: Have you seen John?
     A: Haven't seen him.

136. Q: What about our prime suspect?
     A: Hasn't been seen for days.

Note how it is crucial that the constituent to be dropped occupies first position; if we topicalise *John* (in which case *John*
itself cannot be dropped; presumably because topicalisation in
English, unlike in Dutch and German, necessarily singles out a
new topic from a range of possible topics) as in (137), which is a
possible answer to e.g. the question: *Have you seen John and
Bill?*

137. John I haven't seen.

then we find that *I* can no longer be dropped since it is no
longer in initial constituent position:

137a.*John haven't seen.

   In English it will be systematically the subject that occupies
the 'topic-dropped' position. In Dutch and German, any constituent may be fronted to first position, and it is usual to find the
'topic' of a question (in the sense of 'what the question is
about') in initial position in the answer. Contrary to what
Huang (1984), who based himself on observations in Ross
(1982) suggests, we find that all such first constituents may be
dropped: subject direct object, indirect object, and even adverbial PPs:

138. Q: Heeft Jan je   gezien?
       Hat   Jan dich gesehen?
      (Has   Jan you seen?)
    A: Heeft me   niet gezien.
       Hat   mich nicht gesehen.
      (Has me   not   seen)

139. Q: Heb   jij deze recensie   geschreven?
        Hast du diese Rezension geschrieben?
        (Have you this   review   written?)
     A: Heb ik niet geschreven.
        Habe ich nicht geschrieben.
        (Have I not   written)
140. Q: Heb jij je dochter deze week haar zakgeld gegeven?
        Hast du deiner Tochter diese Woche das Taschengeld
        gegeben?
        (Have you your daughter this week her pocket-money
        given?)
     A: Heb ik deze week geen zakgeld   gegeven.
        Habe ich diese Woche kein Taschengeld gegeben.
        (Have I this week no   pocket-money given)
141. Q: Ben   je al   eens in Disneyland geweest?
        Bist du schon mal in Disneyland gewesen?
        (Have you already once in Disneyland been?)
     A: Ben   ik nog nooit geweest.
        Bin   ich noch nie   gewesen.
        (Have I   never   been)

There are a couple of things that should be noted about such examples. First of all, it is clear that the first constituent has simply been dropped altogether: the answers are simple declarative statements, and yet the verb is in initial position rather than in second position, which is its proper place in Dutch and German declarative main clauses. Furthermore, the subject follows the verb in a number of cases, which is clear evidence that topicalisation has taken place. Therefore, what has been dropped is the first constituent in the sentence.

Note furthermore that it is specifically this first constituent position in the sentence in which topic-drop can take place. One cannot argue that if material is 'known', or 'recoverable from the context', it can simply be left out regardless of its position in the sentence. There is hardly anything that could be more 'recoverable from the context' than the first person subject pronoun in the answer to a yes-no question (139-141): both the discourse context (answering questions) and the syntactic context (first person finite verb form) make it impossible to recover anything *but* the first person subject pronoun following the verb in these sentences. Yet it we drop these eminently recoverable pronouns, the result is systematically bad, like

English (137a) above:

139a. *Heb niet geschreven.
      *Habe nicht geschrieben.
140a. *Heb deze week geen zakgeld   gegeven.
      *Hebe diese Woche kein Taschengeld gegeben.
141a. *Ben nog nooit geweest.
      *Bin noch nie   gewesen.

We can conclude, therefore, that the first constituent position
in a sentence is 'special' in that it will very strongly tend to
contain familiar (known, topic) material, and that such material
in this particular position allows deletions or 'drops' which are
not allowed in any other position; this is at least one significant
correlation with the fact that it is precisely the first constituent
and no other that can be 'ignored' for the purposes of establishing peripherality, which lends further support to our hypothesis.
    There is one other clear instance in which the first constituent
of a sentence must somehow be ignored by a specific grammatical rule in order to ensure its correct application: this time
the rule of 'verb-second' in Dutch and German. As we have
observed before, in Dutch and German, verbs in main clauses
must occupy second position. In declarative clauses, the subject
will occupy first position, unless some sort of topicalisation has
taken place, in which case the topicalised constituent will
occupy first place, the verb second place, and the subject third
place. Now consider a question like:

142. Have you ever been to Amsterdam?

An answer to this question in English might either be (142), in
which the topic *to Amsterdam* is repeated, or (142b), where the
topic is indicated by the demonstrative pronoun *there*:

142a. I have never been to Amsterdam.
142b. I have never been there.

In Dutch (let us restrict ourselves to Dutch for this part of the
discussion), we get the same situation, with the proviso that the
demonstrative pronoun must occupy first position, which the
full PP need not do; the full PP may be either in its usual place
towards the end of the S, or in initial (topic) position.

143.   In Amsterdam ben ik nooit geweest.
143b. Ik ben nooit in Amsterdam geweest.
143c. Daar ben ik nooit geweest.
143d. *Ik ben nooit daar geweest.
       (I have never there been)

It is also possible to have both the demonstrative pronoun and the full constituent in the S, referring to the same place, but in that case the demonstrative pronoun is 'resumptive' for the full constituent, and *must* occur immediately to its right:

144.   In Amsterdam daar ben ik nooit geweest.
144b. *Daar in Amsterdam ben ik nooit geweest.
144c. *In Amsterdam ben ik nooit daar geweest.
144d. *Daar ben ik nooit in Amsterdam geweest.
       (There have I never to Amsterdam been)

There is a number of such pronouns that can function resumptively after the first constituent of the S: *die* (*that*, def. masc./ fem), *dat* (*that*, indef., neut.), *daar* (*there*), *toen* (*then*, past time), *dan* (*then*, future time). All of these behave according to the pattern set out above. But what is relevant to us here is that if the pronoun is resumptive for the full constituent (i.e. immediately follows it), then the verb does not occupy second position, but it must occupy third position:

145.   Jan die ken ik niet.
       (Jan that know I not)
145b. *Jan ken die ik niet
146.   Kaas   dat lust ik niet.
       (Cheese that like I not)
146b. *Kaas lust dat ik niet.
147.   Gisteren toen was ik hier.
       (yesterday then was I here)
147b. *Gisteren was ik toen hier.
148.   Morgen   dan ben ik thuis.
       (Tomorrow then am I at home)
148b. *Morgen ben dan ik thuis

To offer a full analysis for this set of facts is clearly outside the scope of our discussion here, but note that any analysis will have to allow the demonstrative pronoun to function as one constituent, the full noun, PP or adverbial will have to function as one

constituent, and if the two are together they will have to function as one constituent. Whatever the way in which one analyses
these facts (two simple assumptions that spring to mind are to
assume that topic positions may be doubly filled by coindexed
items, or that coindexed items in topic position are reanalysed
as one constituent), the analysis, if it wants to account correctly
for the operation of the 'verb-second' rule, will always somehow
have to capture the fact that two constituents count as one (or,
in other words, that one constituent position is 'ignored') in one
type of initial (topic) position. This situation is not unique for
Dutch: Bernard Comrie (personal communication) has alerted
me to the fact that a similar situation arises in enclitic placement
in Serbo-Croatian. Here, enclitics may have more than one
position in the sentence, but all these possibilities can be
accounted for as 'after the first X': the enclitic may come after
e.g. the first accented word, the first accented constituent, or
after the first accented word or constituent following a pause.
For further discussion, see Browne (1974).

Before we conclude this paragraph, it needs to be pointed
out that there is one clear condition under which a first constituent may be ignored for the purposes of coordinate deletion in
English, Dutch and German, namely that there is a verb in the
deletion target site immediately following the first constituent.
There is a considerable number of languages that has precisely
this constraint in coordinate deletions. There is, however, nothing in the account of coordinate deletions itself that forces this
requirement for there being a verb in the site after the ignored
constituent. In spite of this fact, there are surprisingly few
languages that allow deletion of a medial target that does *not*
contain a verb; the only reasonably well-confirmed instances
that I am aware of are Turkish (Hankamer 1979), although
Koutsoudas (1971) contains statements that cast doubt even on
these observations for Turkish, and Basque. Hankamer
(1979:138) gives us the following example from Turkish:

149.   Ahmet patlɨcanɨ pişirdi, Mehmet yedi.
       (Ahmet the eggplant cooked (and) Mehmet ate)
       Ahmet cooked and Mehmet ate the eggplant.

Later on in the discussion of pronoun-deletion rules,
(1979:313) we find such constructions described as pronominalisation rather than as deletion, and it is indeed not quite clear
whether such constructions should be seen as deletion under

identity or as some sort of null pronominalisation. I shall therefore restrict myself here to noting these constructions, but not
crucially involve them in the discussion of coordinate deletion.
Nor will I offer an explanation for the observation that the
majority of languages require that there should be a verb in the
deletion target site after the first (ignored) constituent. We will
return to these questions in the discussion of coordinate deletions across languages in Chapter 3.

We can conclude that allowing the possibility of ignoring the
first constituent *(0)* in our description of coordinate deletion is
far from *ad hoc*, but has a number of interesting connections
especially with such notions as 'topic'. I shall (again) be content
to note these connections and not attempt to analyse them
further at this point, since it would move us away from the focus
of the discussion here. Let us now go on to some further predictions of the analysis.

2.2.6 Further predictions

The theory as it stands has some very interesting consequences.
It will be clear that, for the data which is most frequently
discussed in the literature as well as for some hitherto undiscussed data, an account which does not refer to any notion of
structure, surface, shallow or deep, but just to the linear surface
order of constituents in a sentence, will achieve a descriptive
adequacy[26] which strongly exceeds that of the accounts
discussed in Chapter 1. A further test of the predictions of this
linear approach to coordinate deletion will now be quite simple:
the behaviour of coordinate deletions should vary with the
linear surface constituent order in the sentence in one of two
ways: either a change in the constituent order affects the *accessibility* of a deletion target site, or it affects the *directionality* of
the deletion: we have not formulated other constraints on the
rule of coordinate deletion.

If one takes, for instance, Dutch (and German, though see
note 25) questions, which are formed by inverting subject and
verb, giving us VSO wordorder, we expect that if there is an
identical subject, this will be deletable in the declarative
sentence, but not in the interrogative sentence: the subject no
longer occupies an accessible position. This prediction is
correct:

150.   Ik houd van kaas en Ø drink   graag   jenever.
       (I love   cheese and and Ø drink with pleasure gin)
150a. *Houd ik van kaas en drink Ø graag jenever?

Likewise, in the irrealis present in Dutch the word order is VSO.
Here again, identical subjects cannot be deleted if they are
preceded by unlike verbs:

151.   Drink ik jenever, dan eet ik kaas.
       (= if I drink gin, then I eat cheese)
151a. *Drink ik jenever, dan eet Ø kaas.

In Dutch, identical subjects in yes-no questions can never be
deleted if they are preceded by unlike verbs. In English, the same
situation obtains in those questions which are formed by inverting
the auxiliary and the subject:

152.   I am ill and Ø must sleep.
152a. *Am I ill and must Ø sleep?
153.   He must go and Ø should not return.
153a. *Must he go and Ø should not return?
154.   John has gone and will not return.
154a. *Has John gone and will Ø not return?

    A second consequence of the fact that linear order of consti-
tuents determines deletion possibilities is that if a deletion target
changes from leftmost to rightmost, then the directionality of
deletion should also change from forward to backward — in
other words, the syntactic function of the constituent in question is not relevant to the application of the coordinate deletion
rule; only the linear position in the sentence which a constituent
occupies is. In Dutch and German, as we have observed before,
constituents may be fronted optionally for stylistic purposes.
The verb will retain second position in the main clause in these
cases [27] This means that if one fronts, in a simple SVO main
clause coordination, the direct object, then the wordorder
changes from SVO to OVS:

155.   Jan aait   de hond.
       Jan streichelt den Hund.
       Jan strokes   the dog.

145

155a. De hond aait   Jan.
      Den Hund streichelt Jan.
      (the dog   strokes   Jan)

If one has a coordination of simple SVO main clauses, identical subjects should delete forwards, and identical objects should
delete backwards. If one fronts the object, then exactly the
reverse situation should hold, and indeed it does:

156.   Men kookt aardappelen en Ø bakt biefstuk.
       Man kocht Kartoffeln und Ø grillt Beefsteak.
       (one boils potatoes and Ø fries steak)
156a. Aardappelen kookt Ø, en biefstuk bakt men.
       Kartoffeln kocht Ø, und Beefsteak grillt man.
156b. *Aardappelen kookt men, en biefstuk bakt Ø.
       *Kartoffeln kocht man, und Beefsteak grillt Ø
157.   Jan kookt Ø en Piet bakt aardappelen.
       Jan kocht Ø und Piet grillt Kartoffeln.
       (Jan boils Ø and Piet fries potatoes)
157a. Aardappelen kookt Jan en Ø bakt Piet.
       Kartoffeln kocht Jan und Ø grillt Piet.
157b. *Ø kookt Jan en aardappelen bakt Piet.
       *Ø kocht Jan und Kartoffeln grillt Piet.

A third consequence of our approach is that we are now led
to doubt Jackendoff's (1972) observations about unlike adverbs
immediately preceding the identical verb blocking the deletion
of that identical verb; according to the theory set out above,
what blocks Gapping in those cases is not the pre-verbal adverb,
but the fact that there is more than one constituent, no matter
what sort of constituent, preceding the verb-site: in determining
the accessibility to deletion of a verb-site, only the first constituent preceding the verb-site may be ignored. In English, there
are normally only two constituents that can precede the verb,
namely the subject, and some adverbs. Adverbs may either
precede or follow the subject, and in both cases they will block
deletion of an identical verb if both adverbs and subjects are
unlike:

158.   *On Monday I bought a car, and on Tuesday John Ø a
       motorcycle.
159.   *I sometimes drink beer and John often Ø wine.

If it is the case that it is not the pre-verbal adverb that blocks Gapping, but the number of constituents preceding the verb, then it should be possible to delete the identical verb if there is an unlike adverb preceding it, provided that this unlike adverb is the only unlike constituent between the verb and the leftmost S-boundary; again, this prediction turns out to be correct:

160. I often drink beer and I sometimes drink wine.
160a. I often drink beer and Ø sometimes Ø wine.

If we do not delete the identical subject in (160), then there will be more than one constituent preceding the verb site, and deletion will then be predicted to be impossible:

160b. *I often drink beer and I sometimes Ø wine.

Note also that a sentence like (160a) makes it quite clear that the CD rule operates linearly and not structurally — it ignores the first constituent regardless of its function and category. This can be made even clearer by taking sentences from German and Dutch in which there is an identical verb, and unlike adverbs, direct objects, and indirect objects, which can all be fronted. In all of these cases, the identical verb will retain second position, and will therefore remain deletable, along with the identical material that follows it:
Subject:

161. Ik geef het boek aan Marie en Jan Ø de plaat aan Klaas.
      Ich gebe das Buch an Marie und Jan Ø die Schallplatte
      an Klaas.
      (I give the book to Marie and Jan Ø the record to Klaas)

Indirect Object:

162. Jou geef ik geen biertje en je vrouw Ø Ø geen zoen.
      Dir gebe ich kein Bier und deiner Frau Ø Ø keinen Kuss.
      (You give I no beer and your wife Ø Ø no kiss)

Direct Object:

163. Bier drink ik niet en wijn Ø Ø maar heel zelden.
      Bier trinke ich nicht und Wein Ø Ø nur sehr selten.
      (Beer drink I not and wine Ø Ø only very rarely)

147

Adverb:

164.   Morgen eet ik ham en overmorgen Ø Ø kaas.
       Morgen esse ich Schinken und übermorgen Ø Ø Käse.
       (tomorrow eat I ham and the day after Ø Ø cheese)

The discontinuity of verbs in Dutch and German also provides interesting evidence: in a sentence such as (165), the past participle *bought* is inaccessible to deletion until the identical subject and auxiliary have been deleted. Thus, we get (165a) and (165b), but never (165c): in the last case, the past participle is not accessible to deletion:

165.   Ik heb kaas gekocht voor Jan, en ik heb vlees gekocht
       voor Klaas.
       Ich habe Käse gekauft für Jan, und ich habe Fleisch
       gekauft für Klaas
       (I have cheese bought for Jan, and I have meat bought
       for Klaas)
165a. Ik heb kaas gekocht voor Jan, en Ø Ø vlees gekocht voor
       Klaas.
       Ich habe Käse gekauft für Jan, und Ø Ø Fleisch gekauft
       für Klaas.
165b. Ik heb kaas gekocht voor Jan, en Ø Ø vlees Ø voor
       Klaas.
       Ich habe Käse gekauft für Jan, und Ø Ø Fleisch Ø für
       Klaas.
165c. *Ik heb kaas gekocht voor Jan, en ik heb vlees Ø voor
       Klaas.
       *Ich habe käse gekauft für Jan, und ich habe Fleisch Ø
       für Klaas.

The linear approach, it will be clear, makes new, non-trivial, and interesting predictions about coordinate deletions. We shall explore some of these predictions a little further in Chapter 3, section 3.4.3, where we will discuss the recovery of linear deletions, and in section 3.5.2, where we shall look at deletion in non-parallel coordinate structures. Before we set off the linear approach against various other approaches discussed in Chapter 1, it will be useful to examine the cases of *overlap* of deletion target sites: quite obviously, verb sites may overlap, partially or totally, either with leftmost sites or with rightmost sites.

148

2.3 SITE OVERLAP

If one examines the definitions of rightmost site, leftmost site, and verb site in 2.2 ff. of this chapter, it will be clear that there are, logically speaking, three *overlap* possibilities between the three sites (where we define overlap as a stretch of material that can be seen as belonging simultaneously to more than one deletion target site). A verb site may overlap with a rightmost site, or with a leftmost site, or a rightmost site may overlap with a leftmost site, in which case it will by definition also overlap with the verb site. This latter possibility we have already mentioned briefly in (2.2.1), where we defined both sites that do not have any material in common, and sites that have all their material in common, as *non-sites*; in such cases deletion cannot take place. If a deletion target site comprises all the material of its sentence, we wish to disallow deletion for a number of reasons: first of all, if we do not disallow total deletion of all the material in a clause, there is nothing to stop us deriving sentences like:

166.   *John ate fish and Ø Ø Ø.

from a coordination of two identical clauses *John ate fish*. Secondly, if we do not disallow total deletion, there is nothing to stop us from postulating, for a sentence that starts with a co-ordinating conjunction like (167), that it is derived from a co-ordination of identical sentences like (167a):

167.   And when you go, could you bring me a six-pack of beer?
167a. When you go, could you bring me a six-pack of beer, and when you go, could you bring me a six-pack of beer?

This is obviously undesirable: coordinating conjunctions also function as connectives in discourse, linking the sentence which they introduce to some earlier sentence. This is how we interpret (167): we do not interpret (167) as making the same statement twice over. What the coordinate deletion rule does, in other words, is to examine a coordination for identical material. If it does not find identical material, it is simply not applicable. If it finds only identical material, it is not applicable either. This latter statement has one interesting consequence: it predicts that if there is only one difference between two coordinated

149

sentences, that difference resides in the first constituent, and the identical material following the first (identical) constituent contains a verb, as in, for instance, (168/169), then the deletion target will qualify as a rightperipheral site, but not as a verb site. When identifying a verb site, the coordinate deletion rule ignores, i.e. does not 'see' the first constituent, and will therefore rule deletion out as inapplicable. When the coordinate deletion rules identifies a leftperipheral or a rightperipheral site, it will 'see' the whole coordination, and will therefore identify both (168) and the coordination of subordinate clauses in (169) as candidates for deletion: both contain accessible like material, and some unlike material. (Forward) verb site deletion should therefore be inapplicable in (168/169), but not (backward) rightperipheral deletion; a prediction which turns out to be correct:

168. John likes   fish   and Bill likes   fish.
     John houdt van vis   en Bill houdt van vis.
     John liebt   Fisch und Bill liebt   Fisch.
168a. *John likes   fish   and Bill Ø Ø.
     *John houdt van vis   en Bill Ø Ø.
     *John liebt   Fisch und Bill Ø Ø.
168b. John Ø Ø and Bill like   fish.
     John Ø Ø en   Bill houden van vis.
     John Ø Ø und Bill lieben   Fisch.
169. Ik geloof dat Karl van vis houdt en Udo van vis houdt.
     Ich glaube, dass Karl Fisch liebt und Udo Fisch liebt.
     (I believe that Karl fish likes and Udo fish likes)
169a. *Ik geloof dat Karl van vis   houdt en Udo Ø Ø.
     *Ich glaube, dass Karl   Fisch liebt   und Udo Ø Ø.
169b. Ik geloof dat Karl Ø Ø en Udo van vis   houden.
     Ich glaube, dass Karl Ø Ø und Udo   Fisch lieben.

Given the existence of site overlap, we need to examine the interactions between the different accessible coordinate deletion sites. So far, I have assumed that the coordinate deletion rule examines a coordination for accessible identical material, and deletes all identical material together in accordance with whether the material is accessible as a rightperipheral site, a leftperipheral site, or a verb site. In the next few sections, we shall see that this assumption is too strong specifically for the directionality of deletions, but that the interaction between the sites provides interesting new insights into the nature of coordinate deletions. In Chapter 3 we shall address the question of directionality of deletions in various languages in some more detail.

2.3.1 Partial deletion

We have already observed, in section 2.1.2.1, that there are serious problems in the interaction of the rules that can effect coordinate deletion that have been proposed as separate and unrelated in the literature. The rule which deletes the identical subject must apply before the rule which deletes the identical verb, or simultaneously with it, but they cannot apply in any order, or the ungrammatical (50) would be generated. Such facts formed part of the motivation for proposing a unitary deletion rule. Let us consider a few more of these examples

170. John hits   the dog   and John hits   the cat.
     John slaat   de   hond en   John slaat   de kat.
     John schlägt den Hund und John schlägt die Katze.
170a. John hits   the dog   and Ø hits   the cat.
     John slaat   de   hond en   Ø slaat   de kat.
     John schlägt den Hund und Ø schlägt die Katze.
170b. John hits   the dog   and Ø Ø the cat.
     John slaat   de   hond en   Ø Ø de kat.
     John schlägt den Hund und Ø Ø die Katze.
170c. *John hits   the dog   and John Ø the cat.
     *John slaat   de   hond en   John Ø de kat.
     *John schlägt den Hund und John Ø die Katze.

The existence of pairs of sentences like (170a/b) makes it quite clear that we cannot assume overall deletion under identity in coordinated structures, and the existence of (170c) makes it clear that the various deletions do not function independently of each other. What we see in the above sentences, where we have an overlap between a verb site and a leftperipheral site, is that the first constituent, the one that is not 'seen' by the coordinate deletion rule when it inspects a coordination for accessible identical material, is the constituent that can be deleted without the rest of the identical material deleting along with it. Let us formulate, on the basis of this observation, the following tentative constraint on the operation of partial deletion:

151

Partial deletion constraint (PDC) Accessible sites are deleted individually. If sites overlap, the material shared between the sites may not delete before the nonshared material.

This constraint predicts, for the three possible overlap situations (sites do not overlap at all, they overlap partially, or they overlap totally), that with no overlap between two sites there will be no interference between the various applications of Coordinate Deletion, it predicts that if there is total overlap between two sites, deletion will take place according to the directionality of one of the sites, and that with partial overlap, nonshared material deletes before shared material.[28] The second prediction has already been shown to be correct; that the first prediction is correct can be seen from (171c), where we have independent sites, and therefore independent deletions:

171.　John hits　the dog　and John kicks　the dog.
　　　John slaat　de hond en　John schopt de hond.
　　　John schlägt den Hund und John tritt　den Hund.
171a.　John hits　Ø and John kicks　the dog.
　　　John slaat　Ø en　John schopt de hond.
　　　John schlägt Ø und John tritt　den Hund.
171b.　John hits　the dog and Ø kicks　the dog.
　　　John slaat　de hond en　Ø schopt de hond.
　　　John schlägt den Hund und Ø tritt　den Hund.
171c.　John hits　Ø and Ø kicks　the dog.
　　　John slaat　Ø en　Ø schopt de hond.
　　　John schlägt Ø und Ø tritt　den Hund.

The third prediction can also quite easily be demonstrated to be correct: if we have, for instance, total overlap between a verb site and a leftperipheral site, as in (172), then partial deletion will be disallowed, but all identical material has to be deleted forward,[29] either by an application as to a verb site, or as to a leftperipheral site:[30]

172.　Shall I　stay　or　shall I　leave?
　　　Zal　ik blijven of　zal ik gaan?
　　　Soll　ich bleiben oder soll ich gehen?
172a.　Shall I　stay　or　Ø Ø leave?
　　　Zal　ik blijven of　Ø Ø gaan?
　　　Soll　ich bleiben order Ø Ø gehen?

172b. *Shall I   stay   or   Ø I   leave?
      *Zal   ik blijven of   Ø ik   gaan?
      *Soll ich bleiben oder Ø ich gehen?
172c. *Shall I   stay   or   shall Ø leave?
      *Zal   ik blijven of   zal Ø gaan?
      *Soll ich bleiben oder soll Ø gehen?

If we have total overlap between a rightperipheral site and a verb site, the facts should fall out the same, which indeed they do: also in this case partial deletion is not allowed. Consider the following subordinate clauses in Dutch and German:[31]

173. Ik geloof dat Jan de hond slaat en Piet de hond slaat.
     Ich glaube, dass Jan den Hund schlägt und Piet den Hund schlägt.
     (I believe that Jan the dog hits and Piet the dog hits)
173a. Ik geloof dat Jan Ø Ø en Piet de hond slaan.
     Ich glaube, dass Jan Ø Ø und Piet den Hund schlagen.
173b. *Ik geloof dat Jan de hond slaat en Piet de hond Ø.
     *Ich glaube, dass Jan den Hund schlägt und Piet den Hund Ø.
173c. *Ik geloof dat Jan Ø slaat en Piet de hond slaat.
     *Ich glaube, dass Jan Ø schlägt und Piet den Hund schlägt.

The predictions which the partial deletion constraint makes are therefore correct. One interesting fact about sentences of the sort discussed in this section is that they provide strong evidence for a deletion-type approach, and against a non-deletion approach to coordinate structures. Consider the following sentence, which is a close parallel of (173b); the only difference is that here, the direct objects are not identical:

174. Ik geloof dat Jan de hond slaat, en Piet de kat Ø.
     Ich glaube, dass Jan den Hund schlägt, und Piet die Katze Ø.

These sentences are perfectly grammatical sentences of Dutch and German; they are regular cases of coordinate deletion applying to a verb site,[32] and can as such be readily accounted for in the present theory. But note how any approach which does not incorporate a notion of deletion (I gloss over the severe difficulties which the non-deletion accounts as we now know them will have in accounting for a sentence like (174) in the first place) will not be able to distinguish between (173b) and (174); they are identical in structure, and to differentiate between them one has to state a constraint on coordination of more or less the following sort: 'there should not be identical material in a coordination, if that material is accessible to deletion and it is part of a single deletion target site, part of which has already been deleted' — but only a deletion-approach incorporates the notions involved in this constraint; hence a non-deletion type of account cannot distinguish between (174b) and (174). One further illustration of this point: if one takes a GPSG-type approach, as set out in e.g. Gazdar (1981), then this approach will be capable of accounting for grammatical simple right-node raised structures like (175) in an elegant way, but it will account equally elegantly for (176) as grammatical, which is, of course, highly undesirable:[33]

175.   John likes Ø and Peter dislikes playing golf.
176.   *John likes Ø and Peter likes playing golf.
176a. John likes playing golf and Peter likes playing golf.

The deletion-account outlined above deals quite naturally with these problems: the PDC will block deletion of JUST the direct object in a sentence like (176a), which would be the source of (176), since the accessible deletion site is either a verb site or a rightmost site; deletion of the verb site is impossible because the only unlike constituent is the first constituent, which is ignored, and partial deletion is disallowed because there is no 'difference' between the two deletion target sites that could be deleted first. I conclude that a deletion account which incorporates the PDC is superior to a non-deletion account and gets the coordination facts crucially right; I also note that this constraint, which rules the interaction between coordinate deletion rules, has been absent from the discussion about coordinate deletion of the last decade and a half.[34] We shall have occasion to return to the PDC and the notion of identity in coordinate deletions in considerable detail in section 3.2 of Chapter 3, where we shall see that the PDC makes some surprising and very interesting novel predictions about disjoint reference in reduced co-ordinated sentences.

2.3.2 Ambiguity

After the publication of Hankamer (1973) and the subsequent somewhat acrimonious debate (see e.g. Langendoen, 1975), linguists lost interest in the phenomenon of ambiguity as a result of coordinate deletion; possibly as a result of the shift of attention away from the Generative Semantics or Semantic Syntax framework, and towards the Extended Standard Theory framework of linguistic research.[35] In Chapter 1, sections 1.3.3 and 1.3.4, I have already observed that, counter to the claim made in Hankamer (1973), coordinate deletions can give rise to ambiguity. A typical example of such ambiguity would be:

177.   John wanted to send Harry to Paris, and Peter to Rome

where the 'gap' is interpreted as either *John wanted to send* or as *wanted to send Harry*.[36] In this, (177) follows a pattern that was established as early as in Chomsky's (1957) *Syntactic Structures*: in order to account for the ambiguity of this sentence, we assign two structures to it, corresponding to the 'full' versions of this sentence, without the gaps. The difference in structure then is lost at surface level through the application of various rules, and we are left with an ambiguous sentence. Obviously, it is the rule of coordinate deletion that has obscured the difference between the two 'full' sentences. Given the constraints we have proposed on the application of coordinate deletion, it is to be expected that ambiguity can only arise under very specific circumstances: the types of ambiguity which can arise must necessarily by defined by the possible applications of the coordinate deletion rule, and the ambiguities will be between two different applications of coordinate deletion.

If we examine the possible sites for the application of coordinate deletion, as in (178):

178. $_S$ [...............] CONJ $_S$ [................]

then, if we look at the case where there is only one remnant left after the application of CD, then this will be either the result of leftperipheral deletion, or of rightperipheral deletion, or of verb-site deletion. If it is the result of rightperipheral deletion (which operates backwards), then the coordinating conjunction will immediately follow the remnant constituent. If it is the result of leftperipheral deletion (which operates forwards), then

155

the coordinating conjunction will immediately precede the remnant constituent. It cannot be the result of verb-site deletion, since V-site deletion cannot leave a single first constituent remnant behind. Given, therefore that with single remnants the place of the coordinating conjunction determines the type of deletion that has taken place, and that leftperipheral deletion and rightperipheral deletion cannot overlap, ambiguity will not arise. It is impossible to interpret (179) with a subject reading for *Bill*, or (180) with an object reading for *Bill*:

179. John accused Simon and Ø Ø Bill.
180. Bill Ø Ø and Simon accused John.

If one takes the situation where there are two remnants after coordinate deletion, then this could have arisen in one of the following ways:

(A) Leftperipheral deletion: either one or more constituents have been deleted. The coordinating conjunction immediately precedes the remnants.
(B) Rightperipheral deletion: either one or more constituents have been deleted. The coordinating conjunction immediately follows the remnants.
(C) Verb-site deletion: either one or more constituents have been deleted. The coordinating conjunction immediately precedes the remnants.[37]

It will be clear that ambiguity will not arise between rightmost deletion on the one hand and leftperipheral or verb-site deletion on the other; the place of the coordinating conjunction will single the deletion out as rightperipheral. There is the possibility of ambiguity arising between leftperipheral deletion and verb-site deletion, however. No ambiguity will arise if a single constituent has been deleted, since that will be the verb if it is verb-site deletion that has applied, and the verb would have remained had leftperipheral deletion applied[38] — the presence or absence of the verb will disambiguate between the applications of coordinate deletion. In order for a potential ambiguity to arise, therefore, more than one constituent will have to have been deleted forwards, either as a V-site, or as a left-peripheral site, and the deletion will in both cases have to involve the verb. Given the restrictions on the application of partial coordinate deletion, it then follows that the ambiguity will be between the first constituent + immediately adjacent verb (by leftperipheral deletion), and verb + immediately following constituent (by verb-site deletion). These predictions are in accordance with the English ambiguous sentences listed in this paragraph and in Chapter 1, sections 1.3.3. and 1.3.4. We can also further test them in Dutch and German; if we take the following two sentences:

181. John kust Marie, en Peter kust Marie ook.
      John küsst Marie, und Peter küsst Marie auch.
      (John kisses Marie, and Peter kisses Marie too)
182. John kust Marie, en John kust Peter ook.
      John küsst Marie, und John küsst Peter auch.
      (John kisses Marie, and John kisses Peter too)

then it will be clear that they meet precisely the conditions we have set out above for the emergence of ambiguous coordinate deletions: in (162), the deletion involves more than one constituent, encompassed in a verb site, and there is a nonidentical constituent besides the first constituent in the second coordinated clause, while in (163), we have a leftperipheral site comprising more than one constituent, one of which is the verb. Deletion should therefore create ambiguity, and indeed it does: sentences like (183) are systematically ambiguous between a subject reading and an object reading for the remnant NP.[39]

183. John kust Marie, en Peter ook.
      John küsst Marie, und Peter auch.
      (John kisses Marie, and Peter too)

In English, this type of ambiguity will not arise, since a verb-site deletion in (181) would require some form of do-support; we shall examine this matter in some detail in the section below concerned with VP-deletion.

It furthermore needs to be pointed out that not all cases where there are two remnant constituents and deletion has operated forward will exhibit ambiguity — if we take just one case, namely German, then it will be clear that the ambiguity observed above will only arise if the remnant NP is a proper name or a mass noun, because these do not show case-marking. Nouns which do show case-marking will only be ambiguous if the subjective case in the remnant noun, which identifies the deletion as verb-site deletion, is not distinct from the non-subjective case which identifies it as leftperipheral deletion. Dutch, which has a much less prolific surface case system, is much more prone to the ambiguity exhibited in (183).

The definition of accessible deletion sites, and their inter-action, predicts precisely and correctly the circumstances under which ambiguity can arise as a result of coordinate deletion; this adds further support to the unitary deletion approach to co-ordinate structures.

2.3.3 VPD and discontinuous deletion

So far in this chapter, I have assumed that there are no substan-tial differences between Dutch, German and English with respect to coordinate deletions. There is at least one area in which this is obviously incorrect: In Chapter 1, section 1.3.9, we have seen that English is different from other languages in that it has a rule of VP-deletion.[40]

Not only is VPD a typical rule of English, it also requires a special statement within the rule of coordinate deletion — as will be clear from a sentence like:

184.   John hasn't eaten his food, and Peter has Ø.

where we have deletion of a site that qualifies both as a right-most site and as a verb site; deletion should therefore operate both forwards and backwards, but the forwards deletion (as for a verb site) should be blocked because the only unlike consti-tuent is the first constituent: yet (184) is clearly a good sentence of English. In Dutch and German, sentences of this sort do not exist: both with and without the finite verb form, the equivalents of (184) are ungrammatical.

185.   *John heeft z'n eten niet opgegeten, en Peter (*heeft).
        *John hat sein Essen nicht aufgegessen, und Peter (*hat).

Nevertheless, we cannot simply abandon the restriction on total identity for V-site deletion; recall that forward deletion (but not backwards deletion) of an identical VP is impossible if the only difference between the conjuncts resides in the first constituent:

186.   John likes fish and Bill likes fish.
186a. *John likes fish and Bill does Ø.
186b. John Ø and Bill like fish.

Observations of this sort have led us to question the formulation of VPD as a rule which operates both in subordinate clauses and in coordinate clauses: a serious problem with VPD in coordinated structures is what one needs in addition to identical VPs in order for VPD to function properly, and this problem does not arise in 'subordinate' VPD. As will be clear from (186/186a), there needs to be something there, but, as we can see from (184), we cannot place some sort of remnant constraint on VPD requiring there to be at least two remnants after the application of VPD. In addition, we find that VPD is just as grammatical if the negation is in the second coordinated clause instead of in the first:

187.   John has eaten his food, and Peter hasn't Ø.

Recall also that in Chapter 1, we observed that VPD does not apply if the VPs are both 'hemmed in' on either side by unlike material: the VPs in (188) inaccessible to deletion.

188.   *Peter once met Mary in London, but Harry didn't ever
       Ø Ø in Biggleswade.

As soon as one of the VPs is accessible, however, deletion is possible again:

189.   John hasn't eaten his food, and Bill hasn't Ø Ø either.

It is not only necessary that at least one VP is accessible, it must be accessible as a rightmost site:

190.   John met Mary in London, and Bill didn't in Biggles-
       wade

This situation can be described as follows: if there is overlap between a rightmost site and a verb site, and at least one site

159

(subsequent or antecedent) is inaccessible from at least one side (i.e. there is unlike material following at least one site, or more than one unlike constituent preceding at least one site), deletion will operate forwards. Schematically represented, this looks as follows:[41]

191. $[0 (X_1) \ldots (X_2)]$ CONJ $[0 (X_1) \ldots (X_2)]$
         Condition: One X2 = Ø
         One X = Ø

In these cases, deletion operates forward, but the tensed verb will be retained unless it is the main verb: in that case, DO is inserted in the place of the tensed verb. This rule, which is specific for English and regulates the interaction of rightmost sites and verb sites, accurately predicts the facts observed above. It also predicts, for instance, that we get acceptable VPD-type structures (but not verb-site deletion) if both X_1-positions are filled, and no X_2 is filled, no matter what the internal constituency of the target site in question. If we take a deletion target which consists only of a verb, then that verb should delete forwards, with no DO-support, if it is a verb site but not a rightmost site, and should delete forwards, with do-support, but not backwards, if it qualifies both as a rightmost site and a verb site. This turns out to be correct:[42]

192.   John lives in Biggleswade, and Mary (* does) Ø in London.
193.   John sometimes fails, but Peter never does Ø.
193a. *John sometimes Ø, but Peter never fails.
194.   John eats fish for its taste, and Mary (*does) Ø for the vitamins.
195.   John sometimes gives alms to the poor, but Peter never does Ø.
195a. *John sometimes Ø Ø Ø but Peter never gives alms to the poor.

The existence of sentences like (193a) demonstrates that Ross's (1970) generalisation that constituents delete according to the directionality of their branching, although extremely perceptive, has shortcomings even for English: Ross would predict that (193a) with the rightmost verb (or VP), which would (presumably) be on a right branch, should delete backwards, or backwards and forwards, but never just forwards. Thus again we see that the DC as it is formulated by Ross is not a good candidate for universal status. In Chapter 3, section 3.5.2, we will observe data from other languages than the ones cited here which systematically allow violations of the DC (such as forward deletions of a rightmost site). The restrictions on the interaction of verb sites and rightmost sites which hold for English quite straightforwardly account for the VPD-type facts, as well as for the difference between English on the one hand, and German and Dutch on the other, where there are no such restrictions on the interaction of these two sites.

Dutch and German are different from English, and might therefore also have their idiosyncratic behaviour. There is one type of data which has hitherto gone unobserved and undiscussed in the literature on coordinate deletions. Dutch and German do not have the equivalent of VPD, but delete identical material without leaving a finite verb form behind:

196. John eet kaas, en Harry eet ook kass.
     John isst Käse, und Harry isst auch Käse.
     (John eats cheese, and Harry also eats   cheese)

When we apply deletion in these sentences, we get the following:

196a. John eet kaas, en Harry Ø ook Ø.
      John isst Käse, und Harry Ø auch Ø.

What we cannot get is the following:

196b. *John eet Ø, en Harry Ø ook kaas.
      *John eet Ø, und Harry Ø auch Käse.

The ungrammaticality of (196b) in Dutch and German, in spite of the fact that deletion has taken place according to the directionality specified for rightmost sites and verb sites, can be attributed to the Partial Deletion Constraint: there is no *difference* between the verb site and the rightmost site which could be deleted first — the PDC can readily be invoked to rule out (196b), but it will not account for the fact of why (196a) is acceptable: here, deletion does not apply to a single site, but to two sites, namely a verb site and a rightperipheral site: the rightperipheral site should have deleted backwards, and the verb site should have deleted forwards. But this will give us precisely (196b), which is prohibited by the PDC — in other words, we seem to have created an unresolvable conflict in the rules and constraints. Before we examine this problem any further, consider the following sentence:

197. Jan heeft vandaag een vrije dag, en Piet heeft morgen een vrije dag.
Jan hat heute einen freien Tag, und Piet hat morgen einen freien Tag.
(Jan has today a free day, and Piet has tomorrow a free day)

This sentence allows both 'bidirectional' deletion, and unitary forward deletion:

197a. Jan heeft vandaag een vrije dag, en Piet Ø morgen Ø.
Jan hat heute einen freien Tag, und Piet Ø morgen Ø.
197b. Jan heeft vandaag Ø, en Piet Ø morgen een vrije dag.
Jan hat heute Ø, und Piet Ø morgen ein freier Tag.

Note that in the case of (197), there is no violation of peripherality, nor is there a violation of the PDC, since there are two separate sites: one verb sites, and one rightperipheral site; what is unusual here is that they are allowed to delete forward as a unity. If we front the time adverbial, which will put the subject after the verb, and will therefore not change the linear sequence or accessibility of the deletion target sites, precisely the same situation obtains: both unitary forward deletion and deletion according to the directionality of the (separate) verb and right-peripheral sites are allowed:

198. Vandaag heeft Jan een vrije dag, en morgen Ø Piet Ø.
Heute hat Jan einen freien Tag, und morgen Ø Piet Ø.
198a. Vandaag heeft Jan Ø en morgen Ø Piet een vrije dag.
Heute hat Jan Ø und morgen Ø Piet einen freien Tag.

Our observations about Dutch and German can be captured as follows:

If a coordination is a candidate for both verb-string deletion and rightmost deletion, deletion may operate forward as a whole.

Cast in the format which we have used in this chapter for deletion target sites, the above statement looks as follows:

199. $_S$[0 .... -V- .... (X) ... -V- ...] $_S$ CONJ $_S$ [O ... -V- ...

(X) ... -V- ...] $_S$

This accounts not only for the Dutch and German data, but also for English sentences in which discontinuous deletion applies. Consider the two grammatical English sentences (200) and (200a):

200. John gave a book to Mary, and Peter Ø a record Ø.
200a. John gave a book Ø, and Peter Ø a record to Mary.

(199) not only gives us the right results, but also immediately makes a number of interesting predictions, and there is no need to state specific constraints on this rule governing the inter-action of rightmost sites and verb sites. Bidirectional deletions in sentences like (196b) are ruled out by the PDC, and (199) provides the opportunity for the deletion rule to operate forwards as a whole. It will allow both acceptable variants of (197) and (198), since there is nothing to block bidirectional deletions here, and (199) allows unitary forward deletion. Now suppose that there are no intervening unlike constituents: after all, the unlike constituents are given as optional in formalisation (199).[43] In that case, we have total site overlap between a verb site and a rightmost site, with, as the only possible unlike consti-tuent, the first (ignored) constituent, and verb-site deletion will then be disallowed under the constraint against total identity (see (95) in section 2.2.1). There can then only be backwards deletion of the rightperipheral site: examples of this type, as in (201), have already been discussed.

201. Ik geloof dat Jan kaas eet, en Piet ook Ø Ø.
      Ich glaube, dass Jan Käse isst, und Piet auch Ø Ø.
      (I   believe that Jan cheese eats, and Piet also Ø Ø)
201a. *Ik geloof dat Jan Ø Ø en Piet ook kaas eet.
      *Ich glaube, dass Jan Ø Ø und Piet auch Käse isst.

If there is more than one unlike constituent to the left of the like material, and there are no unlike constituents intervening, then deletion should be able to operate both forwards and backwards, since the site now qualifies as both a rightperipheral site and a verb site. (199) applies vacuously: forward deletion is allowed anyway, since we have a verb site, and the PDC will block partial deletion in these cases. This situation is borne out by the facts of Dutch and German:[44]

202. Ik geloof dat Jan morgen naar London gaat, en Piet
   overmorgen Ø Ø.
   Ich glaube, dass Jan morgen nach London fährt, und Piet
   übermorgen Ø Ø.
   (I believe that Jan tomorrow to London goes, and Piet
   the day after Ø Ø)

202a. Ik geloof dat Jan morgen Ø Ø, en Piet overmorgen naar
   London gaat
   Ich glaube, dass Jan morgen Ø Ø und Piet übermorgen
   nach London fährt.

If there is only one unlike constituent intervening between two deletion target sites in one of the coordinated clauses, then only forward deletion will apply, since backwards deletion would automatically violate the PDC: an example here is (177) above. If in both coordinated clauses there is material separating the two deletion sites, then either unitary forwards deletion will be allowed, or the deletion will take place according to the directionality of the sites in question.

The constraints we have posited for the operation of co-ordinate deletion are not violated by the specific rules of Dutch, German and English: what we have done is to posit some language-specific constraints which serve only further to define the directionality of deletion in cases of deletion site overlap. The notion of accessibility of deletion sites cannot be violated, nor can the PDC. For the moment, let us conclude the discussion of site overlap and site interaction. In Chapter 3, we shall return to the question of why it should be that English, Dutch and German specifically allow forward deletion in those cases where an S is a candidate for rightmost and V-site deletion.

2.4 CONCLUSION AND EVALUATION

In this chapter, I have developed a theory of the syntax of coordination that seeks to derive both same constituent co-ordination and non-same constituent coordination from sentence coordination. I have opted for this approach rather than a phrase-structural approach as set out in e.g. Dougherty (1970), or Sag *et al.* (1985) because of the essential short-comings of the PS-rule approach: the rule schemata employed for coordination in the PS-rule approach, which claim that it is possible to coordinate *n* same categories *n* times grammatically, is simply a wrong generalisation for at least three reasons: first of all, not only same categories can be conjoined (cf. the results of verb-site deletion, also known in the literature as Gapping), secondly, not all coordinations allow same categories to be conjoined *n* times (only *and* and *or* seem to allow this), and thirdly, even in the cases where it does indeed seem possible to conjoin *n* categories *n* times, it turns out that these coordinations are subject to very different restrictions — *or* cannot occur in *respectively*-constructions, nor can it occur with symmetrical predicates; *and,* however, can occur with both.

The deletion approach which I have outlined in this chapter takes the one generalisation which does seem to be true about coordination, namely that it is possible to coordinate at least two sentences with all coordinations, at least in Dutch, German and English. Some coordinations (and, or) allow more than two sentences to be coordinated, and some coordinations allow identical material to be deleted, while others don't (e.g. *for, denn, want*). The emphasis on the derivation of non-S coordi-nations from S-coordinations does not mean that *all* coordi-nation is S-coordination; some *and*-coordinations behave in the same way that plurals do (notably in symmetrical predicates, and some verb-coordinations) and are therefore best viewed as a special type of plurals.

The deletion approach, which owes a considerable debt to Ross's (1970) approach to Gapping, makes minimal assump-tions — it does not refer to constituent structure, only to the linear left-to-right order of constituents. It can be quite simply stated as: *Delete identical material in coordination.*[45] It applies to three possible target sites (not all of which are necessarily present in all languages, cf. Japanese), namely leftperipheral sites, rightperipheral sites, and medial sites, which we have called verb sites because in the languages which form the main focus of our discussion here, such medial sites will always contain a verb. It is limited by two constraints which, given the data we have inspected so far, are the same for all languages, namely the Peripherality Constraint which states that a site must be peripheral to its S in order to be accessible to the deletion rule, and the Partial Deletion Constraint which regulates the interaction of deletion sites. There are a few things which follow very straightforwardly from the coordinate deletion rule and the way it operates: for instance, it is possible to define the precise locations at which ambiguity can arise as a result of coordinate deletion on the basis of the rule and its two constraints. The rule is furthermore subject to language-specific constraints: For English, a constraint that will give us VPD-type structure, and for Dutch and German, a constraint that will account for 'discontinuous' deletions.

If one compares the deletion approach outlined above with previous approaches in the literature as outlined in Chapter 1, it will be clear that its empirical coverage greatly exceeds any other account: not only does it deal with more deletion patterns than other approaches, it also gets the facts crucially right, and brings to light important bodies of new material. If one compares it at a theoretical level with earlier deletion accounts, one can observe that the increased empirical coverage has led to a simplification of the constraints on deletion rather than a complication thereof. If one compares it with the non-deletion account as outlined in GPSG, the picture is more or less the same, although the theoretical notions employed in GPSG are rather different. There will, for instance, be no need to state constraints on deletion: notably the Peripherality Constraint on forward-deleted leftmost sites and backward-deleted rightmost sites will follow as a theorem from the GPSG approach to coordination.[46] All verb-site deletions are outside the scope of GPSG. However, even non-deletion approaches[47] will need a statement which is equivalent to the Partial Deletion Constraint: notably the PDC facts from Dutch and German will cause a non-deletion account extreme difficulties.

The deletion approach is the most likely to lead to an adequate statement of coordination; the above account is an outline of how one can best approach the syntax of coordination. It makes a number of assumptions and leaves a few questions unanswered; the assumptions, and some unanswered questions, will be the concern of the next chapter.

NOTES

1. See on this matter also 1.3.5 and 1.3.10 in Chapter 1.
2. This is the sort of rule we have encountered in Dougherty (1970); see section 1.2.2 in Chapter 1. For a more sophisticated version of this type of rule, but one that falls victim to essentially the same type of objections, see Gazdar *et al.* (1985), Chapter 7.
3. Even this statement is an oversimplification; the appropriate statement seems to be more or less as follows (a precise formalisation would take us too far afield): a coordination with BUT as a coordinating conjunction is disallowed if the only difference between the two members of the coordination resides in one pair of NPs, and that pair of NPs itself does not differ in more than one respect. Thus, a coordination of any category in which the only difference resides in a pair of NPs which themselves differ only in one pair of articles, or one pair of nouns, will be disallowed, but if adjectives differ, or articles and adjectives, or adjectives and nouns, then the coordination will be allowed:

(a) John is a fine player, but a sensitive player.
(b) I saw one large green animal, but two small red ones.
(c) John is a good cricketer and a fine fellow.

These complications with BUT do not affect the argument.
4. It needs to be observed that none of these problems *disappears* if we opt for a deletion-account, but at least the machinery necessary for dealing with this problem (the notions of deletion, non-identity and identity) are part of the regular machinery which a deletion-account will use: the PS-rule approach will also have to invoke these notions, but they are alien to it. Note also, incidentally, that FOR, WANT and DENN are unusual coordinating conjunctions in that they can only coordinate main clauses: this lends further support to the hypothesis that the coordinating conjunctions have very little in common beyond the fact that they can, under certain circumstances, coordinate sentences: a generalisation like the one expressed in rule (4) is simply far too strong.
5. There exists a hardy race of stylistic purists who insist that a sentence should not be started with a coordinating conjunction. I will not quibble with stylistic preferences, but it is the case that most speakers and writers will quite happily start sentences with a coordinating conjunction (the Bible, for instance, is full of such sentences), and they are definitely well-formed.
6. That this is the correct approach to the subjects of symmetrical predicates is also confirmed by the semantic differences between co-ordinated NP subjects of symmetrical predicates and coordinated NP subjects of other predicates. If the meaning of a coordination is taken to

167

be the intersection of the property-sets of the members of the constituents of the coordination, then this must be clearly incorrect for
sentences like:

Two and two make four.

which have a symmetrical predicate. Symmetrical predicates (a name
which I shall continue to use because it has gained such wide currency)
simply subcategorise for either a plural subject or a coordinated subject,
and the semantics of plurals and coordination are the same in this case.

7. There are some verb coordinations (go and V, try and V, run
and V) which cannot readily be accounted for as derived from S-coordinations. I do not propose to offer an account of these coordinations
here, but a lexical treatment of such constructions seems most appropriate, since these V-coordinations are highly exceptional (only a few of
them exist in English, and German and Dutch do not allow them at all)
and they are not uniform in their characteristics: *try and V*, for instance,
seems not to occur in the past tense, and *and* can be replaced by *to*,
while *go and V* is not so restricted in its occurrence, and *and* cannot be
replaced by *to*, Picking up the point made in the previous note, I do not
consider it at all impossible that further research may demonstrate a
need for a slight readjustment of the balance between S-coordinations
and NP-coordinations for languages other than English, Dutch and
German: it may be preferable, for those languages which have coordinating conjunctions specifically for NP-coordinations (Chinese is a case
in point) to generate these coordinations directly by means of PS-rules.
But note that even such a readjustment will not vindicate the PS-
approach as a whole: there are many languages (again, Chinese is a case
in point) that do not allow coordination of e.g. finite verbs.

8. I have already singled out, in notes (6/7), what these exceptions
are. Symmetrical predicates, which subcategorise for plural or conjoined
subjects, will not be accounted for by means of deletion rules; such
coordinations have essentially different characteristics from deletion-
derived coordinations, as I have already observed in section 2.1.1.

9. By VPD I mean the rule that deletes identical VPs in coordinated structures. For a discussion of why I differentiate between VPD in
coordinated structures and VPD elsewhere, see Chapter 1, section
1.3.9.

10. This example applies to English: neither Dutch nor German
have an equivalent of VPD.

11. These examples cannot be replicated for English since English
does not have verb-final wordorder in subordinate clauses.

12. I assume, in accordance with common practice, that place
adverbials are outside the VP for the purpose of this discussion. See
also, however, section 1.3.9 of Chapter 1.

13. This is the structure employed in van Oirsouw (1983a) for a
discussion of some of the problems raised in this chapter. My earlier
account was seriously inadequate, and I use it here only for the purpose
of illustration.

14. I use the term surface STRUCTURE for convenience only, to

refer to coordinations in their surface form — again, I will not refer to structural configurations within that coordination either in deep or in surface structure, and if I talk about an embedded coordinated clause I talk about the linear sequence of constituents within that embedded coordinated clause, leaving the superordinate clause out of consideration. I must also stress that I do not wish to suggest that structure *per se* is irrelevant; my claim is merely that for stating the constraints on coordination it will not be necessary to refer to structural configurations. On this, see also Chapter 3.

15. One sometimes finds arguments about the structure of a Right-node Raised construction based on the intonation pattern of such structures — Gazdar (1981) suggests that a structure which puts the main constituent break between the 'raised' constituent and what precedes it is the correct structure for RNR. However, as we have seen in note. 28 to Chapter 1, there is no obvious difference between RNR-structures and structures that have not undergone RNR with respect to intonation. In fact, the main intonational break in a Right-node Raised sentence is just before the coordinating conjunction, and certainly not before the Right-node Raised constituent. A sentence like:

John kicked Ø and Bill hit the cat.

simply cannot be pronounced with rises on *John hit* and *Bill kicked* and then a fall on *the cat*; the intonation pattern (in British English) is the same as for the 'non-raised' sentence, namely a rise in the clause before the conjunction, and a fall in the clause after the conjunction.

16. Not all linguists would agree that the three advantages which I mention here are actually desirable consequences — there is a school which attaches more value to a theory the more it limits the form of grammar. This is considered desirable from a psychological point of view: given the enormous range of possible grammars, and given the fact that children acquire language in a rapid and uniform manner on the basis of incomplete and degenerate data, it must be the case that of the host of possible hypotheses that the language-learning child can come up with, many will be eliminated quite rapidly on the basis of incoming primary linguistic data (sentences, words, constructions) — this in turn means that the greater the number of constraints that can be hypothesised on the basis of the primary linguistic evidence, the closer we come to 'explaining' the facts of first language acquisition. This point is well taken: it is one of the primary goals of linguistics to find a descriptively adequate and highly restrictive theory of grammar which can serve as part of the basis for a psychological explanation of the phenomenon of first language acquisition. However, this does not mean that it is always a good research strategy to require of every account of every phenomenon that it should provide the maximum in constraints on the form of grammar — this will often lead to incompatible accounts of different phenomena and no way of deciding between them, or, worse still, to a wilful disregard for certain classes of grammatical phenomena because they are difficult to capture if one wishes to preserve the coherence of one's theoretical constructs. The present

account provides a few clear limitations on the form of grammar which follow from the need to account adequately for a broad range of coordination facts, and aims on the one hand to extend the data-base for accounts of coordination (a highly necessary exercise, as will by now be clear), and on the other to provide a simpler and more adequate account for the phenomena observed in this data-base.

17. I refer here to the linear order of lexically realised constituents; the actual derivation of topicalised constituents in Dutch and German main clauses is not relevant to the argument here.

18. It is an interesting fact that not only German and Dutch disallow deletion of a direct object in SOV order: in Japanese, for instance, deletions of the type SV + SOV are also generally deemed unacceptable:

∗John-ga Ø chyuumonshite Peter-ga raisu-o tabeta.
(John Ø ordered and Peter rice ate)

Furthermore, as we shall see later on in this chapter, this statement is not quite accurate: clausal direct objects in Dutch and German subordinate clauses will follow the verb, and they can then be deleted:

Ik geloof dat Jan wist Ø en Piet vermoedde dat het meisje ziek was.
(I believe that Jan knew Ø and Piet suspected that the girl ill was)

19. This was also observed for German in Ross (1970).

20. By constituent I mean major constituent here: NP, V, Adv.

21. It can be observed here that the verb by itself also qualifies as a verb site; nevertheless, deletion of just the verb is not possible in these examples. We shall return to this matter in considerable detail later on in this chapter.

22. Note that these facts are perfectly parallel to what Jackendoff (1972) observed about deletion of verbs in English with like or unlike adverbs preceding them (see Chapter 1, 1.3.2); this provides further strong support for the unitary approach to coordinate deletions.

23. These examples cannot be replicated in Dutch and German because adverbial positioning is rather different from English in these two languages.

24. It needs to be pointed out that sentences of this type are not unacceptable for a number of speakers of British English. This inconsistency in judgment can be quite elegantly accounted for as follows. For people who accept sentences like (120), adverbials are adjoined as left daughters of VP: the absence of the verb (as a result of deletion) does not affect adverbial movement. For people who do not accept (120), the adverbial is left-sister-adjoined to the verb: if the verb has been deleted, adverbial movement can no longer take place, so that (120) will not be derived. The difference in dialects of English thus do not affect the peripherality constraint, but are the result of the different ways in which speakers may adjoin pre-verbal adverbials. However, the movement of adverbials is a much-underexposed area, and these facts may necessitate further analysis if we assume that deletion only takes place after *all* movement has applied. One possible way of accounting

for this particular variety of English could be to assume that subject + pre-verbal adverb are treated as a single constituent by the coordinate deletion rule: see on this also section 2.2.5. Alternatively, it may simply be the case that in some varieties of English not *all* deletion rules follow *all* movement rules.

25. I am indebted to Nobuko Hasegawa and Makoto Nishikawa for providing the data from Japanese. Note how these observations could also be accounted for quite readily by assuming that Japanese does not allow site overlap (cf. section 2.3 ff.); I hasten to add, however, that this is by no means intended as an adequately detailed discussion of Japanese coordination. One problem is that Japanese is generally more elliptical than e.g. English, which may account for the instances of SOV + SV coordination encountered in e.g. Sanders and Tai (1972), where the 'missing' object in S_2 is construed as strictly coreferential with the overt object, and which some speakers of Japanese accept as marginally correct. Such problems with the dividing line between syntactically conditioned coordinate deletion and contextually conditioned ellipsis are also present in German, which allows a semantically 'empty' subject like *es* (it) to be dropped in *Mir ist schlecht*; correspondingly, we find that for some speakers of German, VSO + VO coordinations are acceptable, though there seems to be a strong preference for the deleted subject to be either a pronoun or a proper name.

26. I use the term descriptive adequacy here advisedly — there are many differing opinions on what constitutes an explanation in linguistics; I do not wish to tie in my discussion of the syntax of coordination *directly* with questions of innateness (see e.g. Lightfoot, 1982) at this point: this I will discuss very briefly at the end of Chapter 3. I adhere to what Seuren (1985:52 ff.) calls the psychological realism of a linguistic description in the following (very minimal) sense: I shall take care not to make claims in my linguistic description which are *incompatible* with findings in psychological research. My view of what constitutes a contribution to explanation is as follows, rather irreverently and informally stated: a contribution to the explanation of a phenomenon will either stop people asking questions about the phenomenon altogether, and thus stop further research (either because the research in question is realised to be fruitless, or because an explanation which fully satisfies a scholarly community has been provided) or make them ask different and more far-reaching questions from the ones they were asking before. This book is intended to provide the second type of (intermediary) 'explanation', which I would prefer to refer to as description, since it provides a broader, more detailed, and better systematised data-base on which to base future grammars, in which phenomena connected with coordination will find a proper place (see e.g. Van Riemsdijk and Williams (1986:175) on the rather cavalier treatment which coordination has received in at least one type of syntactic research).

27. The actual analysis of fronted constituents does not concern us here — if, for instance, one were to derive it by moving the verb into a COMP position, and the focused constituent into a TOPIC position, this structural configuration would be disregarded by the coordinate deletion rule, which simply scans the constituents of a coordination

from left to right.

28. It follows as a theorem that the nonshared material here will always be the first constituent: if one has overlap between either a leftmost site or a rightmost site and a verb site, then this overlap need not be total, but the only possible difference will reside in the first constituent of the S, which is not 'seen' for verb sites. It then follows for rightmost sites that if the only difference between an accessible rightmost site and a verb site is the first constituent, everything but the first constituent will be identical, and deletion of a verb site is then blocked because the coordinate deletion rule will perceive total identity between the members of the coordination, which is disallowed: see also the discussion in 2.2.1 and 2.3. Deletion of the rightperipheral site will still be allowed, because with respect to rightperipheral sites there is no total identity. There will, in other words, never be partial deletion if a verb site overlaps with a rightmost site. Compare the following three sentences: (b) is ungrammatical because verb-site deletion has applied with as only difference between the coordinated Ss the first ignored constituent.

(a) John drinks beer and Bill drinks beer.
(b) *John drinks beer and Bill Ø Ø.
(c) John Ø Ø and Bill drink beer.

29. There is one possible instance where it seems that deletion does not apply to eliminate all of one verb site. Ross (1970) noted that in sentences containing a series of verbs in embedded clauses, it is possible (at least for some speakers) to delete these verbs 'in sequence', i.e. left-to-right. Thus, in a sentence like:

Harry seems to want to try to kiss Sue, and Bill seems to want to try to kiss Margaret.

there are speakers who will accept any of the following:

Harry seems to want to try to kiss Sue, and
— Bill Ø to want to try to kiss Margaret.
— Bill Ø Ø to try to kiss Margaret.
— Bill Ø Ø Ø to kiss Margaret.
— Bill Ø Ø Ø Ø Margaret.

This seems to run counter to our claim that a site is deleted all at once. There are, however, a few things that can be observed about these sentences. First of all, the last sentence, with the 'full' deletion of the V-site, is clearly preferred. Secondly, neither Dutch nor German allow these partial deletions, but only the 'full' ones (note how the infinitival verbs in German are in the mirror image order from the verbs in Dutch; for an account of this phenomenon, see e.g. Evers (1975) or Seuren (1985)):

Jan heeft Piet proberen te leren fietsen, en Marie heeft Susan
Jan hat Piet radfahren zu lehren versucht, und Marie hat Susan

(Jan has Piet bicycling to teach tried, and Marie has Susan)
proberen te leren fietsen.
radfahren zu lehren versucht.
bicycling to teach tried)

Jan heeft Piet proberen te leren fietsen,

— en Marie Ø Susan Ø Ø Ø.
— *en Marie heeft Susan Ø Ø Ø.
— *en Marie heeft Susan proberen Ø Ø.
— *en Marie heeft Susan proberen te leren Ø.

Jan hat Piet radfahren zu lernen versucht,

— und Marie Ø Susan Ø Ø Ø.
— *und Marie hat Susan Ø Ø Ø.
— *und Marie hat Susan radfahren Ø Ø.
— *und Marie hat Susan radfahren zu lehren Ø.

The explanation which immediately suggests itself here is closely related in spirit to what Ross (1970) suggested, namely that for those speakers of English who accept the partial verb-site deletion, the coordinate deletion rule can recognise (albeit with some difficulty, hence the preference for the 'full' deletion) non-finite verbs separated from each other by S-brackets as in:

$$S_0 \ [\cdots \ S_1 \ [\ \text{Vinf} \ S_2 \ [\text{Vinf} \ S_3 \ [\text{Vinf} \cdots]]]]$$

English is unusual in that it (with some difficulty) does allow for partial deletions of this type. Note that it is essential that we have a continuous string of embedded non-finite verbs for this type of partial deletion to occur: it is not possible to have 'partial' VP-deletion:

Peter wants John to talk to Mary, and Harry does Ø, too.
*Peter wants John to talk to Mary, and Harry does John to talk to Mary, too.

Nor does it seem possible to get partial deletions of the auxiliaries:

Peter will have been kissing Sue, and Harry, Ø Belinda.
*Peter will have been kissing Sue, and Harry, Ø have been kissing Belinda.
Ø Ø been kissing Belinda.
Ø Ø Ø kissing Belinda.

30. The Dutch and German translations here are not fully equivalent in meaning here; this, however, does not matter for the purposes of our illustration.
31. I refer to note 28 for these sentences. Since the deletion site qualifies both as a rightmost site and as a verb site, deletion should

operate both forwards and backwards, in accordance with the direction-ality of these sites. However, only backwards deletion is allowed, since the only difference between the coordinated sentences resides in the first constituent.

32. Note that backward deletion is also possible here, since the verb also qualifies as a rightmost site:

Ik geloof dat Jan de hond Ø en Piet de kat slaat.
Ich glaube, dass Jan den Hund Ø, und Piet die Katze schlägt.

This point, which I have already discussed in some detail earlier on in the chapter, is immaterial to the discussion here.

33. For a GPSG account of RNR, see Chapter 1, 1.3.10. There are two possible ways out of this quandry for GPSG, both of which strike at the very roots of the theory: either the PS-rules generating coordinated structures are sensitive to the occurrence of identical material (which would make them non-context-free), or the theory should adopt a rule of deletion under identity as outlined here.

34. The first work to discuss the interaction of deletions in co-ordinated structure was, to my knowledge, Tai (1969). The issues raised there were taken up again in van Oirsouw (1983a, 1985).

35. For a discussion of this shift of attention, see Newmeyer (1980), who takes an unfavourable view of the Generative Semantics enterprise. For a much more favourable discussion, see Seuren (1985).

36. Many speakers seem to find the first reading the more 'natural' one. The reason for this is that it involves the least strain on memory: in order for a hearer to arrive at the second reading, it is required that he remembers the entire preceding coordinated clause *verbatim*, while only the last two constituents have to be remembered in order to arrive at the first reading. This also accounts for the fact why hearers tend to find RNR-type sentences less 'natural' than sentences from which the subject has been deleted; for similar observations to this, see Chapter 1, section 1.2.4. We shall briefly return to this issue in Chapter 3.

37. By remnant we mean, of course, that part of the sentence either to the immediate left or the immediate right of the coordinating conjunction which is not capable of functioning as an independent simple sentence.

38. It is possible for leftperipheral deletion to apply to S-initial verbs, as in auxiliary questions in English, or yes-no questions in German and Dutch — however, there ambiguity will again not arise, since in that case the verb, which is a necessary component of a verb site, is the first constituent, and is therefore 'not seen' by CD when it looks for verb sites.

39. Note how it should be possible, in (178), to delete the subject independently, since this sentence meets the criteria for partial deletion. However, the deletion should then not be ambiguous, because only one constituent has been deleted, and deletion of a single constituent cannot give rise to ambiguity. The predictions turn out to be correct; the following sentence is a good and unambiguous sentence of Dutch and German, equivalent in meaning to (178):

John kust Marie, en kust Peter ook.
John küsst Marie, und küsst Peter auch.

40. Here, as in Chapter 1, I take VPD to involve crucially the reten-
tion (or reinstatement, depending on one's theory) of a finite verb form
after deletion. I know of no other characteristic that could possibly distinguish VPD from other identity deletion rules that operate in coordinated structures.

41. Note how the requirement of one X_2-position not being filled
actually follows from the site overlap requirement.

42. The matter of do-support is an odd one; judgments are not at all
clear in some areas. Thus, it seems that for quite a few speakers, both
(a) and (b) are equally acceptable:

(a) John will come today, and Peter will Ø tomorrow.
(b) John will come today, and Peter Ø tomorrow.

However, in cases like (c/d), there is no doubt that (d) is preferred,
although even here there will be speakers who accept both:

(c) Today, John will come, and tomorrow, Peter Ø.
(d) today, John will come, and tomorrow, Peter will Ø.

I have no explanation to offer for this; note however, that there is nothing to be gained from adopting a structural notion of a node VP in these
cases which either gets pronominalised (see the discussion of Napoli
(1985) in Chapter 3 for such a proposal) or deleted (Sag, 1976). Note
furthermore how this further blurs the distinction between Gapping
(verb-site deletion) and VPD: the existence of a pair of sentences like
(a/b) casts serious doubt on the existence of two separate rules.

43. Trivially, one could also suppose there to be no verbs in the
deletion target sites — if that were the case, then the non-rightmost site
would not be accessible to deletion if the ignored constituent were
unlike, and the rightperipheral site would be deletable as a normal
rightmost site. (199) would then simply not be applicable, since there is
only one deletion target site.

44. This situation can, of course, only arise in coordinations of subordinate clauses: in coordinations of main clauses, there can (because of
the verb-second rule) not be more than one unlike constituent preceding the verb.

45. This statement could easily, and trivially, be simplified into
Neijt's (1979) very general rule of 'Delete' — only one would then have
to restrict it to specific coordinations, one would have to impose a
constraint of identity on it. Until further research shows that significant
improvements in the statement of deletion rules can be achieved by this
simplification, and suitable constraints have been formulated, I prefer
the less general and less opaque statement as I have given it.

46. It is interesting to note in this connection that the ideas
suggested in the paper by Schachter and Mordechay (1983), which are
cast in a GPSG framework, and are specifically concerned with the
notion of peripherality, are not taken up in subsequent GPSG work —

to the detriment of the latter.

47. This also holds for Steedman's approach; PDC-violations are as readily parsable, in his approach, constructions which do not violate the PDC — I therefore conclude that the PDC is a necessary part (whether it is stated as a constraint on deletion or as a constraint against identity in a non-deletion account) of the syntax of coordination.

3

The Notions and Their Consequences

3.1 INTRODUCTION

In the previous chapter, I have given a detailed account of the syntax of coordinate deletion, and I have demonstrated how the linear approach to deletion under identity in coordination provides us with an account which is considerably simpler than previous accounts, covers the same range of empirical data and more, and brings interesting new facts to the discussion of co-ordinate deletions. The very statement of the coordinate deletion rule, *Delete under identity in coordinated structures*, also raises a number of questions of considerable interest, which I have not discussed in the previous chapter, and which now need to be answered.

There is, first of all, the notion of identity — what does it mean for deletion target material to be 'identical'; is this phono-logical, or morphological, or referential identity, for instance, or perhaps a combination of these? The everyday use of the word 'identical', or 'the same' will allow for fairly disparate things to be grouped together. We speak, for instance, of 'identical twins', where the notion of identity will clearly not be something like identity of reference. given that this is so, is it the case that there is one unitary notion of 'identical' for coordinate deletion, or does this vary from situation to situation, or from language to language?

Then, secondly, we have the question of how we are to inter-pret the terms in such a statement — what does *deletion* mean? Does it mean that after deletion, there is absolutely nothing of what has been deleted left, or are there phonologically null categories of some sort which are left behind after the deletion

177

rule? If there are such empty categories, do they then have properties which tell us more about coordination and the constraints we have discussed in the previous chapter? What is the structure of a coordination to which deletion has applied?

Thirdly, I have made an assumption in my account of the syntax of coordination which is not controversial, but which certainly needs to be spelled out and examined: I have assumed that the meaning of a coordination will be the same, whether it has been subjected to deletion or not. This is based on one of the possible views of the semantics of coordination which is well established, simple and attractive: if one has a mechanism for interpreting simplex sentences and coordinations of simplex sentences, then what one needs to do for the interpretation of non-sentence coordination is to trace it back to simplex sentence coordinations (i.e. to 'recover' the deletion). The most important question which this raises in the framework here is whether it will be possible to 'undo' deletions, i.e. to parse non-sentence coordinations in such a way that their relation to S-coordinations is clear and uncontroversial.

Lastly, I have not set out the place of the rule of coordinate deletion in any one model of grammar — I have observed that my (optional) rule of coordinate deletion is incompatible with for instance Generalised Phrase Structure Grammar, because that model of grammar simply does not allow deletion rules. But this means that we still have to define the place of deletion rules in a model of grammar that *does* allow them. Although clearly coordination will not be the only construction to determine the form and nature of a model of grammar[1], it is possible, on the basis of the present account to define, roughly, the place of coordinate deletion in the class of generative grammars[2] that does allow deletion, and to explore the consequences of this.

3.2 IDENTITY

In the second chapter, I have assumed a notion of identity which I there took to mean identity of representation. This raises two questions, namely what the representation that the rule of coordinate deletion refers to is, and secondly, how can one establish whether two representations are identical? To begin with the second question, this is fairly easy to answer.

Generative grammarians have, for decades, written, or typed, or printed representations of the structure of sentences on sheets of paper. Now if we assume that we can define the sort of representation that a rule of coordinate deletion will refer to, then it will be easy enough to define what identity is: two representations will be identical if we can't find any differences between them. This can be visualised as follows: type the representation of one of the conjuncts on a transparent sheet, then type the representation of the second conjunct on a second transparent sheet, using the same type, spacing, etc., and place them on top of each other. Where the representations are legible, they will be identical, where they are not legible, they are not identical.[3]

3.2.1 Establishing identity

This idea of 'superimposition' of representations to see where the identical material is is an old one (McCawley (1968) treats coordination and *respectively*-constructions in a way that is only one step short of being fully three-dimensional, as does Williams (1978)). This suggestion has recently been taken up in Goodall (1984), who, following a suggestion in Chomsky (1982), proposes a three-dimensional representation for coordination along the lines suggested above. Goodall wishes to see coordination represented as a union of trees in which traditional dominance relationships will hold, but not precedence relationships.[4] A 'spellout rule' will then provide the correct linearisation. Goodall's proposal has some fundamental flaws, and it is useful to examine these here, since they will lead to the conclusion that the 'superimposition' of trees on each other as a method of *checking* identity of representation for the deletion rule may be useful, but must be clearly distinct from the deletion rule itself: the deletion rule may or may not apply on the outcome of this checking procedure.

Goodall (1984:32) defines *union of phrase markers* informally as a 'pasting together' of well-formed trees on top of each other, with any identical nodes merging together. This preserves dominance relationships, but not precedence relationships within the tree. Given that sentences are written down in linear order (left-to-right on the page, for instance) or that they are pronounced sequentially, this 'three-dimensional' representation needs to be linearised. The linearisation rule which

Goodall holds responsible for imposing a relation of precedence on distinct elements from different strings is as follows:

> Given an RPM (= Reduced Phrase Marker, RvO) containing distinct terminal strings X1,X2,......Xn, for each element Yi of Xi, Vi not an element of Xi+1, there is an element Yi+1 of Xi+1, Yi+1 not an element of Xi, such that Yi precedes Yi+1. (Goodall, 1984:36)

There are at least two things that one can observe about this linearisation procedure that make it suspect. The first is that it is not this definition which provides the linearisation, but the indexing of the distinct strings: the distinct terminal strings and their elements are indexed (by some method which Goodall does not specify, but certainly not randomly) and an element with a higher index will, according to this definition, always follow an element with a lower index. It is absolutely *essential* that the strings are indexed sequentially, and that the elements in the strings are indexed sequentially in accordance with the indexes of the string of which they are part. Imagine two strings X1 and X2, of which the first (nonshared) element of X1 is the subject, and we index it as V1. The first element of X2 (also the subject) is indexed as V1+1. The second nonshared element in X1 (the object) is indexed as Z1, and in X2 as Z2. Let us call this representation (A). We now have a representation which differs only marginally from a representation in which we do not index the second nonshared element in X1 (the object) as Z1 but rather as Z2, and we index the corresponding element in the other string X2 (again, the object) as Z1: the only difference between this representation (let us call it (B)) and representation (A) is that *index* has been switched between two corresponding objects. But when spellout takes place according to Goodall's method, this difference in indexing turns out to have a profound effect on the surface for of the sentence, as well as on its meaning: the difference between (A) and (B) is precisely the difference between (1) and (2) below:[5]

1.   John kissed Sue and Bill Ø Mary.
2.   John kissed Mary and Bill Ø Sue.

This immediately leads to the conclusion that the 'three-dimensional' representation for coordination which Goodall advocates is three-dimensional in the same way that, for instance, the pages in a book are three-dimensionally arranged: the numbering of the pages is what defines what the book will read like, and not some ordering, linearising, or page-turning principle which readers have to follow.[6] Such representations will specify dominance relationships, and, by force of the indexing, precedence relationships, in the same way that a traditional tree-diagram will: as long as the three-dimensional approach to coordination cannot dispense with indexing, it is at best a notational variant of the two-dimensional approach.

The second thing to note is that if there is a union of phrase markers $Xi.....Xn$, in which all terminal elements will necessarily occur only once, then, given that Goodall's definition makes it impossible to have recurrence of terminal elements (or, to put it in the terms of this book, it is made impossible NOT to delete) then not only can our observations about partial deletion in Chapter 2 not be accounted for, but also the difference between accessible and non-accessible deletion target sites will be lost: in a union of phrase markers in which there is no linear precedence specified, there will be no way of distinguishing acceptable deletions such as (3,4) from unacceptable deletions such as (5,6), and there will be no way of accounting for structures in which deletion has not taken place, as in (7):

3. I am ill and Ø must sleep.
4. Jan slaat Ø en Marie schopt het konijn.
    (Jan hits Ø and Marie kicks the rabbit)
5. *Am I ill and must Ø sleep?
6. *Ik geloof dat Jan Ø slaat en Marie het konijn schopt.
    (I believe that Jan Ø hits and Marie the rabbit kicks)
7. Linus kissed Patty, and Snoopy kissed Lucy.

Even if it were possible to account for the wide array of data on accessibility of deletion and partial deletions that I have presented in the previous chapter in an approach that does not recognise precedence relationships, this would simply re-create one of the central problems in the treatment of coordination, namely the derived vs. base-generated controversy for NPs discussed in Chapter 1. Given that Goodall will derive (8) from the union of representations in (9), there must be some way of making this derivation obligatory for (9), but not for (10), since (11) is perfectly well-formed. This reintroduces precisely the problem which dominated the discussion about coordination in the late sixties and early seventies that we have sought to banish in Chapter 1, namely whether PS-rules or transformations are the source for constituent coordinations. This is obviously an undesirable effect, and it is a problem which we should be anxious to avoid.

8. John and Bill met in the park.
9. John met in the park.
    Bill met in the park.
10. John kissed Sue.
    Bill kissed Sue.
11. John kissed Sue and Bill kissed Sue.

We can conclude that Goodall's three-dimensional approach, which conflates the method of checking for potential deletable material and the actual deletion process is crucially flawed: first of all, the intended elimination of precedence from representations of coordination cannot be brought about, which leaves the three-dimensional approach a (descriptively quite weak) notational variant of a number of early two-dimensional accounts. Secondly, the notion of 'union of phrase markers' will re-create old problems and fail to account for all accessibility facts and all partial deletion facts, as well as for the fact that deletion under identity in coordinated structures is an optional process. In an approach which distinguishes between checking a representation for deletable material and actually deleting this material, the above problems do not arise. The 'super-imposition' method for identifying potentially deletable material is extremely useful, and I will continue to assume it, but it must clearly be distinct from the deletion rule itself.

3.2.2 Relative identity

The above discussion obviously does not answer the question of what identity is; all it gives us is a way of establishing representational parallelism. The type of representational paralellism required for deletion under identity still has to be established. Rather surprisingly, there is not all that much that has been written on the notion of identity required for deletion — Sag's

(1976) definition of identity for the purpose of VPD as 'alphabetical variant in logical form', to be discussed below, stands out as one of the few favourable exceptions. One type of assumption (following e.g. Eisenberg, 1973) is to require that a deletion target be fully identical to its counterpart at all levels of representation, whatever these levels of representation might be; this assumption is tacitly present in quite a lot of work on deletion under identity. This would mean that we would have to get a maximally detailed analysis of a stretch of material, and any point at which a stretch of material X differs from a stretch of material Y will then block deletion. But this position is untenable — as will be clear from (12/13):

12. John goes fishing and his friends go fishing.
13. John had something to eat and his friends had something to eat.

In both cases, deletion is possible — *go* can be deleted under identity with *goes*, so obviously inflection 'doesn't count' in establishing identity for the purposes of deletion in (12). In (13), we can delete *had something to eat* under identity, but whatever identity means here, it will not be identity of reference — John may have been having a pizza, and his friends things like hamburgers and fried chicken, and we may be fully aware of this and still utter either (13) or the reduced version of (13) truthfully — so one might wish to say that neither verb inflection nor reference is of any relevance to the notion of identity employed by the identity deletion rule.

This, however, is inadequate — the present-past distinction is obviously relevant, since we cannot reduce (14) to (14a), or (15) to (15a):

14. John went fishing yesterday and Peter will go fishing tomorrow.
14a. *John went fishing yesterday and Peter Ø tomorrow.
15.. This man will have something to eat and this man has had something to eat.
15a. *This man will have/had something to eat.

As is obvious from the everyday use of the word *identical*, two objects or entities are identical *with respect to* something, rather than fully indistinguishable under all circumstances — a

183

photograph of the Eiffel Tower, for instance, may be an identical print from the same negative as some other, but if one places them side by side they will be different — one will be rightmost, and the other will be leftmost. From the point of view that we're probably interested in, namely the visual representation of the Eiffel Tower that the two photographs give us, this difference will be deemed trivial and irrelevant. A certain difference between objects may be irrelevant for one purpose, but relevant for some other purpose. What one does in establishing identity is not to analyse something for all sorts of potential differences only to establish, through such detailed investigation, that these potential differences either do not materialise or are irrelevant, but one analyses objects or entities as *not distinct for a certain purpose*. In our example, one could be asked to select *a* picture of the Eiffel Tower from a whole collection of pictures laid out on a table. The difference between the rightmost and the leftmost picture would then be irrelevant: the two pictures would be deemed identical in that context. They would no longer be deemed to be identical as soon as one were asked to pick out the leftmost picture of the Eiffel Tower. The same thing can be observed in identity of representations for linguistic rules. Different linguistic operations may be triggered by different bits of the analysis of a structure. A linguistic rule or process will analyse a structure for the *relevant* information and then apply (or not, as the case may be). In (16), the two occurrences of *John* are identical for the theory of coordinate deletion, but not for the theory of Binding (see e.g. Chomsky, 1981): in the second clause, *John* binds the reflexive, which it does not do in the first — a theory of binding will very quickly establish this fact. The rule of coordinate deletion simply does not notice it: whether or not an NP is the binder for the reflexive does not make any difference to its deletability, and therefore the coordinate deletion rule will not analyse for binding relationships.

16.   John kissed her again and John cursed himself.
16a. John kissed her again and Ø cursed himself.
16b. John cursed himself and John kissed her again.
16c. John cursed himself and Ø kissed her again.

The idea of specifically identity being relative to some rule or representation is by no means a novelty — Quine (1962) for instance observes the fact that it is possible and even quite common to use the same utterance to refer to something that changes. On different occasions we can refer to the Los Angeles river, and we will deem it to be the same Los Angeles river on these occasions, even though the water in that river will not be the same water (or might not even be there at all in this case, whereas we know that water is one of the defining characteristics of a river). Quine proposes to relate identity to a specific discourse;

> In general we might propound (this maxim of) the *identification of indiscernibles*: Objects indistinguishable from one another within the terms of a given discourse should be construed as identical for that discourse. More accurately: the references to the original objects should be reconstrued for purposes of the discourse as referring to other and fewer objects, in such a way that indistinguishable originals give way each to the same new object. (Quine, 1962:71)

Lincicome (1974:73) takes up this earlier work by Quine, and observes that 'Criteria for identity of propositions are to be found in each context of discourse about statemental units where qualitatively different units are treated as interchangeable'. Lincicome sees in identity not an absolute concept, but a relative one. 'The' problem of identification (of propositions within a system; for us, of linguistic representations) does not exist, because propositions *(simpliciter)* are not available for identification by means of any one unitary method: what we have instead are a number of different and limitedly applicable sets of criteria for identification relative to a discourse. This idea of identity, of being *indistinguishable in a certain discourse because interchangeable in that discourse,* is precisely the notion of identity we require for *deletion under identity,* since what deletion under identity does is precisely this: in a syntactic construction (coordination) a certain stretch of material is left out because some antecedent or subsequent stretch can be substituted to provide precisely the information supplied in the deleted stretch. Let us explore one or two consequences this notion of identity as NON-DISTINCT (or interchangeable) IN LANGUAGE X OR DISCOURSE Y RELATIVE TO RULE Z for the rule of coordinate deletion.

That the concept of identity is relative to rules will be clear from the discussion above — the principles establishing binding relations will view the two occurrences of *John* in (16) and (16b) as distinct, but the coordinate deletion rule will see them as identical. Such examples could be multiplied *ad nauseam*. What has not yet been demonstrated is that identity is not only relative to a rule, but can also be language-specific; i.e. that something which counts as identical with respect to rule Y in one language will not necessarily be identical with repect to that same rule Y in some other language. One particularly convincing illustration that this holds at the level of the lexicon can be found in Furbee (1974), who discusses the deletion of 'identical' verbs in Tojolabal-Maya. This language has four different transitive verbs of eating; /k'uš/ for meat and crunchy food, /loˀ/ for fruits, vegetables, eggs and other soft food, /weˀ/ for products made from ground corn, and /tiˀ/ for beans. As Furbee points out (1974:299), the use of these four forms is controlled not by specific foodstuffs, but by some characteristic of the foodstuff in question: /k'uš/ for crunchy food /loˀ/ for soft food. /weˀ/ for grainy but contiguous food, and /tiˀ/ for soft and encapsulated foods.[7] In addition to these four, there are two more general 'oral consumption' verbs: /ˀab'/ for tasting something solid, and /ˀuk'/ for drinking (or eating corn gruel). There are strong restrictions on the use of these verbs: an eating verb followed by an inappropriate object eaten yields an ungrammatical sentence: one cannot tiˀ/ meat, for instance, but one must /k'uš/ it.

However, it is possible for the different eating verbs to delete under identity — /loˀ/ and /tiˀ/ have been deleted under identity with /k'uš/ in (17a):

17. S-k'uš-u b'ak'et Hwan sok s-tiˀ-a čenek' Čep sok s-loˀ-o tek'ul
     (he-ate meat John and he-ate beans Joe and he-ate fruit
     Maŋwel sok s-weˀ-a wah Sebastiyan
     Manuel and he-ate tortillas Sebastian)
17a. S-k'uš-u b'ak'et et Hwan, Ø čenek' Čep Ø tek'ul Maŋwel sok Ø wah Sebastiyan.
     (he-ate meat John,Ø beans Joe Ø fruit Manuel and Ø tortillas Sebastian)

Any permutation of the sentences will yield identical results in the sense that any eating verb may be deleted under identity with any other eating verb — even the verb that signifies drinking:

18. S-ti⁷-a čenek′ Čep, Ø peksi Maŋwel sok Ø wah Sebastiyan.
(he-ate beans Joe, Ø Pepsi Manuel and Ø tortillas Sebastian)

What this means for a deletion rule[8] is that specifically any verb to do with eating or drinking in this language is nondistinct for the purposes of the deletion rule: this accounts quite adequately for the facts observed. It will be obvious that English does not allow this type of nondistinctness which ignores extremely obvious differences in the surface forms of lexical items: as has been observed before, morphological identity with the exception verbal number agreement seems to be what we require of a notion of identity in English. Unlike Tojolabal, English does not allow *drink* to be deleted under identity with *eat*:

19. *Joe ate a pork pie, and Peter Ø a pint of beer.

Obviously, there are many notations possible for representing such nondistinctness. Equally obviously, there is no way in which it can be usefully predicted.

But note how the shift from identity to nondistinctness for the purposes of some process or rule within a particular discourse changes the sort of question we need to ask ourselves about deletion — we should not view identity for coordinate deletion as something independent and absolute, a criterion which must be met, at all possible levels of analysis, by two subparts of representations before a deletion rule can apply to them. We should ask ourselves what at which level, two representations will be distinct in such a way that deletion can not apply: this is, if we find, in a particular language, that deletion can systematically not apply under certain circumstances, then the representations must be distinct under those circumstances in a way that is 'seen' by the coordinate deletion rule; this now becomes our focus of interest. For English, Dutch and German, the picture is fairly simple. Differences in morphology will almost always block deletion: only verbal number agreement does not, and in fact, as we shall see later, verbal number agreement is one of the very few rules that interacts with coordinate deletion.

That other morphological differences than verbal agreement will usually block deletion can very easily be demonstrated by means of our now familiar German sentence:

20. Ich bin krank und Ø muss schlafen.
     (I   am ill   and Ø must sleep)

If there is an overt case difference between two otherwise identical NPs in first position, deletion will block:

20a. *Mir ist schlecht und Ø muss schlafen.
     (to me-DAT is bad and Ø must sleep) =
     I don't feel well and Ø must sleep

For similar data from Dyirbal involving ergative/absolutive case inflection, see Dixon (1979: 61-4). It is not necessarily so that overt case differences always block deletions in all languages — recall our discussion of Icelandic sentences (218-219) in Chapter 1, section 1.3.10, where we observed an agreement problem for GPSG. In e.g. sentence (219), repeated below for convenience, the nominative subject *(þeir)* of the second S has been deleted under identity with the oblique subject of the antecedent S; that this is so is clear from the 3rd person plural form of the verb:

219. þeim likar maturinn og Ø borða mikið.
     (them-dat likes-3sg the food and Ø eat-3pl much)

Syntactic configurations do not block deletion: the deletion rule in Chapter 2 has been formulated without appeal to syntactic configurations,[9] so it would be quite surprising to find that syntactic configurations block deletion afterall. We shall not discuss this further here: see, however, section 3.5.2 in this chapter for instances of 'nonparallel' coordinate deletions which make it quite clear that syntactic configurations do not play a role in coordinate deletions. We have established that not all linguistic rules use the same notion of identity, and that not all languages use the same notion of identity. But even for one rule in one language the notion of identity is a relative one, as we shall see below: identity (a term which I shall continue to use in order to avoid the awkward, though more correct term *indistinguishability*) is relative to a *discourse*. It would take us too far afield to define exactly what constitutes a discourse here. Suffice it to say that I use the term here in roughly the same sense in which Seuren (1985) uses the term *discourse domain*: a discourse domain is a sort of cognitive working space which is built up by language users in the course of a particular conversation or piece of prose, and which contains the common knowledge necessary for effective communication in that particular conversation or piece of prose.

3.2.3 An identity problem: alphabetical variants at LF

The one problem of identity for the purpose of deletion which has received considerable attention in the literature is the 'sloppy identity' problem: in a sentence like:

21.   John loves his mother, and Bill does, too.

We construe the 'gap' as *loves his mother*, and *his* then picks out either *Bill* or *John* as antecedent. If we indicate noncoreference by assigning different indices to the anaphor *his* in one of the readings of (21) then these indices will have to be ignored by the rule of VPD. An ingenious way of capturing this was suggested by Sag (1976), who stated VPD as follows:[10]

> With respect to a sentence S, VPD can delete any VP in S whose representation at the level of logical form is a λ-expression that is an alphabetic variant of another λ-expression present in the logical form of S or in the logical form of some other sentence S' which precedes S in discourse. (Sag, 1976:76)

A formula A is an alphabetic variant of a formula B if A differs from B at most in that there are variable-binding operators in A that correspond to occurrences of the same operator (with a different variable) in B. We shall not be concerned with the precise details of Sag's use of λ-calculus here; suffice it to say that λ-notation is a way of expressing properties, in the case of (21) the property of loving someone's mother, this property holds of both John and Bill. The VPs in (20) will come out as alphabetically variant λ-expressions with different variables for *his mother* (in the 'sloppy identity' reading) or as containing a constant (under the 'strict identity' reading) for *his mother* in LF. The λ-operators that the variables are bound by occur within the VPs, and under Sag's definition, VPD can therefore apply on either reading. There is also a third reading, namely where *his mother* refers neither to Bill's mother nor to John's mother, but to a third: in this case, deletion will also still be possible. But note that if we had not said anything about the identity requirement of VPD beyond morphological non-distinctness, precisely the same result would obtain: the morphological identity requirement is met, and what the device of alphabetical variance of LF-representations does in such a case is to *relax* a potentially maximally strict constraint on identity in an appropriate way under certain circumstances — it allows us to *ignore certain differences*; in this case, differences in pronominal reference of *his* in *his mother*. Only if deletion serves to REDUCE the number of interpretations of a sentence could a situation arise in which we may need to have recourse to some representation other than plain surface morphology, for ONLY in that case is it possible that deletion appeals to some sort of semantic representation.

Possibly there is a class of such cases. McCawley (1981:397), in his discussion of the notion of identity employed by Sag (see also Sag, 1976:93 ff.) gives us the following type of sentence:

22. Alan claimed that Betsy had hit him, and Peter also claimed that Betsy had hit him.

He observes that the second clause here is ambiguous between a reading where *him* refers to Peter and a reading where it refers to Alan. According to McCawley (22a) is still ambiguous between these readings, whereas (22b) only allows the reading in which Peter claimed that Betsy had hit Alan:

22a. Alan claimed that Betsy had hit him, and Peter also did.
22b. Alan claimed that Betsy had hit him, and Peter also claimed she had.

This contrast could be accounted for by observing that in the LF-representation of (22a), the λ-operator that binds the variable *him* is within the deletion site, as is its corresponding λ-operator in the antecedent VP, which binds a different variable. This makes the two 'larger' VPs alphabetical variants. In (22b), the λ-operator is outside the deletion target, and the 'smaller' VPs will not be alphabetical variants and can therefore not be deleted if the two occurrences of 'him' have different antecedents: deletion can then only take place if *him* is not a variable but a constant, since then the two VPs will show no distinctions at all, and thus again meet Sag's requirement on identity.

This is a very ingenious solution, but it needs to be observed that the judgement underlying it is a bit elusive. Many people do not find that the ambiguity disappears in (22b); especially if we allow contrastive stress on *Alan* and *him*. (22b) would certainly not be misunderstood in a situation in which both Alan and Peter walk in with a black eye. In most sentences of this type the ambiguity will persist for a large number of speakers, who find, to use a parallel case, (23) as ambiguous as (23a).

23. Patrick got angry when you wanted to talk to him, and Peter got angry when you did, as well.
23a. Patrick got angry when you wanted to talk to him, and Peter did, as well.
24. The parking attendant said that he was just doing his job, and the meter maid said she was, too.
24a. The parking attendant said he was just doing his job, and the meter maid did, too.

Both instances of (23) can convey that Peter got angry when X wanted to talk to Patrick, or that Peter got angry when X wanted to talk to Peter. In (24), what 'alphabetical variant' proposal claims will be the only reading is where the meter maid is doing the parking attendant's job, and this is clearly incorrect — the natural reading is for (24) and (24a) to mean that both meter maid and parking attendant are each doing their own jobs. Even Sag's standard cases of sloppy identity readily fall victim to such observations. If we change, in (21), *loves his mother* to, say, *finished his beer*, the 'sloppy identity' reading disappears altogether.

That the notion 'alphabetical variant at LF' is an inadequate constraint on identity for the purposes of deletion will become clearer still if we tinker a bit with sentence (22). Suppose we replace *Betsy* by *his father*:

22d. Alan claimed that his father had hit him, and Peter also did.

22e. Alan claimed that his father had hit him, and Peter also claimed he had.

For these sentences, we have the familiar sloppy identity vs. strict identity interpretations for the deleted VP: *his father* in the deleted VP in (22d) could be Alan's father, Peter's father, or some third father. In (22e), *his father* in the deleted VP can be (following Sag and McCawley), either Alan's father or some third father. But there is nothing to prevent us from assigning a reading to these cases where *his father* in both antecedent and subsequent VPs is Peter's father rather than Alan's father: this reading will satisfy the identity requirements for both the sloppy identity reading and the strict identity reading. However, in *none* of the VPD cases noted in this section are readings of this type available. Observations of this type cast serious doubt on the usefulness of the notion 'alphabetical variant at LF' as a requirement for deletion under identity.

Nevertheless, the problem persists for those speakers who do detect a systematic difference between sentences (22a) and (22b). For those speakers, we can maintain a suitably adapted version of Sag's requirement of alphabetically variant λ-expressions as an addition to the morphological nondistinctness requirement: in our account outlined above there is no *a priori* reason to reject this as a requirement on identity should it indeed turn out to be necessary for coordinate deletion. This additional requirement is well-defined, unusual and quite restricted: note, for instance, that it involves an island violation. The above sentences on the *nonambiguous* reading involve deletion of the 'smaller' contained within the 'larger' VP. In this deletion operates across a coordinate clause boundary, and into a subordinate clause where a VP is eliminated from the subordinate clause only. The coordinate deletion in sentences (21, 23, 24), in other words, overlaps with that part of VPD which constitutes the 'true' instances of VPD which operates specifically into subordinate clauses. It should therefore not be in principle entirely unpredictable that we find that for a number of speakers in a number of sentences there is a split in judgements, with one set of judgements going the 'VPD' way, and the other set going the 'Coordinate Deletion' way. I shall not explore this dichotomy or its possible description further here;

but note that it is *specific* to these instances of VPD in English. Speakers of Dutch and German, languages which do not have VPD, also allow this type of ambiguity,[11] but do certainly not allow the type of construction in which the ambiguity is eliminated, because these two languages do not allow VPD into subordinate clauses, but only coordinate deletion, which applies to the site in the higher clause containing all of the lower clause, as predicted by the Partial Deletion Constraint formulated in Chapter 2:

25. *Jan zei dat ze hem geslagen had, en Piet zei dat ze ook.
    *Jan sagte, dass sie ihn geschlagen hatte, und Piet sagte dass sie auch.
    (Jan said that she him hit had, and Piet said that she also)
25a. Jan zei dat ze hem geslagen had, en Piet ook.
    Jan sagte, dass sie ihn geschlagen hatte, und Piet auch.
    (Jan said that she him hit had, and Piet too)

(25a) can mean either that: Piet also said that she had hit Jan, or that Piet said that she had hit Piet. It may therefore, in a well-defined set of cases in English, be necessary to appeal to a Sag-type notion of identity for VPD if deletion takes place into subordinate clauses; in this case, this appeal will constitute an additional requirement to *supplement* the requirement of morphological identity for coordinate deletion if it overlaps with VPD. That morphological identity in such cases is a requirement which is *supplemented* by requirements from logical form (something which is not made clear in Sag (1976), who does not discuss this aspect of identity) can quite easily be demonstrated on the basis of the following sentence:

26. That girl loves her mother, and that girl's father does, too.

Here, in spite of the fact that there will be λ-expressions which will be alphabetical variants for a 'sloppy' reading in which that girl's father loves his own mother, this reading is not readily available.

3.2.4 Coordination and quantification

McCawley's discussion of λ-calculus and his illustration of the use made of it by Sag ends with a few very interesting remarks on the nature of identity for coordinate deletion in relation to quantification, which will lead us to the second class of cases in which it might perhaps be argued that the application of co-ordinate deletion has served systematically to *reduce* the number of possible interpretations for a certain type of sentence. He notes sentences like (27) (originally due to Partee, 1970), which seem to contrast with (28) on the requirement of identity: we construe (27) as meaning that the rules that are at the same time explicit easy to read are few, which is not the case in (27a): the latter is construed as meaning that there are few rules that are explicit, and that there are few rules that are easy to read, and nothing is implied about an intersection of these sets. Likewise, in (28) it is not necessarily so that Tom and Dick admire the same few authors, and (28b) does not claim this either.

27.   Few rules are explicit and easy to read.
27a. Few rules are explicit and few rules are easy to read.
28.   Tom and Dick admire few authors.
28a. Tom admires few authors and Dick admires few authors.

This difference, McCawley argues, could be captured as follows: If one assumes that the identity requirement for con-junction reduction is the same as for VP-deletion, namely that two constituents count as identical for conjunction reduction only if they correspond to parts of logical structure that are alphabetical variants of each other, then the VPs in (28) will be alphabetical variants, but not the subjects. He gives us the follow-ing representations (1981: 400-1):

27b. (few rule x) (x, (λy)(y be correct)) and
      (few rule u)(u, (λv)([Δ,(λz)(z read v)],(λw)(w be easy)
28b. (Tom,(λx)(few author y) (x admire y)) and
      (Dick, (λz)(few author w) (z admire w))

The argument runs as follows: If one construes *alphabetical variant* to mean that two expressions are alphabetical variants if we could rename their bound variables and otherwise leave things unchanged, and thus make them identical, without changing their meaning, then the occurrences of (few rule x) and (few rule u) in (27b) are not identical, since one could not change the variables here and preserve the meaning unless one also made other changes elsewhere in the formula. However, he also quite correctly observes that on such an understanding of 'alphabetical variant' two occurrences of a quantified NP will not count as identical, though expressions containing a quantified NP will, and that this creates the situation where 'alphabetical variant of' as a synonym for 'identical' will work for some rules, but not for others: it will rule out the derivation of (27), through coordination reduction, but it will also incorrectly rule out the derivation of (29a) from (29) through Right-node Raising, since the two occurrences of *all operas* will not be alphabetical variants in logical form, in the same way that '[few rule x]' and '[few rule u]' in (27/28b) are not alphabetical variants: we cannot rename the bound variables of just these expressions without also making further changes outside the expressions, namely where the variables recur in LF.

29. Schwartz loves all operas, and Morgenstern hates all operas.
29a. Schwartz loves Ø and Morgenstern hates all operas.

A more serious objection is that this approach does not address the heart of the problem — it provides a convenient way for not deriving (27) from (27a), but it does little more. It will incorrectly block (27c) as derived from (27d), which is exactly the same as (27a), except that the quantifier is now *most*:

27c. Most rules are explicit and easy to read.
27d. Most rules are explicit and most rules are easy to read.

The LF-representation for (27d) will not make the two occurrences of *most rules* alphabetically variant, so deletion will (incorrectly) be blocked, as it would be for other quantifiers like all, every, etc. Nor is it the case that a quantifier like *few* will systematically give rise to problems when they occur in sentence-initial position. In (27e), the two subjects will not be alphabetical variants under McCawley's construction of that term, yet deletion is perfectly possible:

27e. Few people buy Porsches and few people buy Mercedes.
27f. (few people x) (x, (λy) (y buy Porsches)) and
     (few people z) (z, (λq) (q buy Mercedes))
27g. Few people buy Porsches and Mercedes.

The discussion above brings us closer to the idea that identity is a relative notion, and not a constant and unitary one which can be captured by reference to a clearly defined set of structures of representations. It is certainly the case that different rules use different notions of identity: this fact is not only observed in McCawley (1981:401), but also, though for different reasons, in Jackendoff (1983:54-5). Furthermore, there is no *a priori* objection to a situation in which one rule uses two different notions of identity, other than that it is an inelegant solution, and a rather unattractive one for the approach to coordinate deletion as outlined in this book, which attempts to unify coordinate deletion rules as much as possible into one rule which deletes under identity. It would be awkward, though not impossible, to appeal to a number of different notions of identity within one and the same rule. let us see whether we should be committed to such a situation.

If one goes back to Partee (1970), which was the original source for (27),[12] it is made quite clear there that this is to be viewed as a deletion problem, and cannot be accounted for by appealing to some sort of base-generation of the conjoined VPs by means of PS-rules: first of all *both*, which could be inserted in (27), is typical of sentential conjunction and not of phrasal conjunction:[13]

30. Both John and Mary are linguists.
31. *Both John and Mary are a happy couple.

Secondly, *explicit* and *easy to read* are not of the same (deep structure) category, and PS-rules coordinate like categories.[14] The problem is therefore one which has to be resolved by appealing to constraints on identity required for the coordinate deletion rule. A few more examples of such problem sentences are:

32. Someone bought the cigar and someone bought the newspaper.
32a. Someone bought the cigar and the newspaper.
33. Some men are married and some men are happy.
33a. Some men are married and happy.
34. Only the three rules on this page are explicit and only the three rules on this page are easy to read.

34a. Only the three rules on this page are explicit and easy to read.

Partee observes that the conjectured asymmetry between reduced and non-reduced sentences is not consistent for all quantified NPs: requiring e.g. identity for reference or intended reference for deletion of quantified NPs will not do. Sometimes, it is true-that *Someone* or *some men* will not single out the same individual or class of individuals in the nonreduced clause, but will do so in the reduced clause: however, not for all sentences. (35) can be the source for (35a) because here the same rules are singled out, both in the reduced and in the unreduced sentence:

35. The three rules on this page are explicit and the three rules on this page are easy to read.
35a. The three rules on this page are explicit and easy to read.

She suggests (without, however, wishing to expand this suggestion into a fuller theory) that constraints on a meaning-preserving conjunction reduction transformation would have to run (roughly) along the following lines, with the quantifiers at some sort of higher predicate:

> Quantifiers occur as predicates only with indefinite noun phrases as subjects: quantifiers have some other source with definite noun phrases. *Only* occurs as a predicate with both definite and indefinite noun phrases as subject. Conjoined sentences containing formally identical noun phrases may not be collapsed if that noun phrase contains a quantifier unless it also contains a definite article, and not even then if there is an *only*. (Partee, 1970:155-6)

In this formulation Partee's suggestion, which seeks to narrow down the problem to quantified sentences, is suspect — first of all, the observation about *only*, which is based on a contrast between (34/34a) and (35/35a), seems incorrect. If there is a problem here, it is the following 'sloppy identity' one: in both cases *this page* either refers to the same page in the conjoined unreduced clauses, or it does not, and Partee's pretheoretical observations thus seem to mislocate the problem in attributing it to quantification. Secondly, the problems disappear if the quantified phrases are not in initial position:

36.   Matrimony is boring to some men and happiness is boring to some men.
36a. Matrimony and happiness are boring to some men.
37.   The cigar was bought by someone and the newspaper was bought by someone.
37a. The cigar and the newspaper were bought by someone.

In (36a-37a), it is not at all necessarily so that the same men who are bored by marriage are also bored by happiness, or that the person who bought the newspaper also bought the cigar, and the picture is therefore rather more complicated than Partee's remarks suggest: only quantified NPs in a certain position in the S pose problems. Consider also the following two sentences:

38.   A few survivors were electricians and repairmen working on the roof at the time of the disaster.
39.   Few illegal immigrants ever reached San Francisco and Sacramento: most were picked up by a border patrol just before San Diego.

In these two sentences, we have collapsed formally identical quantified indefinite NPs in S-initial position, and yet the proper interpretation of these sentences is one where we surmise different sets of survivors: electricians on the one hand, and repairmen on the other, and different sets of illegal immigrants: those that made it to San Francisco, and those that made it to Sacramento.

At this point, it is useful to go back to the source of the problems observed here, which can be traced back (once again) to Chomsky (1957:35). There, it was observed that if two sentences differ in nothing but one constituent, it is possible to form a sentence containing a conjoined constituent from these sentences. McCawley (1981:17-18) formulates the semantic counterpart of Chomsky's (1957) syntactically motivated observation: conjoined propositions which differ only in one part may also be represented as a proposition containing a conjoined part. The problem with Chomsky's observation was that it is not reversible: it is not the case that for all sentences containing a conjoined constituent there is an equivalent conjunction of sentences not containing a coordination. The main evidence for this is provided by symmetrical predicates, and these turned out to have at least one syntactic property which differs from deletion-derived coordinations: these facts have been discussed in Chapters 1 and 2. We now observe a similar problem of non-reversability from a semantic angle: although there are syntactically well-formed S-paraphrases available for sentences like (27), we do not have semantic equivalence between the S-coordination and the non-S coordination. Before attempting a further delimitation of this problem, let us examine one detailed treatment of the interaction of quantifiers and coordination.

An ingenious approach to quantification and coordination which could be construed as making the claim that, in a deletion account of the type advocated in this book, it is not only left-to-right constituent identity that is needed in coordinate deletion, is presented in Seuren (1985:158 ff.). In a model of Semantic Syntax in which the semantic representation is the input to the transformational component, and in which there is no separate level of deep structure, coordinating conjunctions are seen as truth-functional predicates bearing scope over sentential structures. In sentences like (40/41):

40. The victim was thought to be Jewish and Italian
41. The victim was thought to be Spanish or Italian.

Seuren observes a scope ambiguity which can be brought out by judicious insertion of *both/either*, the ambiguity is essentially of the same type as what McCawley (1981) observed for sentences like (22).

40a. The victim was thought to be both Jewish and Italian.
40b. The victim was both thought to be Jewish and Italian.
41a. The victim was thought to be either Spanish or Italian.
41b. The victim was either thought to be Spanish or Italian.

The way Seuren derives (40/41) is as follows (omitting many details): In a VSO underlying semantic structure for English in which conjunctions and quantifiers are higher predicates, these predicates are lowered cyclically and lose their predicate status in order to become verb, tense, quantifier etc. (Seuren, 1985:141 ff.). There is a constraint (the scope ordering constraint, SOC) which states (again, omitting many details) that lexically represented semantic predicates must, when they are lowered, stay to the left of other semantic predicates that have been lowered on earlier cycles. (40) has two representations: one in which the higher predicate *and* (as a leftmost daughter of SO) precedes a coordination of S1 and S2, also daughters of SO, each with a V *be thought*. These each take as a lower S *be Spanish/Italian the victim*. In the second representation, the higher predicate V *be thought* is a daughter of SO, taking an S1 which has a leftmost daughter the coordinating conjunction, and as its other two daughters the Ss *be Spanish/Italian the victim*. The former representation, in which *thought* is in the scope of *and* will correspond to (40b), the latter, in which *and* is in the scope of *thought*, to (40a). There is a rule of Conjunct Mapping, which collapses representations and eliminates identical material. This process bears some resemblance to Goodall's (1984) 'three-dimensional' approach to coordination, with the following four crucial differences: it is a process rather than a representation, there is a cycle, Conjunct Mapping is optional, and Conjunct Mapping, which applies to material which is peripheral in the representation, is distinct from Conjunct Gapping, which applies to material which need not be medial but which must contain a verb. Because Seuren's rules are optional, and because he distinguishes between conjunct Gapping and Conjunct Mapping, the most serious objections to Goodall's account do not apply to Seuren: see also Seuren (1984) on this matter.

This account of the interaction of quantifiers and conjunction tells us essentially one thing about identity: an existentially quantified expression (or, in the case of passives, the implied agent) which has the coordinating conjunction in its scope is just the single expression which does not recur elsewhere in the representation. It will therefore be 'identical' in the fullest possible sense, under any analysis, since something cannot be distinct from itself. If the coordinating conjunction has the existentially quantified expressions in its scope, then there will be two occurrences of an existentially quantified expression, and these may of course be different: different implied agents may have been doing the thinking in (40b/41b), Not so, however, in (40a/41a), where there is only the one existentially quantified expression: there they are the same. Likewise, there is one buyer for the combination of newspaper and cigar in (32a), but there may have been two buyers, one for the newspaper, and one for the cigar, in (37a). The question which now arises is whether these observations are systematically correct and independent of discourse: if they are, then it could be argued that the coordinate deletion rule does not appeal only to morphological identity, but also to the structure of the semantic representation. There are a number of facts that make it clear that these observations are not independent of the discourse context that they occur in. Our earlier observations about (38/39) above are already strong evidence that they are not. But let us take a further pair of the example sentences which Seuren uses to illustrate the scope of coordinating conjunctions (Seuren, 1985:158):

42. Some critics liked (both) the tenor and the soprano.
42a. (Both) the tenor and the soprano were liked by some critics.

   The first thing to note about these examples is that, especially with the addition of *both* they indeed have a natural reading where, in (42), there is one group of critics who share a liking for the tenor and a liking for the soprano; Seuren suggests that this is the only reading for (42). This reading is also possible in (42a), but there it is not the only reading: there it is also possible that there is a group of critics who like the one singer, but not the other, and vice versa, and the two sets of critics do not intersect. Seuren's observations here are too specific. Although it may be the most *natural* reading for these two sentences in isolation, it is quite possible for (42) to have the readings of (42a). If this sentence is uttered, say, in a context where there has been a song contest of particularly low quality, featuring one tenor and one soprano plus assorted other singers, and one visitor remarks mistakenly to another that none of the critics refereeing the contest liked any of the singers, then the latter could reply with (42), and he would not be considered to provide false information even if there were no critics who liked more than one singer. What he communicates in such a case is that there was liking for two singers, and he does not say anything about possible overlaps between the groups of critics who did the liking. The presence or absence of *both*[15] in these cases may *bias* one reading, but will not *eliminate* other readings. It would therefore strictly speaking be incorrect to assign to it a semantic representation that claims that there is only the one unique reading under all circumstances.
   In fact, it is quite possible to delete even singular existentially

quantified noun phrases in initial position in the S (i.e. where the quantifier will have scope over the entire S in a representation in Seuren's system) without making reference to identity other than morphological identity. Imagine someone who has a kitten to give away, and at the same time wants to sell some things, including a bed. This person therefore places an ad in the local paper giving a list of things for sale, and also says that there is a kitten to be had for free. He duly sells the bed and is relieved of the kitten. Someone who arrives later in the day and who is interested in both the kitten and the bed might very well get the following response:

43. I'm afraid that someone has already both been for the kitten and picked up the bed.

What someone uttering (43) claims is not that there is a single person who, like the person who arrived too late, was interested in both bed and kitten and has taken both, but only that bed and kitten have already gone. We would not say of a person who utters (43), when kitten and bed were taken by different individuals, that he is stating a falsehood. In Seuren's account, (43), like (38/39), would receive a representation in which the one existential quantifier has scope over the coordinating conjunction, and such a representation will claim that it was necessarily the same person who took bed and kitten. This must be weakened somewhat: in a sentence like (43) and its surrounding context the exact identity of the person taking the bed and the kitten, and whether or not they are the same person, is simply not at issue.

If we view (43) as derived by means of deletion of identical *someone* from the second S (under Quine's or Lincicome's construal of identity), we do not claim that it was exactly the same person that took bed and kitten: only that, for the purposes of that sentence in that particular discourse, there were no relevant distinctions between the two. Note also that *someone* can be used to refer to groups of people under certain circumstances. It is quite common to say that 'Someone is coming to visit me at eight' if one knows that there will be more than one person coming. Such a sentence is a perfectly adequate response to a question like 'What are you doing tonight?', and here again it is not the exact number of people or their identity that is at issue, but only the fact that there will be visiting.

Let me give one more example. Imagine a situation in which there has been cyanide tampering with food products and drugs. In such a situation, a manager of a supermarket store could say:

44.   We're still selling quite a lot of both products. This means that many people are still using both Tylenol and Accent.

Yet this sentence cannot be construed as claiming that the same people who use the one product also use the other: the *identity* of the people using these two products is not at issue, let alone whether or not they are the same people: what a sentence like this claims is that there is use of Tylenol as well as use of Accent, and nothing more.

   Something similar can be demonstrated for sentences like (40/41) above. These sentences correspond to Seuren's account. However, a sentence like (45), which will receive exactly the same structure as (40/41), does not have the same interpretations.

45.   Our patients are allowed to smoke pipes and cigars.

Here we can insert *both* in exactly the same way in either the adverbial position or the position immediately preceding the coordinating conjunction as in (40/41), but there is no difference in interpretation:

45a.   Our patients are allowed to smoke both pipes and cigars.
45b.   Our patients are both allowed to smoke pipes and cigars.

In Seuren's account, the verb will have scope over the co-ordinating conjunction in the (b) sentence, and vice versa in the (a) sentence, but there is nothing in the *interpretation* of the sentences that warrants these structural differences. If we construe these sentences in accordance with Seuren's approach, then (45) claims that there was one decree allowing the smoking of both pipes and cigars, while (45a) claims that there were two decrees: one allowing the smoking of pipes, and one allowing the smoking of cigars. Yet this difference in interpretation is not present in these two sentences: they both simply state that patients can smoke pipes or cigars.

   A considerable part of Seuren's observations are valid and must be incorporated. The facts in sentences (32/32a) and (43) can be captured by assuming, in keeping with earlier observations, that if something is deleted under identity within a given discourse, there are no relevant differences between the two occurrences of that identical material in that particular discourse: possible differences in interpretation are not reflected in the structure of underlying representations, but depend on context. In other words, the sentences that Seuren discusses as structurally ambiguous are treated in this account as not specified for the different readings concerned. The different readings are imposed by the contexts in which the sentences occur, in the sense of e.g. Kempson and Cormack (1981).

The observations about *both* and *either* in sentences like (40/41) can be accounted for in the following way: *both* and *either* may be left-attached to a sequence of constituents that is linked by a coordinating conjunction (with the proviso for *both* that it may not be attached to a sequence of sentences). What *both* and *either* do is assert nondistinctness of that part of S that is to their left. This makes it possible for *some critics* in (42) to be a single set of critics, in turn consisting of a set of those who like the tenor and a set of those who like the soprano, and all sorts of opportunity for intersection between these two subsets. I shall not investigate this particular aspect of the material and its ramifications in further detail here, but instead look at two rather different problems before returning to some interesting predictions of the approach to identity outlined in this section.

3.2.5 Two problems

Consider the following three sentences:

46. All cowboys chew tobacco or drink rotgut.
47. No one tried and failed.
48. I don't chew tobacco or drink rotgut.

These three pose interesting problems. First of all, they are not straightforwardly expressible as equivalent conjoined propositions: (46a-48a) are syntactically well-formed, but they are not equivalent to their 'reduced' counterparts.

46a. All cowboys chew tobacco or all cowboys drink rotgut.
47a. No one tried and no one failed.

48a. I don't chew tobacco or I don't drink rotgut.

A normal truth-table for e.g. (46), will be simply at variance with our intuitions. If we take (46) to be derived from a straightforward pair of conjoined sentences like (46a), then (46) ought to come out as true if:

(a) all cowboys chew tobacco and they also chew rotgut.
(b) not all cowboys chew tobacco but they all drink rotgut.
(c) all cowboys chew tobacco but they do not all drink rotgut.

It ought to come out as false if not all cowboys chew tobacco, and not all cowboys drink rotgut. Yet it is precisely this interpretation that we want to get for (46). What this sentence expresses is something like: 'if X is a cowboy, then X chews tobacco or drinks rotgut', and it ought to come out as false only if there are cowboys that neither drink rotgut, nor chew tobacco. In other words, although (46) contains a conjoined proposition, it is itself not straightforwardly paraphrasable as a conjoined proposition. This problem seems somewhat unpredictable: if we change the conjunction in (46) from or to and, it will disappear, and it will also disappear if the quantified expression is not in leftmost position.

I will not attempt to provide a solution for the problem posed by (46) — although one of the solutions that suggests itself is one where we take a single quantifier like all or most to have scope over the conjoined propositions: some version of Seuren's (1985) account outlined above could do this. The reason why I am hesitant to adopt such a solution is that there exist sentences which present similar problems, but which do not readily submit themselves to this type of solution. Let us take a sentence like (47) above. This sentence clearly means something like: 'A number of people who have tried have systematically not failed, so if you try, you will not fail'. So this sentence ought to be true if there is a number of people who tried, and none of the people who have tried have also failed. Here again, we are obviously not dealing with a straightforward pair of conjoined propositions: this sentence certainly does not mean that there is no one who has tried, and that everyone was successful. But even if we propose a straightforward semantic representation of the type: 'there is no X such that X has tried and X has failed', then the truth-table for conjunction will still give us results which are widely at variance with out intuitions, since this will make (47) true if it is true that there is no one who has tried, and (47) just does not mean that. If no one has tried, then it is simply non-sensical to speak of success or failure.

This latter observation strongly suggests that (47) is seman-tically not a conjunction at all, but a conditional: if you try, you will succeed. The semantics of conditional sentences mirror this aspect of the interpretation of (47): in a conditional sentence like (49):

49. If it rains tomorrow, we'll play cards all day.

it does not make sense to speak of the truth or falsehood of the entire proposition if the antecedent is false; i.e. if it does not rain tomorrow. (49) ought to be true if both antecedent (pro-tasis) and consequent (apodosis) are true, and false if the antecedent is true and the consequent is false. Likewise, in (47), if no one has tried, it no longer makes sense to speak of success or failure. Contrast sentence (47) with (50): syntactically, they have exactly the same form, but (50) obviously does not have the conditional interpretation of (47).

50. No one sang and danced.

Furthermore, it seems that sentences of the type (47) only have their conditional interpretation with and: if we change the co-ordinating conjunction to *or*, the conditional interpretation dis-appears:

47a. No one tries or fails.

To my knowledge, conditional coordinations like (47) are quite rare. In English conditional coordinations the prothasis will usually be in the imperative, and the apodosis in the future:

51. Touch my wife and I'll shoot you.
52. Don't touch my wife or I'll shoot you.

Furthermore, it seems impossible in English to get a conditional interpretation on a full S-coordination or a simple NP-coordi-nation, which are the coordinations that all languages seem to allow. If we therefore find cases of non-NP, non-S-paraphrasable coordinations of which the interpretation differs radically from the interpretation of 'normal' coordinations, one cannot but surmise that such coordinations should not fall under a general account of coordination, but should instead be attributed to some other source. Generally speaking, conditional sentences are overtly marked as conditional: in English, most conditional sentences have an *if* or an *unless* somewhere, and cross-linguistically, languages that explicitly mark conditional sentences are in the majority over languages that do not (see Comrie, 1986a). But quite obviously, coordinations can be interpreted as conditional statements, as can a series of negated NPs: all along the California coast one can find restaurants that state their dress code as 'no shoes, no shirts, no service', or even: 'no shoes/shirts/service'. Like the coordination in (47), there are no obvious structural reasons why such statements are interpreted as conditionals: a statement like 'no money, no job, no nothing' is definitely not interpreted as a conditional.

I shall not speculate on the conditions under which coordinations are interpreted as conditionals, but limit myself to observing that conditional coordinations show some clear syntactic and semantic differences with 'normal' coordinations, and leave the description of conjoined conditionals for the future. Let us now turn to the problem posed by sentence (48).

Sentence (48) presents a type of semantic problem which differs from (46) and (47), and which was discussed in some detail for English in Ladusaw (1980). The standard truth-table for disjunction predicts that this sentence will be true if I lack either the vice of chewing tobacco, or the vice of drinking rotgut, or both. But this is not what sentence (48) means: it should *only* be true if I lack *both* vices. This immediately gives us some sort of handle on the problem: (48) can be readily paraphrased as a coordination with the same meaning, provided we change the *or* to *and*:

48b. I don't chew tobacco and I don't drink rotgut.

On the face of it, this leaves us with a small problem. It has generally been assumed that negation cannot gap; see e.g. Neijt (1979) for this point of view. Siegel (1984), however, points out some cases in which it seems that negation *has* gapped; one of these cases is:

53. Ward can't eat caviar and Sue, beans.

If it is the case, as Siegel suggests, that negation can delete, then a question which immediately arises is what happens to the scope of that negation once it has been deleted. If we delete a negation *and* everything to the right of it (i.e. everything that is in its scope), we find that no problems arise: (54) and (54a) are synonymous.

54. The boys don't like fish and the girls don't like fish.
54a. The boys and the girls don't like fish.

But as soon as the negation is deleted and something to its right remains, we find *and* and *or* now both have the conjunctive reading, and there is even a clear preference for *or*:

55. Peter hasn't seen John and Peter hasn't seen Bill.
55a. Peter hasn't seen John or Bill.

The only interpretation of (55a) is as a conjunction, and not as a disjunction: even if we add *either*, which is generally taken to be the marker of exclusive disjunction, and might therefore force a disjunctive reading for (55a), the only possible reading will still be the conjunctive one:

55b. Peter hasn't seen either John or Bill

The same can be demonstrated for Gapping, or for remnants other than NP to the right of the deleted negation: sentences (56) and (57) only have the conjunctive interpretation, as do (56a) and (57a), in spite of the fact that we have changed the conjunction to a disjunction there:

56. John hasn't seen Harry and Bill hasn't seen Sue.
56a. John hasn't seen Harry, or Bill Sue.
57. John doesn't live in Amsterdam and John doesn't live in London.
57a. John doesn't live in Amsterdam or in London.

It is only when a negation has been deleted that we find that the interpretation of *or* changes from disjunctive into conjunctive; if there is no negation involved, *or* retains its disjunctive reading:

58.   John has seen Harry, or Bill Sue.

A sentence like (58) conforms to the truth-table for disjunction: it will be true if John has seen Harry, or if Bill has seen Sue, or if both obtain: only if neither obtain will it be false.

From a logical point of view, the situation described above is not entirely surprising: de Morgan's Law tells us that: 'not P and not Q' is logically equivalent to: 'not (P or Q)'. This has a clear correspondence to the natural language facts observed above: if a negation disappears, and something has to remain to the right of that negation, *and* changes to *or*, and the only reading for that *or* is a conjunctive reading, not a disjunctive one. Pursuing this line, we might ask ourselves what happens if there is a pair of sentences, both containing a negation and linked by *or*, and we delete a stretch of material containing the deletion. If nothing then remains to the right of the negation, the situation is the same as with *and*: no problems arise:

59.   John doesn't like fish or Bill doesn't like fish.
59a. John or Bill doesn't like fish.

But if something remains to the right of the deleted negation, the situation is much less clear. Although 'not P or not Q' is logically equivalent to 'not (P and Q)', it is intuitively very hard to decide whether we can simply reverse the rule for the change of *and* into *or* we have given above. There are certainly sentences like:

60.   You mustn't drink and drive.

which, in spite of the *and*, have to be interpreted as a disjunction, and cannot be interpreted as a conjunction: this is not an injunction against driving *per se* and drinking *per se*, but against doing both at the same time. Likewise, example (53), cited above from Siegel's work (on what she calls the wide scope reading of the negation) is paraphrasable as a full S-coordination with *or* as the coordinating conjunction:

53a. Ward can't eat caviar, or Sue can't eat beans.

Sentence (53a) conveys precisely what (53) means: what these two sentences convey is that it is inappropriate for Ward to eat caviar if Sue eats beans, or *vice versa*.[16] There is therefore some evidence to suggest that, in an *or*-coordinated pair of sentences, *or* changes to *and* if we delete a negation and there is something remaining to the right of the deletion target sites. But there is a clear problem for a proposal that turns *or* into *and* under the same conditions that turn *and* into *or*. If we take a pair of sentences like (61/61a):

61. John doesn't like fish or John doesn't like rice.
61a. John doesn't like fish and rice.

then it is certainly the case that (61) and (61a) will come out as true under the same conditions, namely if (a) John doesn't like fish, (b) John doesn't like rice, or (c) John doesn't like either. Although (61a) could certainly be used to report on a state of affairs where John doesn't like both fish and rice, but likes, say, smoked salmon on toast, or rice pudding, it still seems somehow inappropriate to use sentence (61a) for expressing conditions (a) or (b). This inappropriateness is puzzling: it is clearly the case that *and* in these cases is a disjunction rather than a conjunction, in the same way *or* is a conjunction rather than a disjunction in examples (55-57).

Before returning to one of the most interesting predictions of distinctness in deletion rules, let us subject the above account of the interaction of negation, deletion, and conjunctions to one interesting test. In Dutch, negation (*geen*) will attach as to the direct object of a transitive verb if that direct object is indefinite; if the object is definite, negation (*niet*) will follow the object.

62. Jan rookt sigaren.
     (Jan smokes cigars)
62a. Jan rookt geen sigaren
     (Jan doesn't smoke cigars)
63. Jan rookt een sigaar.
     (Jan smokes a cigar)
63a. Jan rookt geen sigaar.
     (Jan doesn't smoke a cigar)
64. Jan rookt de sigaar (sigaren).
     (Jan smokes the cigar (cigars)).
64a. Jan rookt de sigaar (sigaren) niet.
     (Jan doesn't smoke the cigar (cigars)...)

Given our account of the shift of *and* to *or* in English, we expect that if we have distinct direct objects in *and*-conjoined sentences, it will not turn into *or* if we delete the identical subject plus verb in the indefinite cases, as long as we do not delete *geen*, as in (65). *Of* (= or) should retain its disjunctive meaning, as in (65a). But we do expect *and* to turn into *or* as soon as the negation is deleted as well, and the only reading for *of* should then be the conjunctive reading: this is the case of (66). Given that the negation in the indefinite cases is attached to the direct object rather than to the verb in English, we expect to be able to delete the verb without changing *en* to *of*, since the negation will not be affected by Gapping, as it is in English, as in (67); compare this with its English counterpart. *Of* in such gapped sentences should retain its disjunctive meaning. This is what we find in (67a). Neither do we expect *en* to turn into *of* in the definite cases, since there the negation is rightmost and there will therefore be nothing to the right of that negation: this is illustrated in (68). *Of* retains its disjunctive meaning (68a). These predictions all turn out to be correct, although it has to be observed that the change from *en* to *of* seems to be fully optional in Dutch: the clear preference for *or* or *nor* in English is not paralleled in Dutch.

65. Jan rookt geen sigaren en geen sigaretten.
     (Jan doesn't smoke cigars or cigarettes)
65a. Jan rookt geen sigaren of geen sigaretten.
     (Jan doesn't smoke cigars he doesn't smoke cigarettes)
66. Jan rookt geen sigaren en/of sigaretten.
     (Jan doesn't smoke cigars or cigarettes)
67. Jan rookt geen sigaren en Peter geen sigaretten.
     (Jan doesn't smoke cigars, nor Peter cigarettes)
67a. Jan rookt geen sigaren of Peter sigaretten.
     (Jan doesn't smoke cigars, or Peter doesn't smoke cigarettes)
68. Jan rookt de sigaren en de sigaretten niet.
     (Jan doesn't smoke the cigars or the cigarettes)
68a. Jan rookt dé sigaren of de sigaretten niet.
     (Jan doesn't smoke the cigars, or he doesn't smoke the cigarettes)

I shall not engage in further discussion of this material, but content myself with two observations on the relations between *and, or,* and negation: if deletion applies to a negation in a pair of *and*-coordinated sentences, and something remains to the right of the negation, the only interpretation available for the conjunction is a disjunctive one, and *and* itself changes into *or* or *nor.* The same seems to hold for *or*-coordinations, although there certainly are ample (probably pragmatic) grounds for caution here. let us now turn to one further prediction of the rule 'delete under identity' under the interpretation of identity that we have given earlier in this chapter.

3.2.6 Distinctness

The conclusion of the discussion in section 3.2.4 was of necessity mainly a negative one where structural constraints on identity are concerned. I have demonstrated that there is probably no unified notion of 'identity' that holds across languages or rules, and I have rejected some very specific proposals on this issue, and have replaced them with rather more general proposals; proposals that say that notions of identity (i.e. nondistinctness or substitutability beyond the notion of identity) within a particular language (roughly speaking, morphological identity for English, Dutch and German) for the purpose of coordinate deletion depends primarily on the discourse in which the sentence in question occurs. Since we cannot fruitfully predict contexts of sentences, we cannot make specific claims about the precise nature of identity required for coordinate deletion. But this does not mean that we cannot say anything of interest about identity in coordination. All we need to do is to turn the question around: we should no longer view the problem from the identity angle (where identity is construed as a *prerequisite* for deletion), but from the distinctness angle, where distinctness is what will *block* deletion. This will make some very interesting and eminently testable claims about distinctness in reduced coordinations.

One obvious way in which this makes clear predictions is the following: if deletion has applied to a sentence and has *passed over* seemingly identical material then this material may be distinct in some way — in other words, if something is superficially a deletion target, in the sense in which we have defined deletion target in Chapter 2, and deletion has indeed applied in the sentence in question but not to our deletion target in question, then that deletion target may be highlighted as distinct from the antecedent or subsequent that we might think it is nondistinct from. A brief illustrative example: imagine there are two people at a table in a restaurant, and they have ordered different dishes, ribs and fish. A waiter bringing the food to the table could then be heard to ask:

69.   Who has ordered the ribs and who the fish?

The waiter, in asking this question, does not want to know whether there is perhaps one person at a table who has ordered two things, and who that person might be. What this question conveys is that he assumes that the different orders go to different people, and he wants to know who gets what. Deletion has applied to *has ordered*, but not to *who*. The two occurrences of *who* are therefore distinct in some sense; in the above example, they *must* even be construed as distinct.

Let us explore this line a little further. Let us hypothesise that any failure to delete is to assert distinctness; this would capture our observation for (69), We would then also be committed to always deleting everything that is deletable if we want to avoid asserting distinctness. This must be incorrect: if we have a sentence like:

70.   John kicks the dog and Ø strokes the dog.

where deletion has applied to the subject but not to the direct object, we obviously do not assert distinctness. We do not assert that John kicks one particular dog and strokes another particular dog. Failure to delete is therefore not always to assert distinctness.

As it turns out, one of the constraints of Chapter 2 will give us precisely the class of cases in which distinctness is asserted through failure to delete: the Partial Deletion Constraint. This constraint allows us to delete some material under identity while leaving other identical material behind, and says essentially the following: if two deletion target sites A and B overlap, and B is included in A but not vice versa then the material in A not contained in B may be deleted before the material contained in both A and B, but not vice versa. It does not mention any characteristics of the identical material that is deleted or the material that may be left behind. But what it *does* do is *prohibit* partial deletion under certain circumstances; some identical material may not be left behind if other material is deleted. In other words, it makes deletion *obligatory* under specific circumstances. If we now find that identical material has been left behind after deletion *in apparent violation of the PDC*, and the sentence in question is still well-formed, we must therefore conclude that the superficially identical material is *not* nondistinct in that discourse and has for that reason not been deleted. The PDC applies only in those cases where there is deletion site overlap, and it restricts partial deletion to the *difference* between the sites that overlap — thus, in an SVO sentence where there is an identical subject and an identical verb, the subject may delete before the verb, but not vice versa. This means that if we can leave an (apparently) identical subject behind after deleting the verb, the two occurrences of the subject must be distinct. Sentence (69) is an instance of this; a few more instances would be:

71. Some things are wonderful, and some things Ø awful.
72. Some weeks are good and some weeks Ø bad.

Or, alternatively, a case where there is overlap between a rightmost site and a verb site (overheard during Easter egghunt):

73. I found five and Peter Ø five.

What is clear in these cases is that, in (71) the set of things that is awful is distinct from the set of things that are wonderful, and that the weeks that are good are different from the weeks that are bad, and that the five (eggs) that Peter found are different from the five that the *I* found: reference here is always to *distinct* sets. The speaker uttering these sentences knows that they are distinct, and conveys this. But whether he chooses to refer to a set of objects that he thinks of as wonderful as 'Chicken Florentine, Veal Marsala, and Lobster Thermidor' on the one hand, and to a different set of objects which he thinks are awful as, say, 'greasy hamburgers, soggy pizza, and microwaved apple pie' on the other, or whether he refers to both as 'some things' is obviously at the discretion of that particular speaker within that particular discourse, and such things cannot usefully be predicted. A speaker *may* obviously refer to two different sets of objects, in one and the same sentence, by means

of the same lexical items, but we cannot predict the circumstances under which he will do so. Likewise, we cannot *predict*
whether or not a speaker will apply an optional rule like
coordinate deletion. The coordinate deletion rule as it has been
formulated in Chapter 2 is an optional rule, that is to say, it is a
rule of which we can specify the conditions under which it *may*
apply, but there are no conditions under which it *must* apply:
application or non-application is at the discretion of the
language user, and neither will result in an ill-formed sentence.
But we *can* predict that, under the conditions specified by the
PDC, the speaker will, by not applying deletion to superficially
identical material, overtly identify the remaining part of the
identical deletion target site as distinct; had it been nondistinct,
the PDC would have required that what now remains should
also have been deleted. The situation in which 'some things' is
not deleted under identity with 'some things' is in no way different from the situation in which the speaker uses overtly *different*
lexical items for the subjects in (71/72) and then deletes the
identical verb. In such a case, he will not delete under identity
either: one cannot delete 'Lobster Thermidor' under identity
with 'greasy hamburger'. Nor will a hearer in such a case
construe the nondeleted material as nondistinct from its superficially identical counterpart.

Note that this cannot be accounted for by including some
notion like, for instance, 'nondistinctness of referential indices'
in the definition of identity. If we assume that identity of
referential indices is a prerequisite for deletion, we could indeed
describe a number of these cases. But then we would face a
problem with all sentences where we cannot assign referential
indices to individuals, as in:

74. One or two people drank beer and gin-and-tonics during
     their lunch hour.

We cannot establish individuals here to attach the indices to,
and this sentence certainly does not assert that the people who
drink beer are also the ones who drink gin-and-tonics — what
this sentence says is that there is lunchtime drinking by a
number of people: it does not say anything about who drinks
what. This is reflected in the coordinate deletion rule, which
simply treats the two occurrences of *one or two people* as nondistinct, and does not analyse for distinctness or sameness of

215

indices. Note also that in the cases where deletion does not apply to apparently identical material we are dealing with clearly distinct groups, as in (74a), where there are beer-drinkers and G&T drinkers:

74. One or two people drank beer, and one or two people Ø gin-and-tonic.

If such an observation is *described* in terms of different indices, we have nothing more than a notation which reveals nothing about the nature of distinctness. It is precisely the apparent violations of the PDC that give us the insight into distinctness. Superficially identical material is interpreted as distinct under conditions which are specified precisely by the PDC: natural language uses notions like 'nondistinct' and 'distinct' relative to the operation of some rule.

This point can also be made in a different way. There are a number of ways in natural language in which we can overtly communicate distinctness or nondistinctness; e.g. *the same/ identical* and *some other/else*. What the above account predicts is that in those cases where we have overt nondistinctness and delete in violation of the PDC, the result should be bad (even though in this case one might arguably expect the sentence to be 'saved' by the fact that the deletion targets are not superficially identical), while the result should be good if we overtly state distinctness. The facts here correspond to our expectations in a striking way:

75. *Somebody bought a newspaper and the same guy Ø a cigar.
76. Somebody bought a newspaper and somebody else Ø a cigar.
77. *Harry called someone and Peter Ø the same person.
78. Harry called someone and Peter Ø someone else.

Let us now run through three further examples, each of which will exemplify a different PDC violation. Contrast the following sentences:

79. Who has given arms to Iran and who has given arms to the Contras?
Zaphod Beeblebrox is who!!!

79a. Who has given arms to Iran and Ø Ø Ø to the Contras?
Zaphod Beeblebrox is who!!!

These two sentences illustrate a regular case of coordinate
deletion — the two *who's* in (79) are nondistinct in this particular question. Therefore, reduction to (79a) can take place. But
now note that if we delete just *has given*, the result is quite
different, as is predicted: we cannot interpret *who* as nondistinct
and then 'skip' it in violation of the PDC when we apply
deletion. Under this interpretation, the PDC has been violated
in the following way: there is overlap between a leftmost site
and a verb site, and the leftmost site includes the verb site, but
not vice versa. Deletion has applied to the verb site only, which
is disallowed by the PDC. There is only an interpretation for
(79b) in which the person who has given arms to Iran is different from the person who has given arms to the Contras, and the
question is now made totally inappropriate by the answer
following it, which asserts that it was the same person:

79. *Who has given arms to Iran and who Ø Ø to the
Contras?
Zaphod Beeblebrox is who!!!

Now consider (80), in which we have overlap between a verb
site and a rightmost site. The two sites coincide completely. The
PDC therefore forbids partial deletion, but total deletion is
allowed. The latter part of the prediction is obviously correct:

80. Peter had read that book and Harry has read that book.
80a. Peter Ø Ø and Harry have read that book.

In (80) *that book* may be the same book, or there may be different books. In (80a), however, the books must be nondistinct,
and therefore there is only one book that both Harry and Peter
have read: there is no reading for (80a) in which Harry has
read, say, *So Long, and Thanks for All the Fish*, and Peter has
read *Aspects*. One occurrence of *that book* has been deleted,
and (80a) must therefore be construed as the reading of (80) in
which the two occurrences of *that book* are nondistinct. Now if
we delete in apparent violation of the PDC, we find that exactly
the reverse is the case: for (80b), there is no interpretation
available in which Peter and Harry have both read the same

book. The two occurrences of *that book* now have to be construed as distinct.

80b. Peter has read that book, and Harry Ø that book.

Again, the facts come out as predicted. Let us now take a third case, in which deletion removes either all or part of the left-peripheral site.[17]

81. I have bought this car for you, Ø Ø Ø for you, and Ø Ø Ø for you.
81a. I have bought this car for you, Ø Ø this car for you, and Ø Ø this car for you.

(81) has two interpretations: one car has been bought for three people, or three cars, of the same make and model, have been bought for three people. It does not have an interpretation where three different cars have been bought for three different people. (81a) also has two interpretations: one where three same cars have been bought for three different people, and one where three different cars have been bought for three people. It does not have an interpretation where one car has been bought for three people. This difference in interpretations is again as predicted: the superficially identical material which remains after deletion (both *this car* and *you*) has to be construed as distinct.

Lastly, contrast the following two sentences:

82. *I want beer and I Ø wine.
83. He wants beer and he Ø wine.

The reason why (82) is ill-formed is because the PDC has been violated and there is no way of interpreting the two occurrences of *I* as distinct, whereas in (83), we have an apparent violation of the PDC, but it is possible to interpret the two occurrences of *he* as referring to different people: under that interpretation (and *only* under that interpretation) (82) is well-formed.

There is yet another interesting consequence to this approach. Recall that Sag (1976) stated the identity requirement for VPD as 'alphabetical variant in LF'. This allowed him to deal with 'sloppy identity' cases of VPD. If the approach outlined above is correct, then what we predict is that morphological nondistinctness will suffice as an identity requirement on VPD. Now consider the following case. If we have a sentence in which the VP can be represented as an alphabetical variant of another coordinated VP then, if we take Sag's approach to identity, Sag will allow VPD, even if it is *overtly given* that the VPs contain different variables. In these cases, the 'nondistinctness' approach will predict that deletion is impossible, because the deletion targets are distinct. In example (84), deletion is allowed with 'sloppy identity' (Bill kicked a ball and John kicks possibly, but not necessarily, the same one), since the VPs are alphabetical variants of each other. In our terms, they are accessible and nondistinct from each other, and can therefore be deleted. Likewise, in (85) the VPs can still be construed as alphabetical variants of each other, and under Sag's notion of identity we should therefore be able to delete in a regular fashion.[18] Our approach on the other hand, predicts that deletion should *not* apply, since the two VPs are clearly not non-distinct. The latter prediction turns out to be the correct one:

84. John kicked some ball and Bill kicked some ball, too.
84a. John kicked some ball and Bill did, Ø too.
84b. (John, (λw) (ball y) (kick x,y)) and (Bill,(λw) (ball z) (kick w,z))
85. John kicked some ball and Bill kicked some other ball.
85a. John kicked some ball and Bill Ø some other ball.
85b. *John kicked some ball and Bill did.

Our construal of *identity* for the purposes of coordinate deletion gives us some interesting consequences: it makes a number of crucially correct predictions about a whole class of cases (which, to my knowledge, have hitherto not been observed in the literature) where the 'alphabetical variant' approach to identity falters. It is tempting to examine further cases of how this approach to identity compares with earlier accounts of deletion-related structures using some (usually unspecified or poorly specified) notion of identity, or how a non-deletion based account could explain these facts, but such a discussion would take us too far afield. We can furthermore conclude that the level of analysis at which we establish identity is the surface morphological level, with the proviso that verbal number agreement is ignored for German, Dutch and English. If deletion under identity (with identity construed in the above fashion) fails in violation of the PDC, then we can conclude that the superficially identical material that has been left behind must be construed as distinct in that discourse. Information about distinctness or non-distinctness *beyond* the surface morphological level is ignored by the coordinate deletion rule. Distinctness is, furthermore, a relative notion: something is distinct or non-distinct relative to a particular discourse.

3.3 COORDINATION AFTER DELETION

3.3.1 Empty categories

In the discussion so far, I have avoided the question of what remains after coordinate deletion — there are, of course, the lexical remnants which deletion leaves behind, but otherwise I have made the simplest assumption possible, namely that there is nothing, no nonlexical remnant, left behind at the deletion site itself once deletion has applied to it, and there is no overt evidence at surface structure that the contrary is the case, However, this may be deceptive. Could one perhaps make a case for the position that deletion leaves nonlexical remnants (empty categories, phonologically null strings), or lexical remnants behind? And if such a case could be made, will it perhaps then be more expedient and coherent to base-generate these *in situ*, under the appropriate conditions, as either null or non-null proforms? In answering especially the second part of this question, I shall discuss, in some detail, the case where it seems most obvious that there is a remnant at the deletion site after deletion, namely the auxiliary that we find after VP-deletion in English.

Also, I have demonstrated that a deletion approach which does not rely on structural information, but only on left-to-right order of constituents can provide an adequate and very revealing account of coordinate deletions. However, this leaves open the question of whether there are perhaps processes which operate after coordinate deletion which require information about the *structure* of a sentence after coordinate deletion has applied, rather than just information about the left-to-right sequence of constituents. If there are processes which require such specific information beyond linear sequence, then we will have to define what this structure is, even though the deletion rule itself does not require access to such structural information. In answering this question, I shall discuss the most obvious case of a process that follows deletion, namely subject-verb agreement.

Let us briefly address the empty category problem, restricting ourselves to verbs. Suppose that at the deletion site, there is some type of empty category (let us, following Aoun *et al.* (1986), call it GAP, or, following Saito (1984) call it V_e) left behind after deletion. We should now link the empty categories left behind by movement to those left behind by deletion. The most obvious question which then arises is how this could be done in a way that gives us the essential insight into deletion that has been dominant throughout this book, namely that the deletion target site is nondistinct from its antecedent. The most obvious way in which this could be done is to establish a relation between the deletion target site and the antecedent or subsequent by means of coindexation of the empty category left behind with the 'full' antecedent. Let us assume that a principled way can be found for doing this. If we assume furthermore that such indices, when they are nondistinct, indicate potential or actual coreference at some level of representation, then we have indeed achieved at least one result that is in keeping with our observations so far: there may be coreference between site and antecedent or subsequent (where we have to interpret 'reference' in a very particular way, since verbs do not refer in the sense of the term that is customarily used for nouns). However, this only holds for verbs, and given that coordinate deletion applies to verbs, as well as to nouns and strings of constituents, we would have to extend the indexing procedure to any possible deletion target: obviously a complication, but let us again assume that this can be done in a principled way. What we achieve with this approach is some statement of identity of deletion site and antecedent, but this will be of no obvious help to us in stating any of the constraints on deletion formulated in Chapter 12 in a more insightful way. Such a coindexing will not tell us anything about the crucial constraints on peripherality and directionality. Nor are there obvious similarities between these empty categories and other empty categories familiar from recent work in generative syntax (e.g. *trace* and *PRO*): our novel empty category GAP or V_e is unique in that it does not require a specific *structural configuration* like government or C-command to explain its distribution, but a *parallelism* in a co-ordinated syntactic environment. Also, if one takes one of the essential characteristics of such empty verbs that is stipulated in the literature (e.g. Aoun *et al.*, 1986; Saito, 1984), namely that empty verbs are not proper governors at the level of phonological form (an assumption needed to account for the fact, observed e.g. in Stowell (1981), that gapping a verb will result in ungrammaticality if there is an empty complementiser governed by that gapped verb), then it will be clear that there is no need to assume the existence of a non-governing empty verb to avoid proper government at PF. If there is nothing there at PF at the deletion site, there will also not be anything to govern from the deletion site at PF. Note furthermore that the assumption of an empty verb which lacks governing properties at PF points strongly towards a deletion-type approach rather than *in situ* generation in a GB model: given that a number of processes have to take place under government (e.g. case assignment), the governor (verb) will have to be present at at least one level of representation, and absent (as a governor) from PF.

Such observations of course do not demonstrate that it is *in principle* impossible to resort to empty categories for the description of coordinate deletions, but the discouraging results of even such extremely superficial observations should make us wary of pursuing this line of inquiry. There are in principle no objections to postulating empty categories at a deletion site, but such a hypothesis provides a complication of the grammar and will therefore need to be strongly supported. If it could for instance be demonstrated that an empty verb after Gapping clearly has specific properties, which are furthermore clearly verbal properties, which the full verb does not have, then we have a clear case for postulating an empty verb. For the purposes of this book, I shall assume that after deletion nothing remains at the deletion target site itself. This assumption, which has, apart from avoiding the difficulty of establishing what exactly it is that remains after deletion, the advantage of being the simplest assumption possible, may turn out to be false. But even if this is so, it will not detract from the rules and constraints proposed in this book: hopefully, the proven existence of empty categories after deletion will allow us to find new and insightful ways of stating the rules and constraints here, and possibly even of deriving them from independent principles.

3.3.2 Pro-VP

There seems to be nothing of immediate attraction or urgency in postulating empty categories as a result of deletion. However, there is one case, in one language, in which it seems fairly obvious that something does remain after deletion: as has been observed earlier, VP-deletion in English requires a finite auxiliary to stay behind at the deletion site, and here we can therefore immediately ask the question of whether this finite auxiliary could be viewed as a VP-proform which has been directly generated, whether it must necessarily be viewed as the remnant of deletion, or whether it is 'reinstated' as a result of a language-particular surface rule of filter of some sort. In this book, I have taken the latter position with respect to a part of VPD: I have subsumed VPD in coordinated structures under the coordinate deletion rule. The former position is represented most recently, and in considerable detail, in Napoli (1985). She observes that VPD verb phrases always end in an auxiliary (where *to* is taken as a pro-auxiliary), although this is partly by fiat: she relegates VPD-like structures that do not have the auxiliary, and structures that have the auxiliary but do not have it VP-finally, to other rules. This makes it possible to see the auxiliary as a pro-VP. This has a number of clear advantages over Sag's (1976) VPD account which we shall not discuss in any detail here: I refer the reader to Napoli's original article.[19]

Seeing AUX as a pro-form for VP has a number of interesting consequences. First of all, the occurrence of the pro-form is dependent on the earlier occurrence of a 'full' VP: the pro-VP has to be construed as *kicked the cat* in (86), and not as, say, *visited the Pope in Rome.* Quite obviously, this will require some sort of rule of construal which does essentially what the 'recovery' of a deletion rule would do. Let us assume that such a rule is readily available.

86.   John kicked the cat, and Bill did, too.

What we then find in a considerable number of cases is that the distribution of the pro-VP is not the same as that of the full VP. Time adverbials, for instance, are generally considered to be outside the VP; also by Napoli (1985:286). Yet they can be included in the pro-VP, and sometimes *must* be included in the pro-VP, but *must* sometimes be excluded also:

87. Peter will be leaving tomorrow, and Harry will, too.
88. *Peter will be leaving tomorrow, and Harry will tomor-
     row, too.
89. Peter will leave today, and Harry will, tomorrow

In (87), the pro-VP stands for *will be leaving tomorrow*, and
cannot stand just for *will be leaving*: if it could, we would expect
(88) to be perfectly acceptable, which it is clearly not. Yet we
cannot take this to be an argument for including time adverbials
in the VP: in (89) the time adverbial is clearly outside the VP.
These facts present no problem for the deletion account of
Chapter 2: the Partial Deletion Constraint will rule out (88),
and deletion operates normally to yield (87) and (89). The only
obvious way out for a base-generated pro-VP account would be
to require that a pro-VP is somehow construed as a maximum
expansion of VP plus whatever precedes and follows VP, to the
exclusion of the subject, and this construal will have to take into
account what already precedes and follows the pro-VP, so that
we do not get doubly filled pre- and post VP slots in for
instance those cases where there are unlike time adverbials
following the pro-VP and its antecedent. This is feasible in
principle, but note that, if we achieve this, we have stated
precisely the inverse of a deletion rule incorporating the PDC,
which makes the pro-form account and the deletion account
notational variants with respect to this case.

A second and more problematic instance where pro-VPs
have a different distribution from 'full' VPs involves *neither* and
nor. Recall Napoli's observation that VPD VPs always end in
an auxiliary. if this is so, then the subject in (90) is outside the
VP. But note that in (90a) it is inbetween the auxiliary and the
VP, and may not follow the VP:

90. John didn't want to go, and neither did Bill.
90a. John didn't want to go, and neither did Bill want to go.
90b. *John didn't want to go, and neither did want to go Bill.

Thus, subjects may follow pro-VPs, but not full VPs, which
leaves an inelegant distributional problem for the base-
generated account, which would have to be solved by making
the rules expanding VP in the base context-sensitive. Alternatively, some sort of filter could be invoked specifically for
these cases. This problem will not arise in the deletion approach

advanced in this book: (90) is straightforwardly derived from (90a) by means of forward deletion. Note also the following interesting theory-internal problem that arises in cases similar to these. Consider how a deletion approach would approach this set of sentences. Let us assume a rule for English which raises negation out of a second S to the coordinating conjunction, provided that the first S of the coordination also contains a negative. This rule is optional if there is a finite verb for the negation to attach to, but obligatory if the verb has been deleted. Thus the (a) sentences are derived from the (b) sentences (ignoring many interesting details about deletion, which can be found in Chapter 2):

91a. John doesn't like fish, and neither does Bill.
91b. John doesn't like fish, and Bill doesn't either.
92a. John doesn't like fish; nor does Bill.
92b. *John doesn't like fish, and Bill not.
93a. John doesn't like Bill; nor Bill John.
93b. *John doesn't like Bill and Bill not John.

If it is the case (as is e.g. generally assumed in current Government and Binding models of grammar) that stylistic rules follow deletion rules, this can be seen as a special English stylistic rule, and there are no problems either in accounting for the above sentences or for those versions in which deletion has not taken place. If pro-VPs are based-generated, however, as in Napoli's account, the base rules must have access to the rules they are furthest removed from, namely stylistic rules, in order to achieve the right result: the position of the pro-VPs in the (a) sentences is dependent on whether or not the negation has 'hopped over' the subject.

A third case where the distribution of pro-VPs and full VPs differ is where the pro-VP and the full VP are both preceded *only* by a subject. In those cases, a pro-VP is not allowed, but a full VP is, and it is difficult to see how a base-generation approach would account for these facts, which I have cited earlier as interesting problems for Sag's (1976) account; see Chapter 1, section 1.3.9.

94. John drank beer and Peter drank beer.
94a. *John drank beer and Peter did,

For the deletion approach outlined in Chapter 2, these sentences provide no problem.

In addition to distributional difficulties, the base-generation account as it now stands ignores some differences between pro-VP and other proforms such as pronouns.[20] To give just one example: there is no adjacency requirement on pronouns. Pronouns are allowed to have a possible antecedent intervening between the pronoun and the intended antecedent, and may be in immediately adjacent Ss, but this is not necessary. Pro-VP and antecedent VP, however, *must* be in immediately adjacent Ss, and do not allow a potential antecedent VP to intervene: there is nothing unusual about (95), but (96) is clearly ill-formed. This adjacency requirement is typical of coordinate deletion rules, and not of pronominal rules.[21]

95.   John$_i$ didn't want to go, but Mary$_j$ did, and then she$_j$ drove off without him$_i$.
96.   *John has not yet eaten his dinner and Peter isn't really hungry, but Mary has Ø.

Two more general objections which one could raise against the base-generated pro-VP account are that it misses the obvious generalisations which we have captured in Chapter 2, and that it requires a language-specific base rule which has to be supplemented with a number of equally language-specific filters if it is to achieve the correct result. Recall our earlier observations that we will somehow have to prevent VPD from applying to (97) to yield (97a) and we have to prevent Coordination Reduction from applying to (98) to yield (98a):[22]

97.   John went fishing and Bill went fishing.
97a. *John went fishing and Bill did.
98.   John went fishing and Bill went fishing too.
98a. *?John went fishing and Bill too.

For the deletion approach outlined in Chapter 2, these sentences pose no problem, and constitute strong evidence that VPD in coordinated structures and Coordinated Reduction are very similar processes, which one should try to subsume under one coordinate deletion rule. A base-generation account, however, will have to find some *ad hoc* solution for sentences of the type (97a), where base-generation of pro-VPs is disallowed.

In other words, not only is there an *ad hoc* filter of some sort needed here, but this filter will only serve further to obscure the obvious similarities between some applications of VPD and some applications of Coordination Reduction. Furthermore, problems of this type arise *only* in coordinated structures. This demarcation problem between VPD and coordinate deletion does not arise in subordinate clauses, since coordinate deletion cannot apply in subordinate clauses. It is possible to have VPD in subordinate clauses for VPs which in coordinate clauses would be subject to coordinate deletion and not to VPD. Compare:

99. I will go if you will Ø.
100. *I will go and you will Ø.

That the base-generation account of VPD, if it extends over VPD in coordinated structures, misses out on at least one further obvious similarity between VPD and deletion under identity will also be fairly uncontroversial. A pro-VP must be peripheral (in the sense of Chapter 2) to its S; recall:

101. *Lee drew his gun quickly, but Clint didn't Ø with such speed.

There is more evidence that VPD operates differently in coordinate structures and subordinate structures. Such conclusions can also be drawn from the fact that the pro-form VP is always generated as subsequent to a 'full' VP in structures containing a coordinating conjunction, but not in clauses linked by means of a subordinating conjunction: there the pro-VP may precede the 'full' subsequent VP, as will be clear from the following set of examples:

102. I have kissed Mary, and Bill has, too
102a. *I have, and Bill has kissed Mary, too
103. Unless you kiss Mary, nobody will.
103a. Unless you do, nobody will kiss Mary.

The fact that VPD occurs only in subsequent coordinated Ss and not in antecedent Ss follows from the constraints on directionality of deletion. The only language-specific statement for VPD in coordinated structures that is required in the deletion approach is the one outlined in Chapter 2: in specific cases of deletion target site overlap in English, the AUX is reinstated at the deletion target site, using a form of *do* if the deleted verb is a main verb.[23] As we shall see later, it is not at all unusual for individual languages to vary with respect to the coordinate deletion rule. We have already seen, earlier in this chapter, that the notion of identity may vary between languages. Studies of different languages have made available a set of facts from different languages that make it plain that there is highly specific cross-linguistic variation in coordinate deletion. Later in this chapter, we shall attempt to reduce these differences to specific variations in the constraints on coordinate deletion.

We can conclude that it is in principle not impossible to see VPD-type structures, which in this book have been treated as subpart of coordinate deletion, as cases of base-generated pro-VPs. What will also have become clear, however, is that there are no obvious advantages to the base-generation approach that single it out as more promising: rather, the base-generation account gives rise to some awkward problems which do not arise in the deletion account. To this I have to add, in all fairness, that I will not attempt to provide a clear and improved alternative formulation for that part of VPD which operates in subordinate clauses here. But there are a few observations which can be added that seem to point in the direction of deletion (in the sense of Sag, 1976) rather than base-generation in the sense of Napoli (1985) as the correct approach to VPD in subordinated clauses.

First of all, note that one distributional problem mentioned earlier is not particular to VPD in coordinate structure: if a VP is not peripheral to its S, VPD of an antecedent VP cannot apply, or, to put it in base-generation terms, an antecedent pro-VP cannot occur in between a subject and anything within the same S as the pro-VP:

104. *If you do Ø slowly, I will draw my gun quickly.

Such facts can be tied in with a general constraint on accessibility of syntactic material to rules, of which we have documented many examples in this book specifically for coordination. Secondly, recall that one of the main reasons for positing a deletion rule has always been the perception that a sentence which has been subjected to a deletion rule is 'incomplete' in some sense,[24] and can be completed by rein-stating the deleted material, which will in most cases be present in the same sentence, or possibly in some immediately preced-ing sentence. If we now view, following Napoli, what used to be seen as a deletion rule as a rule for inserting pronouns, we see that the class of deletion rules (at least for English) is reduced by one rule, a rule which by and large conforms to the regular pattern of all deletion rules, but that the class of proforms now has a conspicuous new member which behaves rather differently from e.g. pronouns:[25] intuitively a quite unsatisfactory result. To provide just one example, a pro-VP cannot function as anaphoric to a 'full' VP in discourse in the same way that a regular pronoun functions as anaphoric in discourse. Although there is nothing odd about using the pronoun *they* for *John and Bill* (repeating *John and Bill* constantly would even result in a pretty clumsy story), we cannot use an AUX pro-VP through-out to substitute for *killed two pheasants.*

105. John and Bill killed two pheasants. *After they had, they went home and found the gamekeeper on their doorstep, who complained they had, and turned them over to the police. *They were imprisoned for fourteen days because they had, and after their sentence was over, they both said that that was the last time that they ever had.

This discussion of Napoli's alternative to the deletion approach to VPD cannot explore all the possibilities of any such alternative, and can therefore not be construed as a demonstra-tion that such an approach is impossible in principle. But it will also be clear that it faces serious problems, and that there are no immediate and obvious additional insights to be gleaned from it. A significant number of important observations are readily accounted for by a deletion approach, while they remain highly problematic in a base-generation approach.

3.3.3 Structure

The coordinate deletion rule does not have access to structural information about the coordinations it applies to. It relies crucially on the left-to-right order of constituents, and ignores the structural relations that may hold between these constituents. It may be the case, however, that there are processes that follow on coordinate deletion which crucially require specific information about the structural relations that hold between conjuncts in a coordination. If it is the case that a coordination after deletion clearly has different properties from a coordination before deletion, the question arises whether these properties follow from the *structure* of the coordination after deletion. If this is so, then we must specify what this structural information is, and how it is affected by deletion.

Perhaps the most obvious case[26] of a process following on coordinate deletion, where the coordination before deletion has different properties from the coordination after deletion, is agreement. In English, as in Dutch and German, verbs agree in number with their subjects: a plural subject, or a coordinated subject, will trigger plural agreement. If we therefore have a coordination of Ss with singular subjects, which will trigger singular agreement, and coordinate deletion applies to eliminate everything in the first coordinated S except for the subject, then we have a coordinated subject, which will trigger plural agreement:

106. Johann küsst Mary und Peter küsst Mary.
      Johan kust Mary en Peter kust   Mary.
      John   kisses Mary and Peter kisses Mary.
106a. Johann und Peter küssen Mary.
      Johan en Peter kussen Mary.
      John   and Peter kiss   Mary.

This is a fairly trivial case which seems relatively easy to resolve: a straightforward subject-verb agreement rule, which works for cases of plural subjects, should also work both for coordinated subjects which are derived by means of deletion, and coordinated subjects which are not derived by means of deletion.[27] We could follow e.g. Chomsky (1981:52), and incorporate, as an expansion for *S*, the following rule:

107. S =====> NP INFL VP

If INFL is finite, then it will also have the features person, gender and number: Chomsky (1981) calls this complex AGR (agreement). The agreement relationship between a subject and

AGR can be expressed by coindexing, and INFL, including AGR, can then be related to the verb by means of a standard Affix-Hopping type of rule. Under these assumptions, it will be necessary for agreement to work in the case of coordinated subjects that the features of the coordinated subject NP coincide with those of AGR, and given that neither of the coordinated subject NPs in (106a) will have the feature [+ plural], we will need some sort of 'feature addition mechanism' which will add up [− plural] and [− plural] to make [+ plural] on heads of NPs if there is a higher NP with the coordinating conjunction *and* immediately dominating both NPs (note that *or* will not trigger such agreement). Alternatively, one could make [+ and] a feature of the higher node which has the same agreement effect as [+ plural], and so ensure correct agreement.[28] Such approaches, although undoubtedly inelegant, and not very exciting, are descriptively reasonably adequate for English and a number of other languages. They describe a majority of agreement facts, although they pass over those cases where agreement is optional. Hoeksema (1983) points out that plural subject NPs do not always give rise to agreement:

108. Three defeats in a row was too much for our hero.

Nor do conjoined subject NPs systematically require plural verb agreement:

109. All that beer and wine hasn't helped my headache much.

Since agreement rules of the type outlined above rely on structural configurations in which a higher NP dominates the coordinated NPs, we have to assume that there is some simple restructuring rule (Ross, 1967, has one that will do just fine) that ensures that e.g. English *SVO and SVO* sequences where deletion removes the first VO sequence acquire a new (coordinated) subject node, marked for plurality in this case, that immediately dominates the two original subject nodes.

But it should be noted that there will be little cross-linguistic generality to such an approach. Ken Hale (p.c.) has pointed out to me that in Hopi, verbal number agreement is not with the entire conjoined NP, but only with the last subject NP of the coordination:

110a. 'Itana   niq 'ima totimho 'yam taatapɨy   qöqya.
      (Our father and these boy-pl   cottontails pl-acc killed
                                                  -pl- pl.obj.)
      Our father and these boys killed cottontails.
110b. 'ima totimho 'yam niq 'itana   taataptɨy   qöya.
      (these boy-pl   and our father cottontails-pl-acc
                                             killed-pl.obj.)
      These boys and our father killed cottontails.

Mohammad Mohammad (p.c.) has pointed out to me that in Palestinian Arabic, conjoined subject NPs require the verb to agree fully in person, gender (the masculine overrides the feminine) and number with the entire conjoined NP if the wordorder is SVO, but only with the leftmost NP of the coordination if the wordorder is VSO:

111a. ʔel-walad we-l-banaat gataluu   ʔel-bisse.
      (the boy and the girls killed-3 pl.masc. the cat)
      The boy and the girls killed the cat.

111b. ʔel-banaat we-l-walad gataluu   ʔel-bisse.
      (the girls and the boy killed-3 pl. masc. the cat)
      The girls and the boy killed the cat.
111c. Gatalen   ʔel-banaat we-l-walad   ʔel-bisse.
      (killed-3 pl. fem. the girls and the boy the cat)
      The girls and the boy killed the cat.
111d. Gatal   ʔelwalad we-l-banaat   ʔel-bisse.
      (killed 3sg masc. the boy and the girls the cat)
      The boy and the girls killed the cat.

The question is now whether we will need to refer to some type of structural configuration in order to state subject-verb number agreement in coordination, and the answer to that question is rather obviously 'no'. Agreement in English, Dutch and German at least can be stated in terms of linear sequence just as easily as it can be stated in structural terms:

112. If there is just a deletion remnant subject[29] in an and-coordination, the finite verb which is the corresponding antecedent (or subsequent) to the deleted verb in that coordination must be plural.

Undoubtedly, the above statement is reasonably *ad hoc* as it stands (although certainly not more so than the description appended to (107) above), and it requires improvement. Nevertheless, it has some interesting consequences. Let us first of all see how it accounts for the [± plural] agreement facts of English, Dutch and German. In English, and in Dutch and German main clauses, we have SVO wordorder, and only if we have sequence (113) will (112) be met. In Dutch and German subordinate clauses, we have SOV wordorder, and here (112) will be met only if we have sequence (114). It is also possible to have, after topicalisation of the object, to have OVS wordorder: here (112) will only be met in the case of sequence (115).

113. S and SVO
114. S and SOV
115. OVS and S

In other words, (112) describes the number agreement facts of English, Dutch and German accurately, but seems to have no virtues beyond that: it is a notational variant of the more structure-oriented approaches roughly outlined above.

But there are a few pieces of evidence that seem to favour the linear approach rather than the structural approach to coordinate deletion. The crucial notion of (112) is 'single deletion remnant subject'. There is no inherent reason why it should be that only if there is *just* a deletion remnant subject in a coordination that we get a change in number agreement: we therefore expect to find that languages exist in which there is plural subject-verb agreement, even though there is more than *just* a subject remnant left after deletion. Such a language is Basque; Sjoblom (1980:117 ff.) observes that in SO and SOV coordinations, the verb must agree with *both* subjects:

116. Lindak ardau edaten du ta Anderek esnea edaten du.
     (Linda wine drink 3sg and Ander milk drink 3sg)
117. *Lindak ardau Ø ta Anderek esnea edaten du.
     (Linda wine Ø and Ander milk drink 3sg)
118. Lindak ardau Ø ta Anderek esnea edaten dabez.
     (Linda wine Ø and Ander milk drink 3pl)

Note how these facts can readily be accounted for by the non-structural approach by simply dropping the word *just* from

(112). For the structural approach, such facts are certainly not intractable, but they are rather more awkward: we either have to surmise a language-specific restructuring rule for Basque, plus a language-specific *category* that consists of just a subject and an object,[30] or we have to have a language-specific coindexing procedure that singles out the subjects from these novel categories, coindexes them, and adds their features to [+ plural] if we want to preserve the procedure concomitant with (107).

More evidence comes from inspection of other agreement facts than number agreement. The structural approach relies crucially on some higher node of the same category as the coordinated nodes, which has to provide the appropriate feature complex for agreement. If we look at the facts of Hopi cited above, we see that it is not the higher node that controls agreement, but the NP that is linearly nearest the verb. If we look at Palestinian Arabic, we find again that it is possible to argue that it is a single higher coordinated node that controls agreement for SVO sentences, but this will not account for VSO sentences: there again it is the NP that is linearly nearest the verb that controls agreement.

If we find further instances of languages where not the higher node, but either the first constituent in the linear sequence of the coordinated constituents, or the one linearly nearest the verb the relevant node for the purposes of agreement, then the internal structure of the coordination, and thereby restructuring, is obviously redundant for resolving agreement. Such cases exist; Corbett (1983), which provides a mine of interesting observations about agreement in person, number and gender in a number of languages,[31] gives Czech as a language in which the verb may agree in number and person with the conjunct that is nearest the verb, providing the predicate precedes the verb (Corbett, 1983:179):

119. Půjdu   tam   já a ty.
     will go (1 sg) there I and you.
     (you and I will go there)

In Slovene, the verb may agree with the conjunct that is furthest from it (Corbett, 1983: 180):

120. Groza   in strah   je prevzela vso vas.
     Horror (fem.sg) and fear (masc.sg) has seized (fem. sg)
     the-whole village.

In these two cases, where resolution does not apply,[32] this will obviously have to be accounted for by reference to linear order of conjuncts: such data can be accounted for by simply requiring that the verb agrees in person and number with the leftmost conjunct.

It is also possible for agreement to be rather more selective: Corbett (1983:182-3) cites examples where person agreement is with the conjunct nearest the verb, while number agreement is with both conjuncts; the languages are German and French:

121. ... wenn du und deine Schwester eine tüchtige Portion mehr bekommen werden ...
     when you and your sister a good portion more get will (3pl)
122. ... comme l'ont montré Ferdinand Brunot et moi-même
     as it-have (3 pl) shown Ferdinand Brunot and myself

There is a considerable body of literature on agreement, and the few examples which I have given here cannot do full justice to it. There are many intriguing facts from a large number of languages about agreement that I have glossed over.[33] Neither can they provide conclusive evidence that all structural information is redundant in coordination: it is quite possible that evidence to the contrary will be advanced in the future. It does serve to demonstrate, however, that the most obvious example of a syntactic process that follows on coordinate deletion, and that refers specifically to coordination, provides no evidence that reference to specific *structural* relations between conjuncts is necessary for an adequate account of subject-verb agreement in coordination. We can therefore conclude that, until strong evidence to the contrary is provided, we should not assume a restructuring rule that must apply to coordination after deletion.

The aim of the preceding few sections has been a negative one, and the conclusions are therefore also negative. I have questioned the usefulness of postulating empty category remnants after coordinate deletion, and I have demonstrated that there are no obvious advantages, and a number of disadvantages, to one alternative approach (the base-generation approach) to VPD in coordinated structures over the coordinate deletion approach. Furthermore, I have argued that agreement facts do not dictate that there are particular structural requirements that must be met by a coordinated structure after deletion. These negative conclusions reinforce the strongest and

235

simplest hypothesis about coordinate deletion that can be made, which was advanced in Chapter 2: there is one coordinate deletion rule which is responsible for reduced coordinations. This deletion rule does not leave anything behind at the deletion site. It does not require structural information, nor does it impose a particular structure on its remnants.

3.4 STRUCTURE AND THE RECOVERABILITY OF DELETIONS

3.4.1 Introduction

In section 1.3.3 of Chapter 1, I have briefly quoted Hankamer (1973:17) on the notion 'recoverability of deletion' in the following context: understanding sentences involves hearers determining the underlying representations of sentences which they hear, even if these sentences have undergone deletion. It therefore follows that, if the model of grammar incorporates a deletion rule, the deletions it effects must be recoverable. The passage which is quoted most often on this subject is from Chomsky (1965):

> A deletion operation can eliminate only a dummy element, or a formative explicitly mentioned in the structure index (for example *you* in imperatives), or the designated representative of a category (for example, the *wh*-question transformations that delete noun phrases are in fact limited to indefinite pronouns), or an element that is otherwise represented in the sentence in a fixed position. (Chomsky, 1965:144-5)

The motivation behind this passage will be fairly obvious. Hearers are capable of understanding sentences; i.e. of arriving at some sort of representation of the meaning of a sentence. They are also capable of producing meaningful sentences; i.e. of turning representations of meaning into sentences. This means, under a number of assumptions which have been spelled out and discussed so frequently in the literature that I shall not repeat them here, that there is a set of rules which mediates between the level of representation of meaning (let us call this SR, for Semantic Representation) and the level at which the hearer perceives, or the speaker pronounces sentences; let us call this SS, for Surface Structure. If one now makes a maximally simple (though not crucial) assumption, namely that the rules for production and perception, or encoding and decoding, are the same, and this set of rules includes one or more deletion rules,[34] then there are two ways of ensuring recoverability. Firstly by stipulating that only specific elements may delete, so that there is only one, or maybe a highly limited number of possibilities for 'filling in' a deletion site with the material that has been deleted, and secondly, if a variable deletion target rather than a specific element or class of elements is involved, by making the deletion contingent on a variable corresponding to the deletion target being present elsewhere in the sentence. The latter case is the case of coordinate deletions, or deletion under identity: such deletions apply under identity, and are recoverable under identity. The notion of identity we have discussed in the first section of this chapter, and we shall here not be concerned with identity deletion rules other than coordinate deletion as formulated in Chapter 2.

It needs to be observed that the 'recovery' of a deletion should not be expected to do more than reinstate deleted material: to recover a deletion in a sentence is to restore the sentence to the state it was in before deletion applied. This may seem a trivial point, but it has some quite relevant consequences.

First of all, if we make this maximally simple assumption, that 'recovery' of deletion does nothing more than reverse the deletion process, then, given that the *deletion* rule as stated in Chapter 2 does not appeal to structural configurations between constituents, we do not expect *recovery* of that deletion to make use of structural information either: ideally, deletion and recovery of deletion should make use of the same basic notions.

Secondly, if the above minimal assumptions are correct, then given that deletion under identity can introduce ambiguity (*pace* Hankamer), there must be more than one recovery possible after deletion precisely in those cases where deletion can introduce ambiguity.

The third point is the indirectly related point of the *acquisition* of deletion rules like the one outlined in Chapter 2. There has been a lot of concern in the linguistic literature with the biological foundations of language acquisition, also known as the 'innateness' question: languages are learned, and therefore the rule system underlying individual languages has to be learnable. For the acquisition of deletion this means that the primary data, the *output* of an application of the deletion rule in a particular language has to be analysed by the learner in terms of some previously established method of analysis which either has already been acquired, or which is innate (or maybe a combination of the two), so that the learner can acquire the relevant properties of the deletion rule. Given this, it will be clear that formulating the recovery of deletions is as important and central to our understanding of deletions as is formulating the deletion rule itself: in order to acquire a deletion rule, its effects have to be analysed by the learner, and this analysis will crucially involve the recovery of deletions. Only if the deletion has been recovered will the learner know exactly what has been deleted, and will he be able to formulate hypotheses about the proper formulation of the deletion rule.

3.4.2 Structural recoverability: Williams

To begin with the first issue, Williams (1978), which we have discussed in Chapter 1, section 1.3.6, for its interesting inadequacies as an approach to coordinate deletions, provides a definition of *recoverability of deletion* (ROD) which bears directly and in an interesting way on the structure issue. Recall that Williams (1978:31 ff.) provides what he calls ATB format for coordinate structures, whereby all conjuncts are written on top of each other, and factor lines that split coordinate structures are drawn so as to split all conjuncts of that structure, where *factor* can be seen, for the purposes of this discussion, as any substring of a well-formed labelled bracketing that does not begin with a right bracket or end with a left bracket. Deletion in coordination applies to simultaneous factors, where *simultaneous factor* is a factor that contains part of each conjunct. This deletion must be subject to ROD, which Williams states as follows:

> If a term T is moved or deleted by a transformation, and T consists of simultaneous factors F_1 ..... F_n, then it must be the case that F1= ..... .=Fn. (Williams, 1978:36)

What this says is that if a set of simultaneous factors is deleted, they must be identical, in some sense of that word. *Identical, is a,* or $=$ is stated on that same page as:

> If F is a factor consisting of simultaneous factors F_1 ..... F_n, then F 'is a' X if F_1 'is a' X and .... F_n 'is a' X.

These two definitions beg a number of important questions. First of all, it should be obvious that not an *entire* simultaneous factor can be deleted: at least one *F* needs to remain somewhere. If we do not add this stipulation, (123) will turn into (123a):

123. John gave Mary a book, John gave Sue a box of chocolates, and John gave Selina a bunch of flowers.
123a. *Mary a book, Sue a box of chocolates, and Selina a bunch of flowers.

Once we add that at least one *F* has to remain, we have to stipulate *where* it remains. In (123), the *F* at the *top* of the 'stack' created by writing all conjuncts on top of each other has to remain. In (124), the one at the *bottom* of the stack has to remain:

124. John made, Harry bought, and Peter stole a clothesrack for Mary.

These facts are familiar to us for the discussion of directionality of deletion: let us assume that they could be added to Williams' account to remedy its most obvious shortcomings. Similar objections to the 'directionality of deletion' ones can be raised on the adjacency issue: recall that coordinate deletions apply only to identical material in immediately adjacent coordinated clauses. If there is another coordinated clause in between the clause containing a simultaneous factor, deletion cannot apply:

125. John introduced Sue, Peter invited Mary, and Harry Ø Selina.
126. John introduced Sue, Peter invited Mary, Harry Ø Selina, and Cuthbert turned up with Mavis.

Here, the 'gap' is interpreted as *invited*, not as *introduced*.

From (126), it will be obvious that stating adjacency in an ATB-type format will require a fairly sophisticated notation: we must be able to locate factorisations which are immediately adjacent anywhere in a stack F of factorisations $F_1 \ldots \ldots {}_n$, and within that stack we should then be able to ignore all other immediately adjacent factorisations where the lexical material is not identical ('is a', or '=', in whatever sense is appropriate) to the lexical material contained in the deletion target factorisations. But let us assume that this, too, can be done.

What then emerges is a very interesting problem within the ROD, provided we make one further crucial assumption, which Williams himself mentions in a footnote. Observe that the crucial notion 'is a' outlined above is a notion which needs to be able to refer to lexical material if we want to prevent deleting e.g. different subject NPs in simultaneous factorisations. This may create a problem: Williams' notion of 'is a' is a notion of identity which he leaves unspecified, but which is obviously relative to the level of analysis one employs. For instance, in (127), the deletion target 'is a' WH-term. Deletion applies. In (128), the deletion target 'is a' subject, and 'is a' proper name: here deletion cannot apply, presumably because the proper names are not 'identical' (in whatever sense is appropriate here).

127. Who has eaten my porridge and slept in my bed?
128. Goldilocks has eaten my porridge and Tom Thumb has slept in my bed.

Let us assume that this notion 'is a' can be made sufficiently specific somehow to yield the correct results for (127,128). What then remains is ROD, and ROD has to ensure that a deletion, once it has applied under the conditions which Williams gives, supplemented with the machinery needed to solve the problems briefly outlined above, will be recoverable. It cannot ensure this, and the reason why it cannot ensure this resides in the notion of deletion of a well-formed factor.

For something to be a well-formed factor, it is a prerequisite that it is substring of a well-formed labelled bracketing. Let us interpret 'well-formed labelled bracketing' for English in such a way that, at some level of representation, there is a well-formed labelled bracketing available for every well-formed sentence of English, and ill-formed sentences of English will not receive a well-formed labelled bracketing at R.[35] A well-formed labelled bracketing containing a well-formed simultaneous factor may delete. After deletion and linearisation,[36] what remains will not be a well-formed labelled bracketing for at least one of the conjuncts. A case in point would be:

129. John gave the book to Mary and the record to Sue.

There is no well-formed labelled bracketing for *the record to Sue*, since it is, on its own, not a well-formed sentence of English. There is a well-formed labelled bracketing available for *John gave the book to Mary*, since this is a well-formed sentence of English. In order to 'recover' the deletion, ROD will assume that a well-formed factor has been deleted. This well-formed factor will have been simultaneous with a well-formed factor from the well-formed labelled bracketing that remains in one conjunct; we can therefore 'recover' it from there by taking well-formed factors from it, and supplementing the ill-formed labelled bracketing with these until we find that it becomes well-formed.

This method of 'recovery' will work for a sentence like (129), where there is a well-formed labelled bracketing available for at least one of the conjuncts. If, however, there is no well-formed labelled bracketing available for any of the conjuncts, it will not be possible to define a well-formed factor, since the notion of well-formed factor relies crucially on there being a well-formed labelled bracketing available, and so the deletion will not be recoverable. In a sentence like (130), this type of situation arises in which deletion has destroyed all well-formed labelled bracketings within a 'stack':

130. I always buy and never use such gadgets.

There will be no well-formed labelled bracketing for either conjunct, since neither (130a) nor (130b) are well-formed sentences of English on their own:

130a. *I always buy.
130b. *Never use such gadgets.
130c. I always buy such gadgets and I never use such gadgets.

The deletions that have applied to (130c) to yield (130) are

241

not recoverable, in spite of the fact that (130c) will receive a well-formed labelled bracketing, simultaneous factors have been deleted, and ROD and 'is a' conditions are met. In other words, ROD, in spite of the fact that it has been formulated as a constraint on the recovery of deletions, will fail to ensure recoverability of deletion.

3.4.3 Linear recoverability

But how can recoverability of deletion be ensured? As will be obvious from the remarks in Chomsky (1965), the formalisation of the ROD by Williams, and the statement of Coordinate Deletion in Chapter 2 of this book, *identity* is indeed a crucial notion. But its appeal to *structure* is precisely why the ROD failed: after deletion, no well-formed labelled bracketing could be assigned to the conjuncts, and if there is no well-formed labelled bracketing, there can be no well-formed factors. If we assume, in accordance with the approach which has been consistent throughout this book, that neither the coordinate deletion rule nor the rule or set of rules that recovers deletion makes reference to configurations of constituents, but only to left-to-right order of constituents, we rid ourselves of Williams' recoverability problem: neither well-formed labelled bracketing nor well-formed factorisation will then be notions which need to be appealed to for the actual *recovery* of deletions.

This does not mean that we can dispense with the notion 'well-formed labelled bracketing' altogether. In Chapter 2, we have defined coordinate deletion as applying to coordinations of well-formed sentences themselves not containing a coordination. We will, of course, still need to appeal to the notion of well-formed labelled bracketing in the sense in which that notion defines well-formed sentences of the language. The crucial difference with Williams' approach is that we *first* of all recover a deletion, and only then *check* if the recovery procedure has produced a well-formed sentence (well-formed labelled bracketing). It should therefore be quite clear at the outset that the linear approach to coordinate deletion, and its recoverability, cannot and should not be construed as an *argument against* the structure-dependence of language. Language is structure-dependent: this point is well-established. Chomsky, as the foremost linguist to stress this, recently addressed precisely this point within the larger question of learnability of language and what is generally known as the 'innateness hypothesis/ poverty of stimulus argument' in the following way:

> A great many examples have been given over the years to illustrate what is clearly the fundamental problem: the problem of poverty of evidence. A familiar example is the structure-dependence of rules, the fact that without instruction or direct evidence, children unerringly use computationally complex structure-dependent rules rather than computationally simple rules that include only the predicate 'leftmost' in a linear sequence of words. (Chomsky, 1987:7)

The fact that coordinate deletion rules do *not* involve direct reference to structural configurations of constituents, and that the recovery of deletions does *not* involve direct reference to such structural configurations either detracts nothing from the overall validity of Chomsky's point. Coordinate deletions, and their recovery, are crucially dependent on structure, but not directly so: they are dependent on the notion 'well-formed sentence of a language', and that is a structurally defined notion. It follows that the rule of coordinate deletion, although it does not rely on structural configurations for its definition, does not constitute counterevidence to the structure-dependence of language.

However, in the same way that it does not follow from the linear account to coordination that *all* of language is structure-*independent*, it does not follow from Chomsky's observation that all questions relating to natural language processing are necessarily and directly structure-*dependent*. In pursuing the larger question of the learnability of language to which Chomsky's remark is addressed, we need to be careful not to assume that all natural language processes, or, in our case, all of syntax, are necessarily and directly structure-dependent. Isolating a rule like Coordinate Deletion, which is best stated as a structure-independent, linear rule, and formulating it and its recovery, contributes significantly in two ways to the study of language. First of all, it will create a better understanding of coordination and coordinate deletions, and these are constuctions which are extremely widespread across languages. But perhaps more importantly, it calls our attention to a significant extension of the field of research into linguistic rules. It is true

243

that coordination and coordinate deletion are not primary sources of insight into the structural properties of language. However, they are a primary source of insight into one property of language which is as universal, as uncontested, and as crucial to our understanding of language as the property of structure-dependence referred to by Chomsky, namely that linguistic material is always presented in linear form. Coordinate deletion is a rule which employs this property, and it is through the study of linear rules like coordinate deletion that we gain insight into it.

The syntax of coordinate deletion is a 'derived' syntax: it operates on well-formed sentences of a language which have been coordinated. The notions which it employs are notions which are simple and straightforward, and which will be required in any grammar: it refers crucially to verbs, to constituents, and to leftmost — and rightmost (i.e. the beginning and end of an S). The only notions which are truly particular to it are on the one hand deletion, and on the other hand the notion of 'accessible site'.

If we take the remark in Chomsky (1986) and the linear approach to coordinate deletion seriously, it should follow that, if deletions and their recovery are structure-dependent, recovery should be a computationally relatively simple matter: as a matter of fact, there is no reason why it should not, in the sense of Chomsky (1986), refer only to the predicate 'leftmost' in a linear sequence of words beyond the independently needed notions of 'well-formed sentence' and 'constituent'. In the outline of recovery of deletions below, I shall make use of more than just the predicate 'leftmost', and also use terms like 'to the left of', 'rightmost', and 'to the right of', but only for ease of discussion.[37]

First of all, we need to be able to recover simple applications of coordinate deletions like (131,132):

131. John cooked and Mary ate the fish.
132. John sold his bicycle and bought a car.

Assuming all coordination (with the caveats outlined in Chapter 2)[38] to be sentence coordination, we can assume that what is to the left and to the right of a coordinating conjunction will either be well-formed sentences, or can be traced back to these.[39] Clearly both (131) and (132) do not consist entirely of well-formed coordinated sentences; the former has a deficiency in the first S, and the second has a deficiency in the second S. Let us call the S with the deficiency in it the 'deficient S'. Recovery, which I shall formulate in accordance with the Directionality Constraint here (though see note 39), will now operate in accordance with the method of recovery quoted above from Chomsky (1965) to reconstitute the deficient Ss by reinstating material present elsewhere in the S. For (132), where there is a deficiency to the coordinating conjunction, this will work as follows:

133. Take the leftmost constituent of the antecedent S and copy it as the leftmost constituent of the subsequent S. Repeat with constituents to the left of the last-copied one until the deficient S is well-formed.

Sentence (131) will be recovered in exactly the inverse way:

134. Take the rightmost constituent of the subsequent S and copy it as the rightmost constituent of the antecedent S. Repeat with constituents to the right of the last-copied one until the deficient S is a well-formed sentence.

For the recovery of 'gapped' sentences like (135), a statement like (136) will be needed.

135. John ate fish and Bill rice.
136. Take the first constituent after the first constituent of the antecedent S and copy it as the first constituent after the first constituent of the subsequent S. Repeat with constituents to the right of the last-copied one until the deficient S is a well-formed sentence.

It does not take much to see that this achieves a step-by-step reversal of the coordinate deletion rule outlined in Chapter 2 in a trivial fashion. Given the fact that (133) and (134) are mirror-image formulations, and that the difference between (134) and (136) resides only in that (136) 'skips' one constituent, it will not be too difficult to devise a rather more concise and elegant statement for these rules. For the sake of clarity, however, I shall adhere to the more explicit statements (133), (134) and

(136). In sentences (131, 132, 135), there is only one constituent missing, so rules (133, 134, 136) will apply only once. In (137, 138, 139), they apply twice: once to give the unacceptable intermediate (a) version,[40] and the second time to give the fully expanded (b) version:

137.   John gave a book to Mary and a record to Sue.
137.   *John gave a book to Mary and John a record to Sue.
137b. John gave a book to Mary and John gave a record to Sue.
138.   John gave and Peter sold a book to Mary.
138.   *John gave to Mary, and Peter sold a book to Mary.
138b. John gave a book to Mary, and Peter sold a book to Mary.
139.   John bought a record for Mary, and Peter for Sue.
139.   *John bought a record for Mary, and Peter bought for Sue.
139b. John bought a record for Mary, and Peter bought a record for Sue.

Observe also that this set of rules copes quite readily with sentence (130), which created an impossible situation for recovery by means of Williams' ROD:

130.   I always buy and never use such gadgets.
130a. I always buy such gadgets and never use such gadgets.
130b. I always buy such gadgets and I never use such gadgets.

Both clauses are deficient here, but one application of (133) will give us (130a), which is then still deficient in the subsequent clause. This deficiency is readily recovered by one application of (134), which gives us (130b).

The rules (133, 134, 136), which I shall refer to as the *recovery rules*, are computationally trivially simple. They can readily be implemented in an augmented transition network (see e.g. Winograd (1983) for discussion), given the notions 'constituent' and 'well-formed sentence'. Nor are they intuitively implausible: the existence of constructions like *respectively*, *vice versa*, and the possibility of referring to left-to-right order of coordination observed in Chapters 1 and 2 require a 'pairing' of constituents which is parallel to what constitutes the essential functioning of recovery rules.

Let us test the predictions of the recovery rules further for some rather more complex cases. VPD in English is recoverable under this formulation of the recovery rules:

140. John likes fish, and Bill does, too.
141. John doesn't like fish, but Bill does.
142. John likes fish, and Bill doesn't.

In all of these cases, the deficiency is in the second S. There is only one recovery rule which can apply successfully (140-142); applications of (133) and (134) will not result in a well-formed S, while the application of (136) will, in all three cases.[41]

This brings our attention to another property of the recovery rules: as they stand, they are not ordered, and the application of one recovery rule will not block the application of another recovery rule. The recovery rules will apply until all conjuncts are well-formed sentences. This means that a number of unsuccessful recoveries may be filtered out as non-well-formed sentences by the 'regular' rules of the grammar that check if a sentence is well-formed or not. If we for instance find a deficiency in a subsequent S, and we apply recovery rule (133), and it then turns out that the sentence in question was a regular case of V-site deletion as in e.g. (139), then we can apply rule (133) until we reach the leftmost S-boundary of the antecedent S in (139): even the first application of (133) will give the sentence two subjects. We therefore start again with a different recovery rule; (134) will fail in the same way as (133) did, if only because it recovers in the wrong direction. The only rule that will apply successfully is (136). It is therefore not necessary that the recovery rules have access to information about *where* in the structure or linear sequence of constituents a deficiency occurs; it only needs to be able to determine *that* there is a deficiency somewhere.

Unordered recovery rules give the correct results, and also account quite readily for the ambiguous deletions observed in Chapter 1, section 1.3.3. There, we observed sentences like:

143. Paul put the clothes through the mangle, and Penny in the drier.

This sentence is ambiguous between a leftmost deletion and a verb-site deletion. Both recovery rules (133) and (136) will produce coordinations of well-formed sentences, namely (143a) and (143b) respectively:

143a. Paul put the clothes through the mangle, and Paul put Penny in the drier.
143b. Paul put the clothes through the mangle, and Penny put the clothes in the drier.

There is now one recovery which remains unaccounted for, and that is the recovery of 'bidirectional' verb deletions in e.g. Dutch and German subordinate clauses. The Dutch and German sentences (144) can be recovered by rule (134), but (144a) cannot be recovered by any of the rules stated so far.

144.   Ich glaube, dass Johann Fisch und Willi Reis isst.
      Ik geloof dat Johann vis   en   Willi rijst eet.
      (I believe that Johann fish and Willi rice eats)
144a. Ich glaube, dass Johann Fisch isst, und Willi Reis.
      Ik geloof dat Johann vis   eet, en Willi rijst.
      (I believe that Johann fish eats, and Willi rice)

The directionality of recovery of (134) will ensure the recovery of (144), but it will fail for (144a). We therefore augment (134) to recover forward as well; the revised version now looks as follows:

134a. Take the rightmost constituent of the subsequent S and copy it as the rightmost constituent of the antecedent S, or vice versa. Repeat with constituents to the right of the last-copied one until the deficient S is a well-formed sentence.

This will not only cater for (144a), but it also accounts for some of the VPD-facts of English, namely where the application of VPD has left a rightmost hole in the sentence, as in (131-132). Furthermore, it also accounts quite nicely for the recovery of some of the rather more interestingly complex deletions of Dutch and German. First of all, it will allow recovery of forward-deleted rightmost strings as well as constituents:

145. Ich glaube, dass Johann Maria ein Buch schenkt, und
Peter Susan Ø Ø.
Ik geloof dat Johann Maria een boek geeft, en Peter Susan
Ø Ø.
(I believe that Johann Maria a book gives, and Peter Susan
Ø Ø)

Recovery according to (134a) will first of all replace the verb in
the subsequent S in (145), giving us the unacceptable intermediate:

145a. *....., und Peter Susan Ø schenkt.
*....., en Peter Susan Ø geeft.

A second application will then yield the well-formed Ss:

145b......., und Peter Susan ein Buch schenkt.
......., en Peter Susan een boek geeft.

Secondly, we can now account for discontinuous deletions by
means of a combination of (133) and (134a):[42]

146. Johann hat Maria ein Buch geschenkt, und Ø Ø Susan
eine Schallplatte Ø.
Johann heeft Maria een boek gegeven, en Ø Ø Susan een
plaat Ø.
(Johann has Maria a book given, and Ø Ø Susan a record
Ø)

In sentences like (146), the final past participle may also delete
backwards as a rightperipheral site: again, (133) and (134a) will
recover these deletions. Recall furthermore that (146) is
ambiguous: it can also be interpreted with a non-leftmost gap,
in which *Susan* is the subject of the second S, rather than
indirect object.

146a. Johann hat Maria ein Buch geschenkt, und Susan Ø Ø
eine Schallplatte Ø.
Johann heeft Maria een boek gegeven, en Susan Ø Ø een
plaat Ø.

For sentence (146a), (136) and (134a) will achieve the appropriate recovery. Recall also that sentences like:

147. Johann hat Maria geküsst, und Peter auch.
     Johann heeft Maria gekust, en Peter ook.
     (Johann has Maria kissed, and Peter too)

are systematically ambiguous between a subject interpretation for *Peter*, and an object interpretation. Recovery by means of (133) and (134a) yields the object interpretation, while recovery by means of (136) and (134a) yields the subject interpretation.

Bidirectional recovery may at first sight seem a slightly *ad hoc* move in order to ensure recovery of the bidirectional deletions in Dutch and German. However, note that what we have adapted is the *directionality* of recovery, and it is precisely the *directionality* of deletion which we find is a language-particular phenomenon which can readily be reversed. It is probably not coincidental that (133) and (134) are mirror-images of each other. This raises the question of why it should be (134) rather than (136) or (133) which is reversed in directionality. There is indeed no *principled* reason why not all recovery rules should be reversible in directionality, and we indeed find that they must all three be reversible if we take data from other languages into account. Sanders (1977:246) cites data from an unpublished manuscript by Rosenbaum, in which gappings of the form SO + SVO are presented as grammatical in Zapotec: this requires a reversal of the directionality of (136):

148. xwain been jumE, ne makU been yuu.
     (Juan made a basket, and Marcos made a house)
     xwain Ø jumE, ne makU been yuu

Tojolabal Maya requires a reversal of (133), since it allows Gappings of the type SO + VSO (Furbee, 1974):

149. Ø b'ak'et Hwan, sok yi'a tek'ul Maŋwel
  . (Ø meat Juan, and took fruit Manuel)

We shall return to these data and the directionality of recovery, and suggest a possible method of accounting for the deletion patterns one can observe across languages in the next section;

for the moment, observe that the 'bidirectional' recovery of deletions can very generally be stated as 'reinstate the nearest constituent which occupies a peripheral position'. Languages may differ with respect to the direction of recovery (as they do with respect to deletion), but not with respect to peripherality (I know of no language which systematically deletes from an inaccessible site), or with respect to adjacency of coordinate deletion sites: I know of no languages that allow, in a coordination of 3 Ss, deletion in S_3 under identity with material in S_1 while leaving S_2 intact. Nor do I know of languages that do not have coordination or coordination-like constructions, and all languages allow elliptical utterances of various sorts. This leaves us with an interestingly restricted range of possible variations: languages vary with respect to the directionality of deletion and recovery, and with respect to the conditions they impose on the contents of an accessible deletion site (e.g. whether there must be a verb in such a site, which Dutch, English and German require, but Basque and probably Turkish do not). Languages probably do not vary in any other way with respect to coordinate deletions.

In this section, I have demonstrated that recovery of deletion is a process that does not rely on structure: Williams' (1978) formulation of ROD failed precisely because of its crucial reliance on structure. I have also taken seriously the consequences of a non-structural approach to recovery of deletions, and have demonstrated that recovery of deletions is a computationally very simple and straightforward process which operates only on the linear sequence of constituents in the co-ordination. The recovery process produces coordinations of well-formed sentences, and makes more than one recovery available for ambiguous sentences. This provides further strong evidence that the linear approach to coordinate deletions, which poses severe restrictions both on deletion and recovery of material, is correct.

3.5 COORDINATION AND GRAMMAR

There are two questions which naturally arise when we look at the place of coordination in grammar. The first is the question of where in a particular model of grammar we should expect to

find the rule of coordinate deletion, and how, if at all, it interacts with other rules of the grammar. The second is: how does
the rule of coordinate deletion manifest itself in the grammars
of various languages, and how does it vary across languages?

3.5.1 A late rule

The theoretical question has already been answered to a large
extent. We have assumed that the rule of coordinate deletion,
formulated as 'Delete under identity in coordinated structures',
applies to coordinations of well-formed Ss only. This makes it
one of the 'late' rules in the grammar; one that applies, within
what is usually called the 'Government/Binding' model of
grammar, to surface structure; i.e. after all movement rules have
applied, or, within other models of generative grammar, a rule
that applies late post-cyclically. The evidence for this is simple
and strong, and is quite well-documented.[43] Dougherty (1970)
observes various problems for a PS-rule account, one of the
most important being that, if coordination takes place in the
base, some sort of mechanism will have to be devised to deal
with sentences in which Tough-movement, Passive, and other
such rules have applied. In a sentence like:

150. Mary was easy to please, fun to tease, and known to have
fleas.

we do not have a coordination of base categories (in a Standard
Theory model), but a coordination of derived categories. A
deletion account could solve such problems by ordering the
deletion rule after Passive, Tough-Movement etc. Even if such
rules do not exist, it is easy enough to demonstrate that whatever
rules link deep structure and surface structure, deletion will
have to apply after these. WH-Movement will precede deletion;
in a sentence like:

151. Who did John hug and Bill kiss?

We have forward deletion of a leftperipheral site. Had
deletion operated before WH-Movement, then the site
would have been rightperipheral, and deletion would have

252

operated backwards. This would have given, after WH-movement, which puts the WH-phrase in the COMP of S_2:

151a. *John hug and who did Bill kiss?

The level at which binding relations are checked and parasitic gaps are licensed precedes the level at which deletions take place: the binder for a reflexive may be deleted, as may the licenser for a parasitic gap:

152. John kissed the girl and cursed himself.
153. Which articles did you file without reading properly and John without even looking at?

Likewise, topicalisation will precede deletion. Recall Dutch (or German) sentences of the type SVO+SVO. If we topicalise the object, the verb-second rule will apply to give us the word-order OVS+OVS. If we have identical subjects, these will delete forwards in the non- topicalised sentences, and backwards in the topicalised sentences: the reverse is not possible. Identical objects will delete backwards in non-topicalised sentences, and forwards in topicalised sentences; the reverse is again not possible. If deletion applies after topicalisation, and in accordance with the constraints on directionality as outlined in Chapter 2, these facts are readily accounted for. If deletion precedes topicalisation, it is difficult to see how the ungrammatical (c) sentences could be ruled out in a non-*ad hoc* way.

154. Ik voer de hond en ik aai de kat.
(I feed the dog and I pet the cat)
154a. Ik voer de hond en Ø aai de kat.
154b. De hond voer Ø en de kat aai ik.
154c. *De hond voer ik en e kat aai Ø.
155. Ik voer de hond en Jan aait de hond.
'I feed the dog and Jan pets the dog)
155a. Ik voer Ø en Jan aait de hond.
155b. De hond voer ik en Ø aait Jan.
155c. *O Voer ik en de hond aait Jan.

Likewise, if topicalisation serves to move an inaccessible constituent into an accessible position, deletion can apply to that constituent. If this results in putting an otherwise accessible constituent into an inaccessible position, deletion will fail to apply to that constituent. Compare:

156. Ik geef het boek aan Marie en ik verkoop het schilderij aan Jan.
(I give the book to Marie and I sell the painting to Jan)
156a. Ik geef het boek aan Marie en Ø verkoop het schilderij aan Jan.
156b. *Het boek geef ik aan Marie en het schilderij verkoop Ø aan Jan.
157. Ik herstel het schilderij voor Jan en Jan geeft het schilderij aan Marie.
(I restore the painting for Jan and Jan gives the painting to Marie)
157a. *Ik herstel het schilderij voor Jan en Jan geeft Ø aan Marie.
157b. Het schilderij herstel ik voor Jan en Ø geeft Jan aan Marie.

These facts are not restricted to the three languages that have been the main focus of our discussion so far. Let us take one more illustrative example. Sanders and Tai (1972) provide an interesting analysis of Mandarin Chinese coordinate deletions. Mandarin Chinese, which is an SVO language, is more restricted in the coordinate deletions it allows than English: it does not allow deletion of the identical verb, or deletion of the identical object:[44]

158. *John dǎle nánháizi, Bill Ø nǚháizi.
(John hit   the boy,   Bill Ø the girl)
159. *John dǎle Ø Bill tīle   nánháizi.
(John hit   Ø Bill kicked the boy)

Nor does it allow a pre-verbal adverb to be deleted under identity:

160. *John zuótian   dǎle nánháizi, Bill Ø tīle   nǚháizi.
(John yesterday hit the boy,   Bill Ø kicked the girl)

It does, however, allow deletion of identical subjects:

161.   John dǎle nánháizi, Ø tīle   nǚháizi.
       (John hit   the boy, Ø kicked the girl)

This situation could provisionally be described by stating that
only leftperipheral sites are accessible to coordinate deletion in
Chinese. If this is so, then we expect that anything occupying
leftperipheral position will be deletable under identity. In
passive sentences, where the patient will occupy leftmost
position, deletion is indeed possible:

162.   Nánháizi bèi John dǎle, Ø bèi Bill tīle.
       (The boy by John hit, Ø by Bill kicked)

If we topicalise the direct object, which brings it into leftperipheral position, deletion is possible again:

163.   Nánháizi John dǎle,   Ø Bill tīle.
       (the boy John kicked, Ø Bill hit)

Likewise, if the time adverbial in (160) is leftmost, deletion is
possible again:

164.   Zuótian   John dǎle nánháizi, Ø Bill tīle nǚháizi.
       (Yesterday John kicked the boy, Ø Bill hit the girl)

Facts of this type, which can be duplicated for a number of
languages, demonstrate conclusively that coordinate deletion is
a late rule, which applies to surface structure: i.e. after movement has taken place. This raises a question of a different sort,
namely whether there is interaction of movement and coordinated structures: do movement rules have to specify
constraints specifically for coordinated structures, or do
coordinate deletion rules specifically have to refer to constraints
on movement rules? The evidence and analysis available to date
suggests quite strongly that this is not the case. There has been
some discussion about the interaction between Gapping and
Scrambling which was initiated in Ross (1970), but later work
(e.g. Sanders and Tai (1972), Koutsoudas (1971)) has demonstrated conclusively that this hypothesised interaction is
mistaken. This point is now mainly of historical interest, and we
shall not pursue it here. For some more recent evidence that is
in keeping with the requirement that RNR must be a late rule,

see McCawley (1982) and Levine (1984).

There has been one process, however, which is still relevant and continues to attract attention, and that is extraction out of a coordinated structure. The first and still most relevant observations in this area can be encountered in Ross (1967) under the heading of the *Coordinate Structure Constraint*. I have already made passing references to the CSC, and to the 'Across-the-Board' exceptions to it, earlier on in this book. The CSC says the following:

165. In a coordinate structure, no conjunct may be moved, nor may any element contained in a conjunct be moved out of that conjunct.

This constraint captures the observation that a sentence like:

166. *The nurse who polished my trombone and the plumber computed my tax was a blonde.

is ungrammatical: here *the nurse who polished my trombone* has been moved out of the conjunct in violation of the CSC. There is, as is well known, a class of exceptions to the CSC, namely those cases where movement has applied to *all* corresponding elements if movement applies 'across-the-board' to elements within a coordination, then the CSC may be violated for most coordinating conjunctions (*for, denn, want* do not allow this violation; and, as an anonymous referee has pointed out to me, *aber* in German only seems to allow it if it occurs in between the coordinated clauses):

167. The man whom Harry kissed on the lips and Peter thought was horrible is here.

Now observe that if we assume that Coordinate Deletion applies to well-formed coordinations of surface Ss only, after movement has taken place, then none of the constraints on coordination in this book will rule out either (166) or (167): they simply fail to say anything about the CSC or violations thereof, since the CSC applies to *movement* and the discussion in this book is concerned with *deletion*, which, as we have seen, applies after movement. The CSC will, therefore, have to be preserved in the grammar in some form. I shall briefly outline what is at present the best available formulation of the CSC. This discussion will make it quite clear that the CSC is a constraint on movement which, in its original formulation, stipulates coordination as its *domain of application*, but is neither a constraint on coordination itself, nor a constraint on processes that are particular to coordination. It is therefore to be expected that the CSC can be subsumed under a more general constraint on movement rules that does not specifically mention coordination as a domain of application.

The most successful approach to the particular problem that the CSC addresses, and one that seeks to subsume the CSC under a more general constraint on extraction, is Pesetsky (1982). Pesetsky's general approach, which relies heavily on tree-geometry[45] is concerned with a theory of subsections of a tree which he calls *paths* that link elements within the tree: for instance, a binding relation between a trace and its antecedent. Paths obey a general constraint called the Path Containment Condition, which says that if two paths intersect, one path must be completely nested (contained) within the other. Given this, and assuming an essentially PS-rule approach to category coordination, Pesetsky's approach to the CSC is outlined below. I have assumed much detail that is particular to the Government-Binding framework in which Pesetsky (1982) is written, and omitted much detail from Pesetsky's work itself.

First of all, Pesetsky factors out the CSC into two parts: on the one hand, he assumes a version of the A-over-A condition (see e.g. Chomsky, 1973) which will take care of the part of the CSC that says that no conjunct in a coordinate structure may be moved. This will account for sentences like:

168. *Who did Bill see Mary and.

This seems uncontroversial and correct.[46] The second part of the CSC incorporates a rule that rewrites a category X as any number of coordinately conjoined heads, and more importantly an assumption that conjunctions theta-mark (or: select as arguments) any number of constituents: under an appropriate interpretation which allows for our observations in Chapter 2 (e.g. that *but* will only take two arguments and restricting the rewrite rule to S as an only category), this will not be controversial either. Following a suggestion of Stowell (1981), who sees theta-marking of an argument as a form of Ā (non-argument)-

257

binding, Pesetsky suggests that all the conjuncts will be bound from the coordinating conjunction, and there will therefore be a path (which Pesetsky crucially assumes will be a *single* path) from the coordinating conjunction to every single conjunct. It now follows that no element contained in a conjunct may be moved out of that conjunct: if there is a single path from the coordinating conjunction to all conjuncts, then it will not be a case that the Path Containment Condition is satisfied if one of the conjuncts is moved out of the coordination: the path linking the moved conjunct to its 'new' position will include the part of the path that lies between that conjunct and the coordinating conjunction, but not the part of the path that lies between the coordinating conjunction and the conjuncts that have not moved. The only way in which the Path Containment Condition could be satisfied is by moving all conjuncts: in this way, the entire path which runs between the coordinating conjunction and the conjuncts will be contained in the path that runs between the conjuncts and their 'new' position. This is precisely the Across-the-Board type violation of the CSC that we observe in (167).

Although there are some problems especially with the extensions of the above approach,[47] the approach for the greater part makes the correct predictions and allows Pesetsky to make the CSC part of a more general constraint on extractability rather than to stipulate it for coordinated structures. We shall follow Pesetsky and view the CSC, although it is applicable to co-ordinated structures before deletion applies, as part of a general constraint on extraction, and not attempt to subsume it under a general theory of coordinate deletion.[48]

We can conclude that the late and non-configurationally defined rule of coordinate deletion is, as the case now stands, relatively independent from other (configurational) rules and constraints in the grammar. This is consistent with the dominant models of grammar on which research is currently being carried out. But much more importantly, it is, in view of the wide range of empirical evidence we have discussed so far, correct and accurate.

3.5.2 Coordinate deletion in different languages

As we have observed earlier, Ross (1970) did not intend

primarily to introduce the rule of Gapping, and to explore its formal properties: rather, he assumed that Gapping as a rule exists, and he then proceeded to base a hypothetical linguistic universal on the operation of Gapping, which we know as the Directionality Constraint (DC). Although the rule of Gapping has survived some 30 years of vigorous discussion and has yielded some very interesting insights, the typological aspect of Ross's seminal work has received much less attention. In retrospect, this is hardly surprising: one finds that there are many things wrong with his approach. Just after the publication of Ross's original article, there were some serious objections raised by e.g. Maling (1972), who pointed out various inadequacies of Ross's analysis which are now mainly of historical interest, and which we shall not discuss here.

Furthermore, the restricted selection of almost exclusively Indo-European languages used for this universal seems totally arbitrary. This type objection is difficult to remedy: if we were to follow the guidelines referred to in Comrie (1981) for establishing an ideally representative sample of languages, where representative is to be interpreted as lacking in genetic, areal, or typological bias, then we will simply have to conclude that at present, there is no representative sample of deletion constructions available. Also, it will be difficult to provide such a sample on the basis of linguistic descriptions already available, since very few of these incorporate material on deletions at all, let alone material that would serve our purpose here. It is not my intention to attempt to remedy this deficiency here, and my discussion here should be interpreted in this light. I have used the data on coordinate deletion that is readily available,[49] and have supplemented it with a number of observations of my own. These caveats aside, I am of the opinion that even on the basis of this inadequate and fairly random sample on the one hand, and the account of coordinate deletions outlined in this book on the other, a preliminary classification of possible parameters of variation between languages with respect to coordinate deletion can be set up. This preliminary classification is interesting in the sense that it is quite restrictive and clearly falsifiable; however, I shall not attempt to provide a detailed and independent (e.g. functional) explanation for why languages vary along exactly these parameters and not others. I consider such an enterprise (which is clearly highly important and ultimately more interesting than the classification itself) premature at this stage of research into coordination. It is tempting to conjecture some sort of 'degree of positional resistance', or 'natural constraint on processing' (along the lines of Sanders, 1977) to be responsible for observed patterns in which e.g. languages which forward-delete S-initial constituents are more frequent than languages which backward-delete S-initial constituents. This ties in with Comrie's (1984:88) observations that left-right inversion of strings is often difficult. Given that sentences proceed from beginning to end rather than vice versa, one would expect that deletion, too, should operate in one direction, and then forwards rather than backwards. However, the bidirectional verb-deletion facts of e.g. Dutch and German, where there is no difference in acceptability or naturalness between forward-deleted and backward-deleted verbs, militate against this. At this point it therefore seems to me that to invoke some set of 'naturalness constraints on processing' or the like as the only account for the overall preference for forward-deletion is premature: one should not replace an unexplained classification with an inadequate and equally unexplained metaphor. But it is possible to give some preliminary suggestions on which deletions are more frequent than others.

Apart from factual inaccuracies and problems internal to the analysis, Ross's approach contains at least two unwarranted assumptions. Consider again the central claim of Ross (1970): it assumes that the operation of Gapping is dependent on the order of elements at the time that the rule applies: If the element is on a left branch, Gapping operates forward, if the element is on a right branch, it operates backwards. The term 'element' is interpreted in Ross (1970) in an oddly restricted and seemingly arbitrary manner, namely as 'verb in a transitive clause'.

There is no *a priori* reason why deletion of verbs should be singled out as a natural domain of analysis, nor is there a reason why sentences with transitive verbs should be the only syntactic domain under consideration. Sanders (1977) provides a number of very insightful remarks on this topic. He observes that one difference conjectured in Ross's original article between, for instance, English and Japanese with respect to deletion simply disappears if we take intransitive verbs into account, or deletion of other constituents than verbs. Japanese, which is verb-final, allows, as we have seen earlier, only 'backward' Gapping and no forward Gapping, while English allows only forward Gapping. Thus, English has (169), but not (170), Japanese has (171) but not (172).

169. SVO and SO
170. SO and SVO
171. SO and SOV
172. SOV and SO

However, if we interpret 'element' as 'any constituent', then it will be obvious that the classification changes: neither language allows forward-deletion of a rightmost constituent, and both languages allow backward-deletion of a final constituent. This final constituent will be the verb in Japanese, and the Direct Object in English. Likewise, if we take only intransitive sentences into account, then English and Japanese are again the same: both allow backward deletion of the verb, and both disallow forward deletion of the verb in SV + SV coordinations.

The restricted selection of languages that Ross employs also serves to make it easy to challenge his claims — even if we interpret Ross's proposed universal only in terms of deletion of transitive verbs, it is falsified by Zapotec (Rosenbaum, 1977): recall that this language allows backwards Gapping in SVO and SVO structures.

173. xwain Ø jumE, ne makU been yuu
     (Juan Ø basket, and Marcos made house)

We have also seen that it is falsified by Tojolabal; Furbee-Losee (1976:233) points out that this language, which is predominantly VSO, also allows backward Gapping:

174. Ø b'ak'et Hwan, Ø čenek Čep, y-iʔ-a tek'ul Maŋwel.
     Ø (meat Juan Ø beans Joe took fruit Manuel)

From these facts, and from the discussion of English, Dutch and German in this book, we can conclude (following Sanders, 1977:226) that, in a left-to-right ordering of deletion target sites in a coordination as represented in (175), no deletion is impossible in principle: for every position, we can find one or more languages that will delete there.

175. A B C & D E F

Some examples: Position *A* is accessible to deletion in Tojalabal and other Mayan languages. *B* can be deleted in Zapotec. *C* can be deleted in English, Dutch, German, Turkish and Japanese. *D* can be deleted in Dutch, English, German, Turkish, Japanese and Chinese. *E* can be deleted in Dutch, German, English and Russian. *F* can be deleted in Dutch, German, Russian and Turkish.

Sanders furthermore points out, quite correctly, that Ross assumes some sort of parallelism for Gapping: the subject, object and verb are all in the same order at the time that Gapping applies. This parallelism in construction has always been tacitly assumed in discussions about coordinate deletions (virtually all the example sentences in Chapter 2 of this book, for instance, are parallel constructions) and it is a basic tenet of the 'three-dimensional' approach to coordinations outlined in Goodall (1984), which has no obvious way of handling 'nonparallel' coordinate deletions of e.g. the type OVS & SO. Yet it is by no means necessary that this parallelism should obtain; it certainly does not hold for German and Dutch.[50] Dutch and German allow Gappings of the SVO & OS type:

176. Die grote neem ik, en jij neemt die kleine.
    Den grossen nehme ich, und du nimmst den kleinen.
    (the big one take I, and you take the little one)
177. Die grote neem ik, en jij Ø die kleine.
    Den grossen nehme ich, und du Ø den kleinen.

Sjoblom (1980:128 ff.) takes data from Cherokee, which allows the same Gapping pattern:

178. Asgaya udulika adela, agehya-hno Ø asano.
    (Man   wants money, woman-and Ø dress)
179. Adela udulika asgaya, agehya-hno Ø asano.

The parallelism requirement on coordination therefore also fails to qualify as a potential universal. Given that this requirement is actually crucial to most accounts of coordination, it will be useful to subject it to closer scrutiny.

Observe that the lack of structural parallelism between the Ss in which deletion has taken place and their antecedent Ss in (176/177) weighs heavily against Goodall's (1984) three-dimensional account of coordination discussed earlier, as well as against other accounts of coordination which rely on *structural* paralellism (e.g. Schachter, 1977). Let us focus on the three-dimensional account here. Sentence (177) will be a problem in the following way for this approach: let us make the assumption for Dutch and German topicalised main clauses that the topicalised constituent moves into sentence-initial TOPIC position, and the verb, which has to occupy second position linearly, moves into COMP. If we now have a conjunction of a sentence in which topicalisation has taken place with a sentence in which topicalisation has not taken place, then the verbs in those two clauses will no longer occupy the same structural positions, and we expect that deletion should no longer be able to take palce if structural parallelism matters to deletion. Clearly, the verbs in (177) are deletable.

It is not overly difficult to find further extremely awkward problems for accounts that rely crucially on structural parallelism. The account in Chapter 2 relies on left-to-right linear position for determining deletability, and we therefore expect to find that identical elements that occupy the same accessible linear position should be deletable, even if they fulfil different syntactic functions. It should e.g. be possible to delete a subject under identity with a topicalised object on the linear approach, provided that both occupy the same accessible linear position. Indeed we find that such sentences exist: (180) is grammatical in German:

180. Käse   mag ich nicht, und Ø ist auch nicht gut   für mich.
     (Cheese like I   not,   and Ø is also not   good for me)

In an account that relies on parallelism of *structure*, the existence of sentences of this type is totally unexpected and is highly problematic: a topicalised object and a non-topicalised object will not have the same structural position, and should therefore not be deletable. Nor are sentences of this type restricted to German: we find the same type of data in Dutch, where sentences like:

181. Jan z'n kaas is niet te eten en   Ø koop ik dus niet meer.
     (Jan's cheese is inedible   and Ø buy I therefore no more)

are perfectly acceptable. One occasionally finds them, along with gapped and right-node raised sentences, condemned as

263

stylistically awkward by some stylistic purists, who seek to legis-late against what they call *zeugma* (in Dutch: Tante Betje, 'Aunt Betsy', a term used for 'bad' style), but the fact that such sentences have had the opportunity to incur the printed dis-approval of purists is good evidence that they are normal products of spontaneous speech and writing. For a recent and partly formalised discussion of zeugma, see Roorijck (1986).

Sentences like (180) and (181) provide further evidence against a structurally-based account of deletions. Observe that (181) is totally ungrammatical if the object in the second clause is *not* topicalised: the deletion targets now occupy neither the same linear position, nor the same structural position.

181a. *Jan z'n kaas is niet te eten en ik koop Ø dus niet meer.

The difference between (181) and (181a) is predicted on the linear account, and unexpected on the structural account.

Let us now take one final illustration. I have assumed that topicalised objects in Dutch are moved into a TOPIC position, and the verb then moves into COMP. The only constituent that does *not* move in the topicalisation from an SVO to an OVS sentence is the subject — that still occupies its original structural position, although its linear position has changed from S-initial to S-final. If what matters for deletion is parallelism of structure, we expect identical subjects to be deletable in both [SVO and SVO] coordinations, as well as in [OVS and SVO] coordin-ations. If linear position is what matters, then the latter deletion should be unacceptable.

182.   Jan bakt vis en kookt aardappelen
       (Jan fries fish and boils potatoes)
182a. *Vis bakt Jan en kookt aardappelen.
       (fish fries Jan and boils potatoes)

The linear approach again turns out to make the correct predic-tions: (182) is acceptable, (182a) is not.

But what can we then hypothesise about the nature of coordination taken across languages? Obviously, the Direction-ality Constraint is not a candidate for universal status, and the typology of deletion ought not to have been restricted to trans-itive verbs in the first place. Secondly, there is clearly no univer-sal structural parallelism requirement. Thirdly, as observed in

Koutsoudas (1971) and Sanders and Tai (1972), not all languages allow coordination of all major constituent types. Notably finite verbs can often not be coordinated. However, it is clearly not the case that 'anything goes' across languages as far as deletion under identity in coordinated structures goes — as a matter of fact, if we look at the potential variation across languages with respect to coordinate deletion, only a fairly restricted part of this potential variation actually shows up. In principle, there is no *a priori* reason why any constituent anywhere in a corodination should not be deleted under identity with some other constituent in the same coordinated set of Ss.

I shall not attempt to provide a classification of conjunctions across languages — that is a task for the future. Suffice it to say that very many coordinating conjunctions have highly idiosyncratic properties, and vary widely across languages. They may vary within languages in the deletions they allow: *for* in English, *want* in Dutch, and *denn* in German do not allow deletion at all, although they must clearly be classified as coordinating conjunctions. Furthermore, we find considerable variation across languages with respect to the number and properties of their coordinating conjunctions. There are languages that have only very few coordinating conjunctions, if they have them at all, individual conjunctions can appear only under very restricted conditions, and not always in between the coordinated constituents. Chinese, for instance, has *gen* for NP coordinations, and it occurs inbetween the coordinated NPs, or postposed. Turkish has a suffix *-la* for NP-coordinations, and it is appended to the first coordinated NP (Hankamer, 1979:84). But although the number and distribution of overt coordinating morphemes may vary considerably from language to language, all languages seem to have coordination of at least S and NP, and many languages allow deletion identity in coordinated structures.

Such a statement is an observation to which one can add little — it will be proved false or inadequate if it turns out that there are languages which do not allow coordination of either NP or S.[51] Also, it seems to do little more than provide maximum liberty for the coordinate deletion rule — possibly all languages have coordination, and very many allow deletion. Yet this maximum liberty does not show up in all languages: it seems that the coordinate deletion rule is restricted in quite specific ways. There are three restrictions on coordinate deletion that

seem to be correct for all languages: there are, to my knowledge, no languages which do not obey these constraints.

(A) All languages delete at most at the three accessible sites
we have identified: leftmost sites, sites which are leftmost
if the first constituent is ignored, and rightmost sites. Not
all languages necessarily allow deletion at all three sites.
(B) A deletion target site and its antecedent or subsequent
have to occupy the same sites; i.e. deletion target and
antecedent or subsequent have to be both leftmost,
leftmost after the first constituent, or rightmost.
(C) If a single site allows both forwards and backwards
deletion, it either contains a verb or is a rightmost site.

The first statement is one that restricts the possible coordinate
deletions across languages quite rigorously: anything outside the
three sites we have identified does not classify as a possible
deletion target. We have found this to be clearly and very
convincingly true for English, Dutch and German, as well as for
a number of other languages: the *third* constituent in a linear
sequence of constituents is, if it is the only identical constituent
in a coordination, not accessible to deletion. Nor have we found
evidence of the existence of languages that systematically allow
deletion outside the accessible sites we have defined. Picking a
few more languages, more or less at random, we can see that
this observation remains correct: Neither Vietnamese[52] nor
Japanese allows deletion of only a *third* identical constituent:

183. *John đã đu a cho Mary cuôń sách và Bill đã bán Ø dia
hát.
(John past give to Mary a book and Bill past sell Ø a
record)
184. *Tokyo-de raisu-o John-ga tabeta shi, London-de biiru-o
Ø nonda.
(In Tokyo rice John ate and in London beer Ø drank)

Languages can vary as to whether they allow deletion at medial
sites or at rightmost sites. An example of a language that does
not allow deletion of a medial site is Vietnamese: languages that
do not seem to allow either rightperipheral or medial deletion
are Palestinian Arabic and Lebanese Arabic.[53] The following

two examples are from Lebanese Arabic (Sanders and Tai, 1972):

185. John ḍarab il walad wa Bill ḍarab il   bint.
     (John hit   the boy and Bill hit   the girl)
186a.*John ḍarab il walad, wa Bill Ø il bint.
187. John ḍarab il walad, wa Bill rafas   il walad.
     (John hit   the boy   and Bill kicked the boy)
187a.*John ḍarab Ø wa Bill rafas il walad.

In Vietnamese, (188) is ungrammatical, while (189) can only mean that John gave a record to Peter: i.e. the sentence can only be interpreted with a leftperipheral deletion site, and not with a medial deletion site.

188. *John đã đã con chó và Peter Ø con mèo.
     (John past kick the dog and Peter Ø the cat)
189. John ã đu a cho tôi cuoń sách và Peter điã hát.
     (John past give to me a book and Peter a record)

While on the subject of Vietnamese, let us engage in a brief diversion to demonstrate how a preliminary classification of coordinate deletions will assist in describing and accounting for coordination across languages. Coordination in Vietnamese can very readily and straightforwardly be characterised in exactly the same way as in English, German and Dutch, with just the proviso that it does not allow the first constituent to be ignored: in other words, it does not allow medial deletion. It allows both leftperipheral and rightperipheral deletion of either single constituents or sequences of constituents: leftperipheral sites delete forward, and rightperipheral sites delete backwards. Compare:

190. John Ø Ø và   Bill đã   đánh con chó
     (John Ø Ø and Bill past hit   the dog)
191. John đã   dánh Ø và   Bill đã   đá   con chó
     (John past hit   Ø and Bill past kick the dog)
192. John đã bán cuôń sách và Ø đã mua điã hát.
     (John past sell a book   and past buy a record)
193. John đã đu a cuôń sách cho Mary và Ø Ø hoa cho Sue
     (John past give a book to Mary and Ø Ø flowers to Sue)

267

If we take the ungrammatical sentence (184) and move *to Mary* to rightmost position, then it becomes deletable again as a straightforward rightmost site; these facts are exactly parallel to the peripherality facts we have observed for English, Dutch and German:

194. John đã du a cuòn sách Ø va Bill đã bán điã cho Mary.
(John past give a book Ø and Bill past sell a record to Mary)

Statement (B) serves to restrict possible deletions even further: although it will be clear from the examples from Dutch, German and Cherokee above the full parallelism in the order of constituents between the coordinated clauses is not a necessary prerequisite for deletion, deletion targets have to occupy the same type of site in the linear sequence of constituents — sentences like (182) above, which could be multiplied at will, demonstrate this conclusively. Note that it is not so much the formulation of the deletion rule itself that motivates such a constraint, but rather the recovery of deletions: the procedure for 'finding' identical material we have outlined in this chapter will not operate correctly to reinstate identical material if the two occurrences occupy different positions in the linear sequence of constituents. Likewise, the recovery procedure outlined in this chapter can only reinstate deleted material in the 'deficient' clause in the same linear position this material has in the antecedent 'nondeficient' clause. It is possible to delete a (topicalised) leftperipheral site under identity with a (non-topicalised) leftperipheral site, even though these have different grammatical functions, and such deletions will be readily recoverable. But we have already found that it is impossible to delete e.g. and rightperipheral site under identity with a (topi-calised) leftperipheral site: this is what (182) illustrates. It is not restricted to Dutch: German mirrors Dutch in this respect, as will be clear from (195). English shows the same effect: a left-peripheral subject may not be deleted under identity with subject that has moved to post-auxiliary position as a result of subject-aux inversion, as in (196):

195. *Jan geloof ik en Piet vertrouwt Ø.
    *Jan glaube ich und Piet vertraut Ø.
    (Jan believe I and Piet trusts)
    (= I believe Jan, and Piet trusts him)
196. *Never have I seen such a thing, and don't want to, either.

(A) and (B) are restrictions on the linear *position* of deletion
target sites. (C) is quite different in that it states a restriction on
the circumstances under which the same site may either delete
forwards or backwards freely; i.e. on the *direction* of deletion.
Let us explore this a little further. The languages that allow bidirectional deletion in (AD) and (BE) positions (using the position letters from (175)) seem to be quite restricted in number
and geographical area; Tojalabal and a number of other Mayan
languages (see Furbee-Losee, 1976) allow (AD) bidirectional
deletion, while (BE) deletion seems to be restricted to Zapotec
(see Rosenbaum, 1977). Both these types of bidirectional
deletion are restricted to verbs. (CF) bidirectional deletion can
be encountered in quite a few more languages, and is not
restricted only to verbs for all languages: we have already seen
that Dutch, German and Russian allow bidirectional deletion of
verbs in (CF) position. Turkish is another language that allows
bidirectional deletion of verbs, but it is exceptional in that bidirectional deletion is not restricted to verbs: this language,
according to Hankamer (1979), allows bidirectional deletion of
both verbs and objects in rightmost position.[54] He provides the
following examples:

197.   Hasan yumurtayɨ yedi, Ahmet patlɨcanɨ   yedi.
       (Hasan the egg   ate, Ahmet the eggplant ate)
197a. Hasan yumurtayɨ Ø, Ahmet patlɨcanɨ yedi.
197b. Hasan yumurtayɨ yedi, Ahmet patlɨcanɨ Ø.
198.   Mehmet pişirdi yumurtayɨ, Hasan yedi yumurtayɨ.
       (Mehmet cooked   the egg, Hasan ate the egg)
198a. Mehmet pişirdi Ø, Hasan yedi yumurtayɨ.
198b. Mehmet pisirdi yumurtayɨ, Hasan yedi Ø.

Nevertheless, we can conclude that, in bidirectional deletions,
there seems to be a strong preference for the deletions to
involve verbs rather than some other category.[55]
    Let us now look at unidirectional deletion. Here we find that
the parameters along which languages can vary are already

quite restricted as a result of our earlier obervations. There seem to be no languages that allow only backward deletion of positions (A) and (B) in (175); the languages that allow (A) and (B) to be deleted at all allow this only as part of a bidirectional (AD or BE) deletion. There is no variation with respect to position (D): all languages allow deletion of (D). This means that variation in unidirectional deletion is restricted to sites (C,E,F). The possible types of variation that are open to these sites are: whether the site deletes at all in a particular language, and whether there is a restriction on the particular type of constituent that must occur or may not occur at these sites in order for deletion to apply. Japanese has backward (C) deletion, as does English, while Swahili has forward (F) deletion (Vitale, 1981), as does Bolivian Quechua (Pulte, 1971).

199. John-ga raisu-o Ø Bill-ga sushi-o tabeta.
    (John rice Ø Bill sushi ate)
    John ate rice and Bill sushi.
200. ni-li-taka lolipopi ile lakini Halima a-me-kwishe kula Ø.
    (I-pst-want lollypop that but Halima she-per-finish eat)
    I wanted that lollypop but Halima has already eaten it.
201. Juanito rik"un alquta, Tiyucataq uyarin Ø.
    (Juanito sees dog-acc, Tiyuca-and hears Ø)
    Juanito sees and Tiyuca hears the dog.

As we have seen earlier, neither Vietnamese nor Chinese allow (E) deletion, while Dutch, German, Russian, Turkish and English do. Dutch, German and English restrict (E) deletion to sites containing a verb, while Turkish does *not* allow deletion of verbs in that position (Hankamer, 1979).

202. Ahmet patlıcanı pişirdi, Mehmet Ø yedi.
    (Ahmet the eggplant cooked, Mehmet Ø ate)
    Ahmet cooked and Mehmet ate the eggplant.
203. *Ahmet pişirdi patlıcanı, Mehmet Ø yumurtayı.
    (Ahmet cooked the eggplant, Mehment Ø the egg)
    Ahmet cooked the eggplant, and Mehmet the egg.

Basque allows deletion in (E) position, and there is no requirement that (E) should be a verb:

270

204. Jonek txakurra ikusi du   eta Peruk Ø jo du.
     (John the dog   saw 3sg acc. and Peter Ø hit 3sg acc.)

The classification of variation in directionality of deletion
outlined above gives only very few parameters along which
coordinate deletions will vary: first of all, whether they allow
bidirectional deletion, and if so, whether a verb must be deleted
in a rightmost bidirectional site. Secondly, whether a language
allows medial or rightmost deletion, or both, whether a verb
must or may not be deleted in a medial site, and whether a
rightmost site deletes forwards or backwards.

Further statements could be added. It seems, for intance, that
if a language has bidirectional deletion, then it has deletion of
verbs. Again, this statement is correct for the languages
examined, but because of the limited number of languages I
have examined in this book I shall leave the further classification of coordinated structures, and especially the validation
and explanation of this classification for the future. For the
moment, it is sufficient to conclude that of the possible deletion
patterns that could occur across languages, the majority *never*
seems to occur (i.e. deletion outside the accessible sites defined
in Chapter 2, deletion of nonparallel sites, deletion in coordinated sentences which are linearly not immediately adjacent), a
few patterns are very specifically restricted (bidirectional
deletions), and the remaining patterns also vary only along a
very small number of parameters. The patterning of coordinate
deletions across languages presents itself as an interesting area
for further investigation.

3.6 CONCLUSION

In this chapter, I have addressed four questions of major interest
within the deletion approach: I have discussed the notion of
identity required for coordinate deletion, whether coordinate
deletion leaves nonlexical remnants, how deletions should be
recovered, and what the place of coordinate deletions is in
grammar.

I have demonstrated that the notion of identity we require for
coordinate deletions is a relative one — different languages may
employ slightly different definitions of 'identical', although
superficial morphological nondistinctness, with a few notable

271

THE NOTIONS AND THEIR CONSEQUENCES

exceptions (verbal number agreement), plays a major role in the majority of cases. From this it follows that we should not see identity at some level of analysis as a prerequisite for deletion, but that we should attempt to discover when distinctness will block deletion. This has brought into focus an interesting new range of facts, namely the circumstances under which superficially nondistinct material in coordinated structures is obligatorily construed as distinct, usually in the sense of 'disjoint in reference'.

I have also examined what *deletion* means — and I have come to the conclusion that there is no *a priori* reason to deviate from the simplest possible interpretation of the word 'deletion': deletion means that the deleted material disappears altogether, without leaving nonlexical traces. Nor does deletion impose a specific structure on its remnants. The one case (VPD) in one language (English), which could perhaps be argued to require a description as a case of a base-generated pro-form, has been examined in some detail, and we have found no advantages and a number of disadvantages to such an approach.

Thirdly, I have demonstrated that the recovery of the sometimes quite complex deletions effected by the rule formulated in Chapter 2 is a trivially simple matter. This point, which has in general been neglected in the literature, considerably strengthens the non-configurational deletion approach: elliptical coordinated constructions do not require complex special rules of recovery or interpretation, but only a straightforward step-by-step reversal of the deletion.

Lastly, I have defined a place of the coordinate deletion rule in the grammar: it is a late rule, and one which requires no access to levels of structure beyond linear, left-to-right order of constituents. I have also observed that the possible variation in coordinate deletions across languages is quite limited, and suggested a way in which we might begin to account for these limitations. The detailed formulation of the coordinate deletion rule for English, Dutch and German, and its recovery, reflect these limitations on variation quite clearly.

If one adds up the discussion in the three chapters of this book, the conclusion is the following: a thorough evaluation of the research done on the syntax of coordinated structures in the last 20 or so years has shown that a deletion account is clearly to be preferred over other approaches. It is possible to formulate a unified, simple and quite straightforward coordinate deletion rule, which deals elegantly with old problems and new observations alike. This rule relies on a small number of well-defined concepts, is quite restricted in its application, has a specific place in the grammar, and is readily recoverable.

NOTES

1. This remark does not mean that I consider this point to be of minor importance — to determine the precise form of the theory of grammar is one of the main goals of linguistics. There are, however, far too many accounts available which rashly purport to 'determine the nature of grammar or grammatical representation', in an ill-argued and cavalier way, which lacks empirical motivation (for an example, see Goodall, 1984, discussed in this chapter). I will not add to their number by making unwarranted claims about the consequences for the theory of grammar of the account of coordinate deletion: there is, however, a need for a rule of coordinate deletion in generative grammar, and one or two things need to be said about the place that this rule will occupy in such a grammar.

2. The term 'generative grammar' is sometimes incorrectly taken to refer exclusively to particular trends within versions of the theory of grammar associated with the important work of Noam Chomsky and his immediate followers (for instance the Government-Binding theory; see Chomsky, 1981). I use the term to refer to generative grammar in the sense of Chomsky (1986: 3), where 'generative' means nothing more or less than 'explicit'.

3. This metaphor for establishing identity was suggested to me by Pieter Seuren (personal communication); he himself uses a slightly more formalised version in his rule of Conjunct Mapping (see e.g. Seuren, 1985). It glosses over a number of details, but the metaphor is too attractive not to use it.

4. For very a clear and attractive discussion of the separation between dominance and precedence relationships, see Gazdar *et al.*, (1985), chapter III.

5. Note how 'gapped' sentences pose a further special problem for the three-dimensional approach, because without special provisions, the linearisation principle outlined here will order both subjects before the verb, and both objects after the verb, as in:

John and Bill kissed Mary and Sue.

for which Goodall, incidentally, surmises an (unlikely and unnatural) *respectively*-reading. In order to get 'gapped' structures, he has to treat the remnant subject + object as one unit (1984: 105), which is a clearly undesirably *ad hoc* analysis, since there is no other rule than Gapping which requires this sort of treatment.

6. For the convenience of the reader, the pages in a book are

(usually) bound in sequential order. It is, however, not at all impossible to read a book of which the pages are bound in random order, provided that the numbering of the pages determines a unique order for reading. The extreme importance of order is not at all recognised by Goodall; he fails to observe that it is the indexing of elements rather than his linearisation principle that is responsible for the correct sequencing outcome of 'superimposed' representations of coordination. What he does recognise, however, in a footnote to the linearisation principle, is that linear precedence will often determine temporal precedence: (a) is clearly different in what it conveys from (b):

(a) She died, and we buried her.
(b) We buried her, and she died.

To account for this fact, he suggests assuming that the ordering of component sentences in a union of phrase markers is present in all levels of the grammar (1984: 125) — which commits him to the impossible situation in which representations are, at the same time and at the same level of representation, both superimposed and therefore linearly unordered, and linearly ordered.

7. As Furbee points out, /ti'/ is a bit problematic in that the feature specification for this eating verb is very difficult to give. This difficulty is not relevant to our argument.

8. Note how these facts cast doubt on the usefulness of the unordered (ID/LP) GPSG-type solution for coordination outlined in Gazdar, *et al.* (1985) (see also Chapter 1). Following Gazdar (1981), this might rely on unordered coordination of S-O sequences with a 'raised' verb (which somehow has to be made to appear on the left, which is not a regular instance of coordination in GPSG anyway), but it would then also somehow have to select the right verb to go with all these different foodstuffs. The verb that has to be selected is the one that subcategorises for the object of the *first* S-O in the left-to-right sequence, and that again would mean that a sequence has to be linearised before the feature specification of the verb can be derived.

9. Note that syntactic configuration could play a role in the sense that the coordinate deletion rule, if construed in a strict sense will apply only to coordinated sentences. In a configuration like:

$$[...... [------]]_S]_S \text{ CONJ } [....... [------]]_S]_S$$

deletion of e.g. identical verbs will not apply to the 'innermost' Ss, since they are, strictly speaking, not coordinated; only the matrix Ss are: this can be construed as a straightforward A-over-A violation, or, in the sense of Koster (1978), as a Bounding violation. I know of no cases, however, where we clearly need to appeal to this type of structure: the constraint on peripherality of deletion sites will successfully rule out e.g. Gapping into subordinate clauses which are not directly coordinated, while allowing RNR out of subordinate clauses. Bernard Comrie (p.c.)

has furthermore pointed out to me that sentences like (a) are definitely odd, if not ungrammatical:

(a) ?? Yesterday I went for a walk and was beautiful.

Here one might be tempted to argue that it is the fact that *yesterday* fulfils different functions in the antecedent and the subsequent S that is responsible for this oddity. It is not clear, however, that we should seek a syntactic solution for these cases: (b), in which deletion has not applied, is not obviously better than (a):

(b) Yesterday I went for a walk and yesterday was a beautiful day.

Observe furthermore that this sentence improves considerably, both in the reduced and in the unreduced versions, if we reverse the order of the two clauses:

(c) Yesterday was a beautiful day and yesterday I went for a walk.
(d) Yesterday was a beautiful day and I went for a walk.

Although I offer no account for this problem, it seems clear that a solution should not be sought in the rules and constraints in this book. In this connection, see also Saiki (1985) for some observations about Japanese.

10. For a brief expository discussion of λ-expression, see e.g. McCawley (1981), chapter 13.

11. Dutch and German will most certainly have ambiguity here, but it is a different type of ambiguity from the one encountered in English — given that neither language has VPD or the do-support concomitant on VPD, there will be ambiguity between the subject reading and the object reading for *Piet* in a sentence like:

Jan zei   dat ze hem geslagen had, en Piet ook.
Jan sagte, dass sie ihn geschlagen hatte, und Piet auch.
(Jan said   that she him hit   had, and Piet too)

For a discussion of this type of ambiguity, see Chapter 2.

12. The original intent of Partee (1970) was an explicitly negative one, namely to disprove the thesis (originally due to Katz and Postal, 1964) that some level of deep structure determines semantic interpretation, and so to provide a counterargument to the Generative Semantics movement, which sought to do away with the distinction between semantic representations and deep structure, and to muster support for Interpretive Semantics, where surface structure plays a crucial role in determining semantic interpretation. Partee's paper does not provide any detailed surface structure analaysis of the problems discussed, and it is therefore very interesting and informative to read Lakoff's (1970) reply to Partee.

13. For a discussion of these issues, see Chapter 1. It is interesting to see that neither Partee, nor McCawley (1981: 401), nor Seuren (1985:

164), who also discusses problems of this type, makes any reference to where items like *both* and *either* are to come from: they are absent from the semantic representations of the coordinations which these authors provide. I shall follow their example and also assume that they can be inserted under the appropriate circumstances without committing myself to what exactly these circumstances are.

14. In later versions of GPSG (see e.g. Gazdar *et al.*, 1985) it is possible to circumvent this requirement by allowing the PS-rules to conjoin underspecified categories; for further discussion, see Chapter 1.

15. Seuren's account of the distribution of *both* and *either* is dependent on the difference in structure between representations where the coordinating conjunction is the highest scope-bearing predicate, and those representations where it is not. This ignores the fact that there are certain distributional differences between *both* and *either* which cannot be so accounted for; *either* can take up sentence-initial position in a coordination of full Ss, which *both* cannot do:

Either you shut up or I'll see to it that you get into a lot of trouble.
∗Both you kept on talking and you are in a lot of trouble.

The distribution of such items as *both* and *either* are an interesting question for which no satisfactory answer has yet been given. For an attempt, see Neijt (1979), chapter I.

16. Siegel's squib is intended to discredit a deletion-based approach to Gapping. Although it contains some interesting observations, the data presented are extremely elusive, and sometimes doubtful in places. Furthermore, the deletion approach to Gapping outlined there is somewhat disingenious: for this reason, I shall not discuss the squib here. One of the main questions it leaves unanswered is why wide-scope interpretation of negation should be possible for the examples she cites in which deletion has taken place, but not in the cases where no deletion has applied:

Ward can't eat caviar, and Sue can't eat beans.
Ward can't eat caviar and Sue beans.

Quite apart from this, the two above sentences are not equivalent in meaning in the first place.

17. Note that the 'full' version of the sentence will also be interpreted as at least referring to different *you's*. This is accounted for by the constraint against total nondistinctness observed in section 2.2.1 in Chapter 2.

18. It should be noted that this argument does not necessarily discredit the 'alphabetical variant' approach to identity entirely. It would be easy enough to save such an approach by construing the VPs in question as expressing two clearly distinct properties: one of kicking one ball, and another, quite different property, of kicking some other ball. The VPs in question would then no longer be alphabetical variants, and deletion would therefore be blocked.

19. Most of the problems Napoli cities for Sag are related to the notion of alphabetical variant: a notion which we have demonstrated to

be too specific and too strong as a condition on recoverability. Many of these problems do not arise if we assume the approach advocated in the first section of this chapter. Also, a lot of Sag's observations are rather subtle and fail to generalise. In many of Sag's examples, using a different conjunction (e.g. *whenever* instead of *when*) or a different tense (present vs. simple past), which should not affect the interpretation of alphabetically variant VPs, actually does affect them. Sag's main theory-internal problem, namely that a deletion rule which operates at the level of Phonological Form has to be recoverable at the level of Logical Form, which the 'T-Model' of grammar advocated in e.g. Chomsky (1981) does not allow, will not arise either in the approach in this book or in Napoli's approach. See also the discussion of recoverability later on in this chapter: given that deletion applies to PF, it must be recoverable at PF.

20. To contrast the anaphoric properties of pro-VPs and pronouns would take us too far afield here; Napoli also leaves this problem to future research. Suffice it to say that there are a number of obvious differences between pro-VPs and pronouns, and one of the tasks of the pro-VP approach will be to account for these differences in anaphoric properties. In the deletion account, this problem does not arise: here we have to account for the similarities and differences between the various deletion rules.

21. I have marked this sentence with (?*) because for many native speakers, it is acceptable and will not receive either a star or a question mark. For speakers of this dialect, the finite auxiliary is completely optional, which creates an additional interesting problem for the pro-VP account; not only will a pro-VP have to be base-generated, but also an empty category VP. Note also that Napoli's account needs even more additions in this area: if VPD is 'the same rule' in both subordinate clauses and coordinate clauses, we have no explanation why AUX is not obligatory for a number of speakers in coordinate clauses, but is absolutely obligatory in non-coordinate claues:

(a) *I will go if you Ø.

22. I take the defining characteristic of VPD to be that there is deletion of a VP which leaves behind a finite auxiliary. I know of no language other than English that allows this process.

23. For some dialects of English, this rule will be optional (see also note 21).

24. See e.g. the collection of papers edited by Meyer-Hermann and Rieser (1985). Most work on ellipsis focuses on the notion of completeness/incompleteness: it is precisely this notion which defines concepts like ellipsis and deletion. Note also that the possibility of VPD between immediately adjacent Ss, even if the two sentences are pronounced by different speakers, is sometimes construed, like the (occasional and restricted) possibility of Gapping across sentences as evidence that VPD and Gapping are 'discourse rules' and therefore not the concern of sentence grammar. However, the fact that a process can, under very special circumstances, occur across immediately adjacent sentences (i.e. *can*

occur in discourse), is no evidence whatsoever that this process is of relevance only to some sort of non-specified 'discourse grammar'.

25. Napoli (1985: 309 ff.) observes some similarities between VPD and cases in which the specifier of the head of the major category occurs without the head and can be construed as having pro-form status. However, these cases could also be construed as deletion, and true pronouns are absent from the discussion.

26. Another obvious candidate is the rule that reinstates the tense-carrying AUX after deletion in (English) cases of VPD. As can be seen from Chapter 2, this rule does not employ *structural* information.

27. That is, those cases where a predicate subcategorises for a plural or coordinated subject (e.g. *meet, be a nice pair*); I have discussed these in the previous two chapters under the heading of 'symmetrical predicates'.

28. Note how agreement provides us with yet another argument against approaches to coordination which look for generalisations in rule schemata of the sort:

$$X ======> \text{conj. } X_n$$

This type of rule provides no account for the fact that *and* is the only coordinating conjunction which can force agreement between the subject head nouns which it coordinates and the verb. *Or* cannot force agreement:

Beer and wine don't help when you've got the blues.
Beer or wine doesn't help when you've got the blues.

Given that *but* cannot coordinate heads of NPs, and that *for* can only coordinate *S*s, they will never give rise to subject-verb agreement. Conjunctions behave differently also with respect to agreement and therefore should not be lumped together under one agreement rule.

29. Rather obviously, we still need the notion 'subject' to state subject-verb agreement, just as we need the notion 'verb', and 'subject' is a notion that is quite frequently (though not necessarily) structurally defined. If one wants to be puritanical about this rule and its failure to refer to structure, therefore, one would be committed to a non-structural definition of subject.

30. In GPSG, such categories will not present a problem: they would simply be S/V; 'S with a V-hole in it'. For an approach which relies on deletion and subsequent restructuring, however, it is an additional theoretical construct.

31. Corbett's (1983) bibliography contains a number of original works from which his example sentences have been taken; I refer here only to the data in Corbett's article.

32. Corbett's (1983) paper is primarily concerned with resolution of agreement conflicts between conjuncts, and he makes it abundantly clear that there there is no simple syntactic solution for agreement. What this means for the remark quoted from Chomsky (1981) in this context is that if AGR is coindexed with the subject (or subjects) of the

S, then resolution of the features carried over from the subject(s) will have to take place within AGR.

33. For one thing, I have referred only to subject-verb agreement. Chomsky (1981: 229, fn. 61) assumes that other agreement of e.g. adjectives and determiners, can be determined by percolation of features from NP, AP and VP (where VP absorbs the features from INFL). This seems essentially correct, and is not incompatible with the present non-structural approach to coordination: person, gender and number features on the subjects are resolved in AGR, and then percolated to the appropriate place.

34. I am fully aware of the 20 or so years of controversy that surrounds these few remarks: for a fairly detailed, though biased, outline, see Newmeyer (1980). Note that for the discussion here, it does not matter whether we use the Generative Semantics term 'Semantic Representation', or its closest Government-Binding equivalent 'Logical Form'; both need rules to mediate between the level of representation of meaning (or the level of representation from which the representation of meaning is 'read off'). Nor does the nature of the rules that mediate between the level matter, or indeed the directionality of mapping between the levels: as long as there are the two distinct levels of meaning representation (which we have called SR, and) the level at which such sentences are produced (which we have called SS), and as long as there are deletion rules, the argument will go through.

35. This amounts no more than saying that there is a level of representation at which the grammar differentiates between those sentences that are sentences of English, and those that are not. The argument outlined here does not hinge on whether this level is unitary or not, and is not sensitive to the manner in which the grammar assigns and checks representations. Recall that Williams assumes that factorisation, deletion and ROD apply to deep structure (Williams, 1978: 42); a position I have rejected in Chapter 1, section 1.3.6.

36. Williams, like Goodall (1984) needs a linearisation rule for the conjuncts written 'on top of' each other. His representation, and the subsequent linearisation rule, make covert reference to linear order in the same way that Goodall does; see Williams, 1978: 42.

37. As a matter of fact it is a trivial exercise to translate 'left and right' into 'left'; an exercise which I shall not engage in here.

38. I refer to what we have called 'symmetrical predicates' in earlier discussion: as soon as it becomes clear that the predicate of a coordinated subject is a symmetrical predicate like 'be similar', 'be a nice couple' etc. the recovery procedure should be aborted. The recovery procedure can also be aborted if the coordinating conjunction is *for*, since no deletion will have taken place in that case. Needless to say, this assumption relies crucially on the grammar making available the notion 'well-formed sentence of L' to the coordination rule: this rule needs the notion both for deletion, and for recovery of deletion.

39. This will work for languages which coordinate by means of coordinating conjunctions in between the conjuncts. Some languages will require some sort of special provision, since they do not place the coordinating conjunction between the conjunct, but, for instance after

the first constituent of the second S (Quechua; see e.g. Pulte, 1971).

40. Note that the (a) versions are unacceptable since they are systematic violations of the PDC. Given that the recovery rules are written not to respect the PDC, and that the PDC is formulated as a constraint on the proper operation on *deletion*, this is hardly surprising. Note also, that if deletion has been partial, and the PDC has been obeyed, the deletions are recoverable in the regular fashion outlined here.

41. Under the assumption, of course, that the form of *do* which was inserted after the application of VP-deletion is eliminated.

42. Note that here there will be a number of unsuccessful recoveries, since the application of any one recovery rule will not result in a well-formed S in these cases of discontinuous deletion. Recovery will be readily achieved, though, if we iterate not the application of one rule, but single applications of two rules. Two applications of (133) and one application of (134b) will achieve the right result. Note that we still do not have to order the recovery rules: If we apply (134b) once, and (133) once, and then (134b) once again, recovery will not succeed and will be filtered out. If we start with (133), then (134b), and then (133) again, recovery will succeed.

43. The only work that I am aware of that explicitly assumes otherwise is Ross (1970), who claims that Gapping is an 'anywhere' rule, i.e. a rule that can apply anywhere in the derivation of a sentence. This must clearly be wrong: for counterarguments, see e.g. Hankamer (1979).

44. Chinese does allow the equivalent of 'Right-node Raising', but only after it has been Right-dislocated. Thus, while 'normal' RNR is impossible, we do get (b):

(b) Wo dǎle ta Ø, ni tǐle ta, nèige nánháizi.
     (I hit him Ø, you kicked him, that boy)

Something similar to this process, which is intuitively somewhat odd (why have right-dislocation if the constituent being dislocated is already rightmost anyway?) also occurs in Modern Greek (Koutsoudas, 1971: 343), where RNR of an object is impossible unless there is a dependent pre-verbal object pronoun for both objects. Thus, while (c) is impossible, (d) is grammatical:

(c) *To koritsi iðe Ø ke to peði xitipise tin γata.
     (the girl saw Ø and the boy hit the cat)
(d) To koritsi tin iðe Ø ke to peði tin xitipise tin γata.
     (The girl it saw Ø and the boy it hit the cat)

45. The fact that the most fruitful approach to the CSC relies so heavily on tree-structure, while deletion refers only to left-to-right constituent order, is a further strong suggestion that the CSC is part of a general constraint on movement rather than a specific constraint of coordination: the CSC and deletion/recovery are essentially different.

46. For the motivation of this separation, which is largely internal to Pesetsky's argument, see Pesetsky, 1982: 443 ff. In the approach in this

book, which will relate non-S coordinations to S-coordinations, such illicit movement will most profitably be subsumed under Subjacency, since in a structure like:

Bill saw Mary and Bill saw *wh*.

which underlies (116), *wh* will have to cross two S-boundaries:

*Who$_1$ did Bill see Mary and Bill see e_1?

Note also that if *wh* crosses one boundary, to COMP of S_2, the result is not ungrammatical, although it may be somewhat odd to follow a statement with a question which could answer the statement:

?Bill saw Mary and who did Bill see?

That this is not a violation of a movement constraint will be clear from:

You are in search of a reliable second-hand car and what do you do? You go to Honest Joe to get the best deal in town.

For the rest Pesetsky's account of the CSC, although based on a more PS-rule oriented account, can be taken over into the deletion account without major adaptations.

47. There are two extensions that may cause problems. The first is the elimination of 'subject-object asymmetries', first discussed in Williams (1978), and the second is with the path running from [TNS] in COMP to INFL. A full discussion of these problems and Pesetsky's treatment would take us too far afield, but he makes the following prediction with respect to subject-object asymmetries (1982: 453 ff.): if ATB WH-movement yields a gap in the highest subject position of one conjunct, and a gap lower than VP in the other conjunct, the result must be ungrammatical, since here the paths involved in the movement will overlap but neither path will include the other, in Pesetsky's analysis. Yet it is not too difficult to find cases where this is precisely what has happened, but the result is well-formed:

(A) Mr. McPresident, who$_1$ e_1 hates travelling and several people have tried to kill e_1 during his travels, still travels a lot.
(B) John, who$_1$ e_1 hated his boss and several people have seen e_1 repeatedly at the scene of the crime is one of the prime suspects.

The second problem concerns Pesetsky's (1982: 459ff.) prediction that tensed Ss cannot be conjoined with infinitival Ss because there will be a path between [TNS] and COMP in a tensed S, but not between [TNS] and COMP in a non-tensed S. But here again, examples can be found where this prediction is too strict:

(C) I'm wondering which books$_1$ to buy e_1, or rather you should buy e_1, because I want to read them and I have no money.

I shall merely list these observations for future reference and not attempt an alternative formulation to the PCC here. For a further interesting set of primarily semantic observations on the CSC, see Goldsmith (1985).

48. Pesetsky (1982) gives an outline of how the approach he outlines might be extended to Gapping. As I have observed earlier, however, his is a very tentative and preliminary proposal, and he himself notes a few quite forbidding problems. For these reasons, I have not included a discussion of his Gapping proposal.

49. The only attempt at typological characterisation of coordinate deletions that employs a fair selection of languages that I am aware of is Koutsoudas (1971), who examines some thirty-odd languages. Unfortunately, he lists very little of his data, his observations seem just straightforwardly incorrect in some cases, and are overly restricted in other cases. For instance, he lists Chinese as not allowing object deletion, something which is disconfirmed by Sanders and Tai's (1972) observations, and he lists Mam as not allowing verb deletions, which is disconfirmed by Furbee-Losee (1976: 234). He lists Swahili as not allowing object deletions, which is disconfirmed by Vitale (1981: 61-2). He also lists German as an SVO language that allows verb deletion and object deletion. As will be clear from the discussion in Chapter 2, there is just as good a case to be made for calling German an SOV language which does *not* allow object deletion: the picture is grossly oversimplified by Koutsoudas' classification. Furthermore, since he is only concerned with forward verb deletions and object deletions, which is a highly restricted class, the approach loses most, if not all, of its value. Furthermore, if one examines the descriptive grammars of less well-known and well-described languages for information on coordination, one tends to find little, and even less on what we now know as 'Gapping' and 'Right-node Raising' constructions, although all languages seem to have rules of coordination and deletion.

50. To my knowledge, the first to observe that parallelism is not a requirement for German is Walter (1975).

51. Observe the correlation with our observations in Chapter 2: for an adequate account of the coordinate deletion facts in English, Dutch and German alike we found that it was necessary to be able to conjoin sentences (both because full sentences do appear in coordinations, and because they are the basis for most non-S coordinations, and NPs for those cases of coordinated NPs which occur with so-called 'symmetrical predicates'. A crucial case may well be found in those languages in which it is not obvious that there is a process of coordination that is distinct from subordination, e.g. languages which link sentences by means different from subordination and cocordination, such as switch-reference.

52. I am indebted to Anne and Vinh Vuong for the examples from Vietnamese.

53. Note that here the approach we have chosen tends partly to obscure one point; there may be languages (Lebanese Arabic being a case in point) that do not allow rightmost deletion but do allow coordinated NPs in subject position, which we claim can be derived from sentence coordination through rightmost deletion. This creates an undesir-

THE NOTIONS AND THEIR CONSEQUENCES

able asymmetry. The account I have given for Dutch, German and English coordination assumed a minimal role for NP-coordination, and relied heavily on S-coordination and deletion from S-coordinations. This choice was partly a formal one, and it will not be too difficult to rephrase it for e.g. Lebanese Arabic in such a way that there is a greater role for NP-coordination, and less reliance on deletion from SD-coordination without detracting from any of the essential insights of Chapter 2. Dutch, German and English, however, do not provide the crucial date for a conclusive decision either way. There is a clear possibility that detailed examination of other languages may also necessitate an adjustment of this balance between S-coordination and NP-coordination. There is, however, no evidence that coordination of categories other than S and NP is necessary for an adequate account of coordination across languages.

54. I am somewhat hesitant about Turkish; while Hankamer (1979) claims that it allows SOV & SO, SVO & SV, SO & SOV, SV & SVO, and SOV & SO, Koutsoudas (1971) lists two dialects of Turkish: one that does not allow either object deletion or verb deletion, and one that allows both. Although there is reason to doubt Koutsoudas' classification of facts such remarks lead me to suspect that there may indeed well be significant dialectal differences for deletion in Turkish.

55. Recall that for the analysis of Dutch and German coordinate deletions, it was not necessary to stipulate that rightmost sites, if they contain a verb, allow 'bidirectional' deletion: the fact that bidirectional deletion of S-final verbs is allowed in Dutch and German followed from our analysis. More detailed analysis of bidirectional deletions may show that bidirectionality for deletion sites need never be stipulated for any individual language.

References

Aoun, J., Hornstein, N., Lightfoot, D. and Weinberg, A. (1986) *Two types of Locality*, Ms., University of Maryland

Austin, P. (1981) *A Grammar of Diyari, South Australia*, Cambridge: Cambridge University Press

Bierwisch, M. and Heidolph, K. (eds) (1970) *Progress in Linguistics*, The Hague, Mouton

Bouton, L. (1970) 'Antecedent-contained pro-forms', in *Papers from the Sixth Regional Meeting of the Chicago Linguistic Society*, Chicago, Ill.: Chicago Linguistic Society

Browne, W. (1974) 'On the Problem of Enclitic Placement in Serbo-Croatian' in R.D. Brecht and C.D. Chvany (eds): *Slavic Transformational Syntax*, Ann Arbor: University of Michigan

Chomsky, N.A. (1957) *Syntactic Structures*, The Hague: Mouton

——(1964) *Current Issues in Linguistic Theory*, The Hague: Mouton

——(1965) *Aspects of the Theory of Syntax*, Cambridge, Mass.: MIT Press

——(1973) 'Conditions on Transformations', in S. Anderson and P. Kiparsky (eds), *A Festschrift for Morris Halle*, New York: Holt, Rinehart & Winston

——(1981) *Lectures on Government & Binding*, Dordrecht: Foris Publications

——(1982) *Some Concepts and Consequences of the Theory of Government and Binding*, Cambridge, Mass.: MIT Press

——(1986) *Knowledge of Language: Its Nature, Origin and Use*, New York: Praeger

Comrie, B.S. (1981) *Language Universals and Linguistic Typology*, Oxford: Basil Blackwell

——(1984) 'Form and Function in Explaining Language Universals', in B. Butterworth, C. Comrie and O. Dahl (eds), *Explanations for Language Universals*, Berlin: Mouton

——(1986a) 'Conditionals: A Typology', in E. Closs Traugott, A. Ter Meulen, J. Snitzer Reilly and Ch. A. Ferguson (eds), *On Conditionals*, Cambridge: Cambridge University Press

——(1986b) 'Review of Finer (1985)', *Linguistics*, vol. 24, pp. 439-46

Corbett, S. (1983) 'Resolution Rules: Agreement in Person, Number and Gender' in G. Gazdar, E. Klein and G. Pullum, *Order, Concord and Constituency*, Dordrecht: Foris Publications

Creider, C.A. (1981) 'Thematisation in Luo', in P. Werth (ed.), *Conversation and Discourse*, New York: St Martin's Press

Curme, G. (1931) *A Grammar of English: Syntax*, Boston: D.C. Heath & Company

Dik, S. (1968) *Coordination: Its Implications for the Theory of General Linguistics*, Amsterdam: North-Holland Publishing Company

——(1980)'Seventeen Sentences: Basic Principles and Application of Functional Grammar', in E.A. Moravcsik and J. Wirth (eds), *Syntax and Semantics, vol. XIII: Current Approaches to Syntax*

Dixon, R.M.W. (1972) *The Dyirbal Language of North Queensland,* Cambridge: Cambridge University Press

——(1979) 'Ergativity', *Language,* vol. 55, pp. 59-139

Dougherty, R.C. (1970) 'A Grammar of Coordinate Conjoined Structures, pt. I', *Language,* vol. 46, pp. 850-98

——(1971) 'A Grammar of Coordinate Conjoined Structures, pt. II', *Language,* vol. 47, pp. 278-339

Eisenberg, P. (1973) 'A Note on Identity of Constituents', *Linguistic Inquiry,* vol. 4, pp. 417-20

Evers, A. (1975) *The Transformational Cycle in Dutch and German,* Doctoral Dissertation, University of Utrecht

Finer, D.L. (1985) *The Formal Syntax of Switch-reference,* New York: Garland

Furbee, L. (1974) 'Identity in Gapping and the Lexicalisation of Verbs', *Linguistic Inquiry,* vol. 5, pp. 299-304

Furbee-Losee, L. (1976) *The Correct Language: Tojalabal,* New York: Garland Press

Gazdar, G. (1981) 'Unbounded Dependencies and Coordinated Structure', *Linguistic Inquiry,* vol. 12, pp. 155-82

——Pullum, G., Sag, I. and Wasow, T. (1982) 'Coordination and Transformational Grammar', *Linguistic Inquiry,* vol. 13, pp. 663-76

——Klein, E., Fullum, G. and Sag, I. (1985) *Generalised Phrase Structure Grammar,* Oxford: Basil Blackwell

Gleitman, L.R. (1965) 'Coordinating Conjunctions in English', *Language,* vol. 41, pp. 260-93

Givón, T. (1979) *On Understanding Grammar,* New York: Academic Press

Goldsmith, J. (1985) 'A Principled Exception to the Coordinate Structure Constraint', in *Papers from the First Regional Meeting of the Chicago Linguistic Society,* Chicago, Ill.: Chicago Linguistic Society

Goodall, G. (1983) 'A Three-Dimensional Analysis of Coordination', in *Papers from the 19th Regional Meeting of the Chicago Linguistic Society,* Chicago, Ill.: Chicago Linguistic Society

——(1984)*Parallel Structures in Syntax,* Doctoral Dissertation, University of California at San Diego.

Grice, H.P. (1975) 'Logic and conversation', in P. Cole and J.L. Morgan (eds), *Syntax and Semantics, vol. III: Speech Acts*

Halliday, M.A.K. (1967) 'Notes on Transitivity and Theme in English, II', *Journal of Linguistics,* vol. 3, pp. 199-244

Hankamer, J. (1972) 'On the Non-existence of Mirror-Image Rules in Syntax', in J.P. Kimball (ed.), *Syntax and Semantics, vol. I,* New York: Seminar Press

——(1973) 'Unacceptable Ambiguity' *Linguistic Inquiry,* vol. 4, pp. 17-68

—— (1979) *'Constraints on Deletion in Syntax,* New York: Garland Press

Harries, H. (1973) 'Coordination Reduction', *Stanford University Working Papers on Language Universals,* no. 11

Hermann, E. (1985) 'Zur Verbal (Phrasen) Ellipse im Modernen Russischen', in Meyer-Hermann and Rieser (eds), *Ellipsen und*

285

Fragmentarische Ausdrücke, Tübingen: Max Niemeyer

Hoeksema, J. (1983) 'Plurality and Conjunction', in A. ter Meulen (ed.), *Studies in Modeltheoretic Semantics*, Dordrecht: Foris Publications

Hornstein, N. and Lightfoot, D. (eds) (1981) *Explanation in Linguistics*, London: Longmans

Huang, C-T. James (1984) 'On the Distribution and Reference of Empty Pronouns', *Linguistic Inquiry*, vol. 15, pp. 531-47

Hudson, R.A. (1976) 'Conjunction Reduction, Gapping, and Right-node Raising' *Language*, vol. 52, pp. 535-62

——(1982) 'Incomplete Conjuncts', *Linguistic Inquiry*, vol. 13, pp. 547-50

Jackendoff, R.S. (1972) 'Gapping and Related Rules', *Linguistic Inquiry*, vol. 2, pp. 21-35

——(1977) *X̄-bar Syntax: A Study of Phrase Structure*, Cambridge, Mass.: MIT Press

——(1983) *Semantics and Cognition*, Cambridge, Mass.: MIT Press

Katz, J.J. and Postal, P.M. (1964) *An Integrated Theory of Linguistic Descriptions*, Cambridge, Mass.: MIT Press

Keenan, E. and Faltz, L. (1985) *Boolean Semantics for Natural Language*, Dordrecht: Reidel

Kempson, R.M. (1977) *Semantic Theory*, Cambridge: Cambridge University Press

——and Cormack, A. (1981) 'Ambiguity and Quantification', *Linguistics and Philosophy*, vol. 4, pp. 259-309

Kooij, J. (1983) 'Review of Neijt (1979)', *Language*, vol. 59, pp. 196-201

Koster, J. (1978) *Locality Principles in Syntax*, Dordrecht: Foris Publications

Koutsoudas, A. (1971) 'Gapping, Conjunction Reduction, and Identity Deletion', *Foundations of Language*, vol. 7, pp. 337, 386

Kuno, S. (1976) 'Gapping: A Functional Analysis', *Linguistic Inquiry*, vol. 7, pp. 300-18

Ladusaw, William A. (1980) 'Affective *or*, Factive verbs, and Negative Polarity Items', in Papers from the 16th Regional Meeting of the Chicago Linguistic Society, Chicago, Ill.: Chicago Linguistic Society

Lakoff, G. (1970) 'Repartee', *Foundations of Language*, vol. 6, pp. 389-421

——and Peters, S. (1969) 'Phrasal Conjunction and Symmetric Predicates', in D. Reibel and S. Schane (eds), *Modern Studies in English*, Englewood Cliffs: Prentice Hall

Lakoff, R. (1971) 'If's, And's and But's about Conjunction', in C.J. Fillmore and D.T. Langendoen, *Studies in Linguistic Semantics*, New York: Holt, Rinehart & Winston

Lang, E. (1984) *The Semantics of Coordination*, Amsterdam: John Benjamins

Langendoen, D.T. (1975) 'Acceptable Conclusions from Unacceptable Ambiguity', in D. Cohen and J. Wirth (eds), *Testing Linguistic Hypotheses*, Washington: Hemisphere

Levin, N.S. (1978) 'Some Identity-of-sense Deletions Puzzle Me. Do They You?' in *Papers from the 14th Regional Meeting of the*

Chicago Linguistic Society, Chicago, Ill: Chicago Linguistic Society, pp. 229-40

——(1979) *Main-verb Ellipsis in Spoken English,* Doctoral Dissertation, Ohio State University

Levine, R.D. (1984) 'Right-node (non) Raising', *Linguistic Inquiry,* vol. 16, pp. 492-7

Li, Ch.N. and Thompson, S.A. (1978) 'An Exploration of Mandarin Chinese', in W.P. Lehmann (ed.), *Syntactic Typology* Hassocks, Sussex: Harvester Press

Lightfoot, D. (1982) *The Language Lottery,* Cambridge, Mass.: MIT Press

Lincicome, D.V.C. (1974) 'Systematically Ignored Differences and the Identity of Propositions', *Foundations of Language,* vol. 12, pp. 73-101

Maling, J.M. (1972) 'On: Gapping and the Order of Constituents', *Linguistic Inquiry,* vol. 3, pp. 101-8

Matthews, P.H. (1969) 'Review of S.C. Dik, *Coordination',* *Lingua,* vol. 23, pp. 349-71

McCawley, J.D. (1968) 'The Role of Semantics in a Grammar', in E. Bach and R.T. Harms: *Universals in Linguistic Theory,* New York: Holt, Reinhart & Winston

——(1981) *Everything that Linguists have Always Wanted to Know About Logic (But were Ashamed to Ask)* Oxford: Basil Blackwell

——(1982) 'Parentheticals and Discontinuous Constituent Structure' *Linguistic Inquiry,* vol. 13, pp. 91-106

Meyer-Hermann, R. and Rieser, H. (eds) (1985) *Ellipsen und Fragmentarische Ausdrücke,* Tübingen: Max Niemeyer Verlag

Napoli, D.J. (1985) 'Verb Phrase Deletion in English: A Base-generated Analysis', *Journal of Linguistics,* vol. 21, pp. 281-319

Neijt, A.H. (1979) *Gapping: A Contribution to Sentence Grammar,* Dordrecht: Foris publications

Newmeyer, F.R. (1980) *Linguistic Theory in America,* New York: Academic Press

van Oirsouw, R. (1982a) 'Review of Neijt (1979)', *Journal of Linguistics,* vol. 18, pp. 184-8

——(1982b) 'Gazdar on Coordination and Constituents', *Linguistic Inquiry,* vol. 13, pp. 553-7

——(1983a) 'Coordinate Deletion and N-ary Branching Nodes', *Journal of Linguistics,* vol. 19, pp. 305-21

——(1983b) 'Coordinated sentences' *Lingua,* vol. 60, pp. 135-45

——(1984) 'Accessibility of Deletion in Dutch', *Journal of Semantics,* vol. 3, pp. 201-27

——(1985) 'A Linear Approach to Coordinate Deletion', *Linguistics,* vol. 23, pp. 363-90

——(1986) 'Syntactic Ambiguity', in A. Swedek and D. Kastovsky (eds), *A Festschrift for Jacek Fisiak,* Amsterdam: Benjamin

Partee, B.H. (1970) 'Negation, Conjunction and Quantifiers: Syntax Vs. Semantics', *Foundations of Language,* vol. 6, pp. 153-65

Pesetsky, D.M. (1982) *Paths and Categories,* Doctoral Dissertation, MIT

Postal, P.M. (1974) *On Raising,* Cambridge, Mass.: MIT Press

Pullum, G.K. (1976) 'The Duke of York Gambit', *Journal of Linguistics*, vol. 12, pp. 83-102

Pulte, W. (1971) 'Gapping and Word Order in Quechua', in *Papers from the Seventh Regional Meeting of the Chicago Linguistic Society*, Chicago, Ill.: Chicago Linguistic Society

Quine, W.V.O. (1962) 'Identity, Ostension, and Hypostasis', in W.V.O. Quine, *From a Logical Point of View*, 2nd ed., New York: Harper & Row

Quirk, R., Leech, G., Svartvik, J. and Greenbaum, S. (1972) *A Grammar of Contemporary English*, London: Longmans

Reinhart, T. (1981) 'Pragmatics and Linguistics: An Analysis of Sentence Topics', *Philosophica*, 27, pp. 53-94

Van Riemsdijk, H. and Williams, E. (1986) *Introduction to the Theory of Grammar*, Cambridge, Mass.: MIT Press

Rögnvaldsson, E. (1982) 'We Need (Some Kind of a) Rule of Conjunction Reduction', *Linguistic Inquiry*, vol. 13, pp. 557-61

Roorijck, J. (1986) 'Gapping-Zeugma in French and English: A Non-deletion Analysis', *Linguistic Analysis*, pp. 187-229

Rosenbaum, H. (1977) 'Zapotec Gapping as Counterevidence to Some Universal Proposals', *Linguistic Inquiry*, vol. 8, pp. 379-95

Ross, J.R. (1967) *Constraints on Variables in Syntax*, Doctoral Dissertation, MIT

——(1970) 'Gapping and The Order of Constituents', in M. Bierwisch and K. Heidolph (eds), *Progress in Linguistics*, The Hague: Mouton

——(1982): *Pronoun Deleting Processes in German*, Paper presented at the Annual Meeting of the Linguistic Society of America, San Diego

Saiki, M. (1986) 'On the Coordination of Gapped Constituents in Japanese' in *Papers from the 21st Regional Meeting of the Chicago Linguistic Society*, Chicago, Ill: Chicago Linguistic Society

Saito, M. (1984) *Three Notes on Syntactic Movement in Japanese*, Ms., MIT

Sag, I.A. (1976) *Deletion and Logical Form*, Doctoral Dissertation, MIT

——Gazdar, G., Wasow, T. and Weisler, S. (1985) 'Coordination and How to Distinguish Categories', *Natural Language and Linguistic Theory*, vol. 3, pp. 117-71

Sanders, S.A. (1977) 'A Functional Typology of Elliptical Coordinations', in F.R. Eckman (ed.), *Current themes in Linguistics: Bilingualism, Experimental Linguistics, and Language Typologies*, Washington: Hemisphere

——and Tai, J. H-Y(1972) 'Immediate Dominance and Identity Deletion', *Foundations of Language*, vol. 8, pp. 161-98

Schachter, P. (1977) 'Constraints on Coordination', *Language*, vol. 53, pp. 86-103

——and Mordechay, S. (1983): 'A Phrase Structure Account of "Nonconstituent" Conjunctions', in M. Barlow, D. Flickinger and M. Wescoat (eds), *Proceedings of the Second West Coast Conference on Formal Linguistics*, Dept. of Linguistics, Stanford

Seuren, P.A.M. (1984) 'Operator Lowering', *Linguistics*, vol. 22, pp. 573-627

———(1985): *Discourse Semantics*, Oxford: Basil Blackwell

Siegel, Muffy, E.A. (1984) 'Gapping and Interpretation', *Linguistic Inquiry*, vol. 15, pp. 523-30

Sjoblom, T. (1980) *Coordination*, Doctoral Dissertation, MIT

Smith, C.S. (1969) 'Ambiguous Sentences with *and*', in D. Reibel and S. Schane (eds.), *Modern Studies in English*, Englewood Cliffs: Prentice Hall

Steedman, M. (1985) 'Dependency and Coordination in the Grammar of Dutch and English', *Language*, vol. 61, pp. 523-68

Stillings, J.T. (1975) 'The Formulation of Gapping as Evidence for Variable Types in Syntactic Transformations', *Linguistic Analysis*, vol. 1

Stockwell, R., Schachter, P. and Partee, B. (1973) *The Major Syntactic Structures of English*, New York: Holt, Rinehart & Winston

Stowell, T. (1981) *Origins of Phrase Structure*, Doctoral Dissertation, MIT

Stump, G.T. (1978) 'Interpretive Gapping in Montague Grammar', in *Papers from the Fourteenth Annual Meeting of the Chicago Linguistic Society*, Chicago, Ill.: Chicago Linguistic Society

Tai, J. H-Y (1969) *Coordination Reduction*, Doctoral Dissertation, Indiana University

Vitale, A.J. (1981) *Swahili Syntax*, Dordrecht: Foris Publications

Walter, H. (1975) 'Gapping, Wortstellung und Direktionalitätshypothese', Arbeitspapier no. 30, Universität Köln, Institut für Sprachwissenschaft

Webber, B.L. (1979): *A Formal Approach to Discourse Anaphora*, New York: Garland Press

Wekker, H. and Haegeman, L. (1985): *A Modern Course in English Syntax*, London: Croom Helm

Williams, E. (1977) 'Discourse and Logical Form', *Linguistic Inquiry*, vol. 8, pp. 101-39

———(1978) 'Across-the-Board Rule Application', *Linguistic Inquiry*, vol. 9, pp. 31-43

Winograd, T. (1983) *Language as a Cognitive Process Vol. I: Syntax*, Reading, Mass.: Addison-Wesley

Wise, H. (1975): *A Transformational Grammar of Spoken Egyptian Arabic*, Publications of the Philological Society, XXVI, Oxford: Basil Blackwell

Name Index

Aoun, J. 221-2
Austin, P. 137

Bierwisch, M. 91n25
Bouton, L. 64
Browne, W. 143

Chomsky, N. 5ff, 75, 87, 89nn2
   & 11, 91n28, 155, 179, 184,
   198, 236, 237n2, 242ff, 257,
   277n19, 278n32, 279n33
Comrie, B. 73, 143, 207,
   259-60, 274n9
Corbett, G. 234-5, 278nn30 & 31
Cormack, A. 204
Creider, C. 137
Curme, G. 89n7

Dik, S. 9, 30ff, 70, 89n1, 92n35
Dixon, R. 137-8, 188
Dougherty, R. 6, 9, 15, 20ff,
   26ff, 33, 70, 84, 88, 89n4,
   90nn18 & 19, 93n40, 103,
   165, 167n2, 252

Eisenberg, P. 183
Evers, A. 172n29

Finer, D. 73
Furbee, N. 186, 250, 261, 269,
   274n7, 282n49

Gazdar, G. 6, 9, 58, 70ff, 88,
   89n8, 93n42, 96n62, 97nn65
   & 66, 98nn68 & 69, 99nn71
   & 72, 103-4, 109, 116, 154,
   167n2, 169n15, 273n4,
   274n8, 276n14
Givón, T. 137
Gleitman, L. 6ff, 19, 64, 67, 71,
   75-6, 87, 89n5, 103
Goldsmith, J. 281n47
Goodall, G. 26, 48, 82, 179ff,
   200, 262, 273nn1 & 5,
   279n36

Haegeman, L. 109
Hale, K. 73, 231
Halliday, M. 137
Hankamer, J. 9, 34, 38ff, 59,
   92n34, 96n58, 113, 143,
   155ff, 236-7, 265, 269-70,
   280n43, 283n54
Harries, H. 9
Hasegawa, N. 171n25
Heidolph, K. 91n25
Hermann, E. 48, 122
Hoeksema, J. 14, 231
Hornstein, N. 93n43
Huang, J. 139
Hudson, R. 27ff, 90n20, 96n62,
   107

Jackendoff, R. 9, 34ff, 44, 63,
   66, 82, 91n28, 92nn32 & 36,
   95n53, 114, 131, 146,
   170n22, 196

Katz, J. 275n12
Kempson, R. 204
Kooij, J. 94n47, 95n52
Koopman, H. 108-9
Koster, J. 95n51, 274n9
Koutsoudas, A. 9, 108, 113,
   143, 255, 265, 280n44,
   282n49, 283n54
Kuno, S. 9, 45ff, 63, 88,
   92nn35 & 37, 100n79

Ladusaw, W. 207
Lakoff, G. 10ff, 32, 89n7,
   275n12
Lakoff, R. 8, 89n5
Langendoen, D. 9, 43ff, 63, 78,
   88, 128, 155
Levin, N. 9, 35
Levine, A. 256
Li, Ch. 108
Lightfoot, D. 93n43, 171n26
Lincicome, D. 185, 202

290

McCawley, J. 14-15, 25ff, 179,
190ff, 256, 275nn10 & 13
Maling, J. 9, 34, 259
Matthews, P. 30
Meyer-Hermann, R. 277n24
Mohammad, M. 232
Mordechay, S. 9, 70, 76ff,
98n68, 100n76, 175n46

Napoli, D.J. 175n42, 223ff,
276n19, 277n20, 278n25
Neijt, A. 9, 56ff, 67, 88, 93n47,
50, 95nn53 & 54, 118,
175n45, 207, 276n15
Newmeyer, F. 92n34, 174n35,
279n34
Nishikawa, M. 171n25

Oirsouw, R. van 76, 78, 88,
89nn5 & 8, 90n13, 92n33,
94n47, 95n52, 98n67, 123,
168n13, 174n34

Partee, B. 194ff, 275nn12 & 13
Pesetsky, D. 257ff, 280n46,
281n447, 282n48
Peters, S. 10ff, 32, 89n7
Postal, P. 59, 96n63, 275n12
Pullum, G. 19
Pulte, W. 100n75, 270, 280n39

Quine, W. 184-5, 202
Quirk, R. 96n59

Reinhart, T. 137ff
Riemsdijk, H. van 99n74,
171n26
Rieser, H. 277n24
Rögnvaldsson, E. 71ff
Roorijck, J. 264
Rosenbaum, H. 250, 261, 269
Ross, J. 9, 13, 31, 33ff, 49, 52,
56, 62-3, 76, 79-80, 82,

87-8, 90n20, 100n75,
101n81, 123, 134, 138-9,
160-1, 165, 170n19,
172n29, 231, 255ff, 280n43

Sag, I. 6-7, 9, 56, 58, 64ff, 70,
76, 80-1, 88, 95nn55 & 56,
96n62, 99n75, 109, 165,
175n42, 182, 189ff, 218,
223ff, 276n19
Saiki, M. 275n9
Saito, M. 135, 221-2
Sanders, G. 16, 108, 250,
254-5, 260-1, 265, 282n49
Schachter, P. 9, 70, 76ff, 85, 88,
98n68, 100n76, 175n46, 263
Seuren, P. 83, 100n78, 171n26,
172n29, 174n35, 189, 199ff,
273n3, 275n13, 276n15
Siegel, M. 207ff, 276n16
Sjoblom, T. 233, 262
Smith, C. 8ff, 18, 87, 103
Steedman, M. 46, 76, 83ff,
96n62, 100nn76 & 79,
101nn80 & 81, 176n47
Stockwell, R. 9, 91n24
Stowell, T. 222, 254
Stump, G. 82, 96n62

Tai, J. 9, 15ff, 24-5, 28, 31, 34,
44, 49, 76, 89n15, 108, 113,
174n34, 254-5, 265, 282n49
Thompson, S. 108

Vitale, A. 270, 282n49
Vuong, A. and V. 282n52

Walter, H. 9, 282n50
Wekker, H. 109
Williams, E. 8-9, 52ff, 63, 75,
93nn40, 41 & 42, 99n74,
171n26, 179, 238ff, 251,
279nn35 & 36, 281n47
Winograd, T. 246

Subject Index